ETHICS AND THE UNIVERSITY

Ethics and the University brings together two closely related topics, the practice of ethics in the university ("academic ethics") and the teaching of practical or applied ethics in the university.

The volume is divided into four parts:
- a survey of practical ethics, offering an explanation of its recent emergence as a university subject, situating that subject within a wider social and historical context and identifying some problems that the subject generates for universities;
- an examination of research ethics, including the problem of plagiarism;
- a discussion of the teaching of practical ethics. Michael Davis explores how ethics can be integrated into the university curriculum and what part particular cases should play in the teaching of ethics; and
- an exploration of sexual ethics.

Ethics and the University provides a stimulating and provocative analysis of academic ethics which will be useful to students, academics and practitioners.

Michael Davis is Senior Fellow at the Center for the Study of Ethics in the Professions, and Professor of Philosophy, Department of Humanities, Illinois Institute of Technology. He is the author of *Thinking Like an Engineer: Essays in the Ethics of a Profession* (1998).

PROFESSIONAL ETHICS
General editor: Ruth Chadwick, Centre for
Professional Ethics, University of Central
Lancashire

Professionalism is a subject of interest to academics, the general public and
would-be professional groups. Traditional ideas of professions and professional conduct have been challenged by recent social, political and
technological changes. One result has been the development for almost
every profession of an ethical code of conduct which attempts to formalise
its values and standards. These codes of conducts raise a number of questions about the status of a 'profession' and the consequent moral
implications for behaviour.

This series seeks to examine these questions both critically and constructively. Individual volumes will consider issues relevant to particular
professions, including nursing, genetic counselling, journalism, business, the
food industry and law. Other volumes will address issues relevant to all
professional groups such as the function and value of a code of ethics and
the demands of confidentiality.

Also available in this series:

ETHICS AND THE UNIVERSITY

Michael Davis

London and New York

First published 1999
by Routledge
11 New Fetter Lane, London EC4P 4EE

Simultaneously published in the USA and Canada
by Routledge
29 West 35th Street, New York, NY 10001

Typeset in Times by Routledge
Printed and bound in Great Britain by
MPG Books Ltd, Bodmin, Cornwall

British Library Cataloguing in Publication Data
A catalogue record for this book is available from the British Library

Library of Congress Cataloguing in Publication Data
Davis, Michael
Ethics in the university / Michael Davis
p. cm – (Professional Ethics)
Includes bibliographical references (p.) and index.
1. Education, Higher – Moral and ethical aspects – United States.
2. Ethics – Study and teaching (Higher) – United States.
3. Research – Moral and ethical aspects – United States. 4. Sexual
Ethics – United States
I. Title. II. Series.
LB2324. D38 1999
174`. 937 – dc21   98 – 27141
                                                CIP

ISBN 0–415–18097–X (hbk)
ISBN 0–415–18098–8 (pbk)

CONTENTS

CONTENTS

PREFACE

This book brings together two closely related topics, the practice of ethics in the university ("academic ethics") and the teaching of practical (or applied) ethics in the university. The topics are related in at least three ways. The first is historically: a discussion of academic ethics seems to belong to a wider "ethics boom" in teaching professional ethics, social ethics, and business ethics. The second is substantively: some fields of professional (or institutional) ethics, especially the ethics of scientific research, overlap substantially with academic ethics. Because about half of all scientists employed in research are employed by universities, many questions of research ethics are questions of academic ethics as well. The third is causally: teaching professional ethics, social ethics, or business ethics can itself generate questions of academic ethics (or, at least, of "professorial ethics"). For example, if teaching medical ethics is a kind of inculcation of proper values, how can an academic committed to freeing the mind of mere inculcation ethically teach medical ethics? *Ethics and the University* works at the intersection of these historical, substantive, and causal relations. Its purpose is both to clarify the field and extend discussion on certain central topics.

Part I provides a high-altitude survey of the field, marking distinctions important throughout the book. Chapter 1, "The ethics boom, philosophy, and the university," offers an explanation of the emergence of practical ethics as a university subject, putting that subject into a wider social and historical context. This chapter distinguishes several senses of ethics and explains the sense in which the ethics boom is new, generating new problems for the university that wishes to make room for it. Academic ethics is a special topic within the complex of topics now identifiable as "the ethics boom."

Chapter 2 considers the relation between academic freedom,

academic ethics, and "professorial ethics." Academic ethics is a form of institutional ethics (just as is business ethics or research ethics); professorial ethics is a form of professional ethics. Neither of these is congruent with academic freedom which is mostly about the rights of academics (professors and students), not about their obligations (except insofar as the rights carry obligations).

In Part II, Chapters 3–6, focuses on research ethics. Chapter 3 offers a survey of the field, both historical and topical. Why now? Why these topics? Chapter 4 considers the possibility of deriving special standards for researchers entirely from consideration of the purpose, function, or status of "science" or "scientific research." It concludes that such an attempt will fail. What is required are conventions, whether specific to a particular field of research or discipline or covering scientific research generally. A code of ethics is not a discovery but an invention. Chapter 5 considers a specific set of problems posed by the increasingly close relationship between business and university research. What standards should be imposed on that relationship? Why? Chapter 6 considers in depth a case, a plagiarism complaint, in which academic ethics seems to need both new standards and new procedures.

Having thus defined the field of practical ethics, we are ready for Part III, Chapters 7–10, the subject of which is teaching practical ethics. Chapter 7 describes a program to integrate professional (and institutional) ethics into a wide range of courses across the university, everything from first-year calculus to senior design or research projects. Since "the case method" plays a large part in this program – and, indeed, is now the preferred method of teaching professional ethics – Chapter 8 attempts to explain what the case method is, ending up not with one method but several. Chapter 8 also illustrates important differences between methods and provides considerable advice on how to develop and use cases. Chapter 9 considers a problem of professorial ethics that teaching practical ethics seems to generate. Teaching ethics changes teaching – or at least brings out parts of teaching we tend to forget. Chapter 9 suggests how much remains to be done to clarify the ethical presuppositions of university teaching in particular – and academic ethics in general. Chapter 10 argues against one approach to a certain range of questions now hotly contested. Trying to think of questions of "sexual ethics" as closely related is likely to make them harder, not easier, to resolve.

Few books owe no debts, but this one owes more than the usual. Many are paid in individual endnotes. Three, I think, deserve a global acknowledgement. This book began as a series of invited talks, with my host assigning the topic, or with some other form of external stimulus, for example, being asked to write a grant proposal on a certain topic. But for those external stimuli, I would, I think, have devoted my time to other topics, missing the opportunity to explore a field both rewarding in itself and of practical importance to my own profession. So, one global debt I want to acknowledge is to all those people, both at IIT's Center for the Study of Ethics in the Professions and outside, who at one time or another wanted to know what I thought about ethics and the university.

A second debt is to the Ethics Center's staff: to the present librarian (and information specialist), Jing Li, for helping to check, complete, and correct my citations; and to our secretary, Rebecca Slaughter (until recently Newton), and her student helpers, for getting the early papers back on computer. Technical help, though easily forgotten, made the difference between completing this work on time – and perhaps not completing it at all.

The third global debt is to my family: my lawyer wife for helping to assure the financial security that allowed me to write, my son for tolerating a father who thinks looking at words on a computer screen is fun, and my loyal dog for sleeping at my feet on cold mornings as I followed arguments where they led.

Though each of the first nine chapters has been published in one form or another before, none has been published in the form it has here. I have tried to update text whenever appropriate, to improve arguments when I saw a way of doing so, and to make explicit connections between chapters wherever that seemed appropriate. Nevertheless, I think it appropriate to acknowledge places of prior publication. Chapter 1 (under the title "The Ethics Boom: What and Why") first appeared in *The Centennial Review* (Spring 1990), vol. 34, pp. 163–85; Chapter 2 (under the title "Wild Professors and Sensitive Students: A Preface to Academic Ethics") in *Social Theory and Practice* (Summer 1992), vol. 18, pp. 117–41; Chapter 3 in *International Journal of Applied Philosophy* (Spring 1990), vol. 5, pp. 1–10; Chapter 4 in *Professional Ethics* (Spring 1995), vol. 4, pp. 49–74; Chapter 5 in *Journal of College and University Law* (Summer 1991), vol. 18, pp. 29–38; Chapter 6 in *Accountability in Research* (Spring 1993), vol. 2, pp. 273–86; Chapter 7 in *Teaching Philosophy* (September 1993), vol. 16, pp. 205–35; Chapter 8 (under the title "Developing and Using Cases to Teach Practical Ethics") in *Teaching Philosophy* (December

1997), vol. 20, pp. 353–85; and Chapter 9 (under the title "On Teaching Cloistered Virtue: The Ethics of Teaching Students to Avoid Moral Risk") in *Teaching Philosophy* (September 1991), vol. 14, pp. 259–76.

SERIES EDITOR'S
PREFACE

Professional Ethics is now acknowledged as a field of study in its own right. Much of its recent development has resulted from rethinking traditional medical ethics in the light of new moral problems arising out of advances in medical science and technology. Applied philosophers, ethicists and lawyers have devoted considerable energy to exploring the dilemmas emerging from modern healthcare practices and their effects on the practitioner–patient relationship.

But the point can be generalized. Even in healthcare, ethical problems are not confined to medical practitioners. Beyond healthcare, other groups are increasingly thinking critically about the kind of service they offer and about the nature of the relationship between provider and recipient. In many areas of life social, political and technological changes have challenged traditional ideas of practice.

The Professional Ethics series seeks to examine ethical issues in the professions and related areas both critically and constructively. Individual volumes address issues relevant to all professional groups, such as the nature of a profession and the function and value of codes of ethics. Other volumes examine issues relevant to particular professions, including those which have hitherto received little attention, such as accountancy, general practice and health care management.

It is particularly demanding to reflect upon the ethics of one's own profession, but this volume attempts to do just that. Those who work in ethics professionally are usually, though not exclusively, academics working in a university environment. Michael Davis works in a Center for the Study of Ethics in the Professions at a higher education institution, and explores ethical issues related to the university. As he explains in his preface, this involves two closely related topics, both the practice of ethics in the university as it might arise for example in research; and the teaching of applied ethics. The latter will be of particular relevance to the practice of the growing number of specialists in applied ethics, while also having wider implications about the nature of ethics itself; the former touches upon issues of importance for all who work in an academic environment.

Part I

INTRODUCTION

1

THE ETHICS BOOM, PHILOSOPHY, AND THE UNIVERSITY

> It was the best of times, it was the worst of times, it was the
> age of wisdom, it was the age of foolishness,...we were all
> going direct to Heaven, we were all going direct the other
> way – in short, the period was so far like the present, that
> some of its noisiest authorities insisted on its being received
> for good or for evil, in the superlative degree of comparison
> only.

With these words Charles Dickens began *A Tale of Two Cities*,
rebuking all those "noisy authorities" who would claim for their age
some priority over others. No age is without some experts to declare
it the best of times and others to declare it the worst. Yet, Dickens
would not, I think, deny that times change. His rebuke must, then,
be directed at those who, without good evidence, declare that their
age differs in some important way from others. The age in which
one lives always looks different from those of which one knows
little or nothing.

I have, I admit, a personal stake in this reading of Dickens. I
want to claim that our present concern with "ethics" distinguishes
this age from others. I am therefore a candidate for Dickens' rebuke.
To avoid it, I shall proceed in this way. I shall begin this chapter by
considering what the "ethics boom" is supposed to be; then examine
the evidence for the boom; and, having shown the boom to be real,
explain why we are having it. The boom's novelty, its connection
with academic philosophy, is a corollary of that explanation and an
appropriate way to introduce our subject; ethics and the university.

What boom?

Looking back over the last three decades, what I seem to see is not one boom but many. The first is in medical ethics. By the early 1960s, physicians were already struggling with many questions they did not feel prepared to answer. Medical technology made it possible to keep patients alive long after they had no hope even of consciousness. What did doing one's best for the patient mean in such circumstances? When, if ever, may a physician justifiably cease trying to preserve life when there is hope of preserving it?

Medical technology was also becoming increasingly expensive. Physicians confronted hard questions of distribution. Do we buy a dialysis machine to keep a few dozen patients alive or instead spend the money on an outpatient clinic that will serve many more people but perhaps save no lives? How do we decide who gets dialysis if we can't provide dialysis for all who need it? Should physicians make such decision? If not physicians, who?

Medical technology was also changing the practice of medicine. The old personal relationship between physician and patient, the symbol of which was the house call, was becoming increasingly impractical. The progress of medicine seemed to force physicians to specialize more, to depend more on tests that could only be performed in an office or at a hospital, and to cooperate more closely with other physicians. The lone doctor with their little black bag was going the way of the passenger train and the forty-acre farm. In this less personal environment, traditional practices like giving a placebo looked much harder to defend. Lying to an old friend for his or her own good seems one thing; lying to a helpless stranger, another.

Physicians spoke of these changes in the way they practiced medicine as raising issues of "medical ethics."[1] At first, they talked about these issues among themselves. Soon, however, they recognized that they were not equipped to resolve them. So, as befits an era of increasing specialization, they began looking for help from specialists in ethics. Medical schools had no such specialty. But every university had courses with "ethics" in the title. Usually, these were taught by philosophers. So, going for help to philosophers seemed to make sense. And, at a few universities, that is what members of the medical faculty did.

They were surprised by what they found. Philosophers, it turned out, taught moral theory, not practical ethics. And the moral theory to which they devoted most of their time was far from practice. The philosophers liked to call it "meta-ethics." A whole course might concern a question like whether "good" is a natural or a non-natural property. Some philosophers openly doubted that philosophy could "bake bread."

But, at a few universities, philosophers and physicians agreed to talk anyway. They focused on particular cases the physicians found troubling. Soon the philosophers saw connections between their traditional concerns and problems the physicians were posing. For example, philosophers had long studied personal identity, the criteria by which we may decide when, despite apparent change, I remain the same person and when I have become someone or something else. Criteria of personal identity seemed relevant to questions of terminating life support. If, for example, personal identity presupposed the possibility of consciousness, a physician might be justified in terminating life support as soon as the patient's brain died. The patient would have ceased to exist as a person.

By the late 1960s, the conversation between physicians and philosophers had advanced enough to become institutionalized. The first clear evidence came in 1969 with the founding of the Institute of Society, Ethics, and the Life Sciences in Hastings-on-Hudson, just north of New York City. The Hastings Center, as it is commonly known, is still the most important think tank for medical ethics in the world. The Center was conceived as an inter-disciplinary enterprise, one in which theologians, lawyers, and social scientists, as well as philosophers and physicians, were to work together on the problems facing medicine (and related fields). Yet, from the beginning, philosophers were central to its work.

About the time the Hastings Center was getting started, philosophers elsewhere, either alone or teamed with a physician, began teaching courses in medical ethics. These courses – whether a seminar in a medical school or in a graduate or undergraduate program – tended to mix moral theory with specific problems that concerned physicians. A good mix proved hard to find. The first philosophical text in medical ethics did not appear until 1976.[2] Most of the early texts took a form already popular in philosophy, the anthology of primary sources, arranged by "problem," and designed to provoke discussion.

The boom in legal ethics has a different history. The central event is certainly Watergate. John Dean's observation that lawyers seemed shockingly over-represented among those appointees of President Nixon guilty of criminal wrongdoing struck a chord with lawyers. In 1974, some states decided to require a course in legal ethics as a condition for admission to the bar. Others followed quickly. The requirement took many law schools by surprise. Legal ethics had until then been an optional course struggling to survive in an increasingly rich curriculum. My own experience will illustrate the difference between the way legal and medical ethics developed.

In the spring of 1974, I was a young assistant professor of philosophy in a department that had one of the earliest courses in medical ethics. One day my departmental chair called me into his office and asked what I knew about legal ethics. "Nothing," I replied. "No matter," he said. "You're smart. You do ethics and philosophy of law. The rest you can learn."

He had, he said, received a call from the law school. They needed a three-credit course in legal ethics by next spring. No one on their faculty could teach it. They hoped the philosophy department would do for legal ethics what it had done for medical ethics. He was asking me because the medical ethics people were too busy and I was the only member of the department besides himself who knew much about law. The law school was prepared to pay handsomely. They would give me the fall to teach myself what I needed to know. All they asked was that the course be given next spring to the senior class. When I hesitated, he smiled, "I know what you're thinking. What can a philosopher tell lawyers about their own ethics? Don't worry, lawyers are like doctors: if they're desperate enough to ask a philosopher's help, they need it." Thus began my initiation into professional ethics.

I went over to the law school that fall. What I found surprised me. Lawyers needed much less help than physicians had. The legal literature was significant (though not philosophically sophisticated).[3] Lawyers had been teaching legal ethics for some time. There were a few good texts.[4] Lawyers had specialists in ethics in a way physicians did not. Indeed, the law school was already planning to hire one of those specialists for the following year.

Still, lawyers were not so different from physicians. In 1970, the American Bar Association (ABA) had replaced its model "Canons of Ethics," originally adopted in 1908 but much amended since, with a new "Code of Professional Responsibility." The Code distinguished between "canons," "mandatory rules," and "ethical considerations." There was a good deal of confusion about the distinction. Underlying this confusion were deeper questions: Was there a difference between legal ethics and professional responsibility? Was the Code just another statute or something else? If something else, what? How did the answer to these questions affect the way the Code should be interpreted? How did it affect what a lawyer should do?

When most people think of Watergate, they think only of lawyers and politicians. But I think of engineers too. Spiro Agnew resigned as Vice President of the United States not because of what he had done as Nixon's Vice President but because of what he had done while holding office in Maryland. He had solicited bribes from civil engineers seeking state contracts. Many had paid. Engineers all over the country were appalled that so many engineers could be involved in such a flagrant violation of professional ethics. The scandal contributed to the unease engineers already felt about the part engineers had had in the then-recent controversies surrounding the faked testing of Goodrich's A-7D airbrakes, the Ford Pinto's exploding gas tank, and the DC-10's misdesigned cargo door. Many were also concerned about what was happening to the engineers who had warned the public of the danger posed by the Bay Area Transit Authority's computer controlled trains.[5]

In 1975, an anonymous donor offered the Illinois Institute of Technology (IIT) $500,000 to improve the philosophy department. IIT's president, a chemist, convinced the donor to give the money to establish an "ethics center" to do something about the ethics of engineers, scientists, architects, and other professionals. The model was to be the Hastings Center. The following year the organization at which I now work, the Center for the Study of Ethics in the Professions, was established. Perhaps only by coincidence, the University of Maryland established its Center for Ethics and Public Policy in the same year.

IIT's work in professional ethics followed the pattern of medical ethics, beginning with engineering. Faculty in philosophy, engineering, and the social sciences met to discuss engineering ethics, using cases like the DC-10 cargo door to understand the part engineers had (or could have) in what were ultimately corporate decisions. Soon the philosophers and engineers were team-teaching a course. Eventually, the philosophers taught it alone. Similar courses in architecture ethics and computer ethics followed.

The boom in business ethics seems to date from this period as well. Other professions – accounting, nursing, journalism, financial analysis, public administration, dentistry, and so on – each have their own story. For example, interest in the ethics of scientific research seems to have become significant only in the early 1980s. Only in the last few years has it begun to have the proportions of a boom (as I shall explain in Chapter 3). And only in this decade has interest in academic ethics become noticeable. Any boom is yet to come.

Evidence of the boom

This is the "boom" we are talking about; an increased interest in ethics spreading unevenly from one profession or occupation to another. What evidence is there that this boom is more than apparent?

One feature of the ethics boom seems to be a growth in codes of ethics. What evidence do we have of this growth? In 1980, the Ethics Resource Center (ERC) surveyed 105 corporations they knew to have a code of ethics. Of those responding, fifty-eight percent indicated that their code was *less* than *four* years old.[6] When the ERC repeated its survey in 1990, they identified 1,700 companies with a code of ethics.[7] Clearly, there has been a boom in corporate codes of ethics. What about codes of ethics for professions?

My center collects professional codes. In 1981, we had 241 professional codes on file. By 1989, we had 338; by 1997, the number had risen to 764.[8] Though not as dramatic as the growth in business codes, the growth in professional codes is still substantial. But that growth seems to be due almost entirely to the organization of new professional societies rather than to the adoption by existing societies of codes where none existed before. That is not surprising. Generally, adopting a code of ethics is part of organizing a profession. Organizing a profession is itself part of the ethics boom.

Looking through our files, I noticed an interesting pattern. Many of the present codes were adopted during the last twenty-five years, replacing codes adopted before 1920. So, for example, not only did the ABA replace its Canons of Ethics with the code of Professional Responsibility in 1970; in 1982, it replaced that code with the "Model Rules of Professional Conduct." The Institute of Electrical and Electronic Engineers (IEEE) did something similar. In 1978, it replaced a code of ethics dating from 1912 with an entirely new document; and then, in 1990, replaced that document with another.

The two ABA codes have at least one other feature in common with the two new IEEE codes, one shared with most of the codes adopted in the last twenty-five years. The new codes bear surprisingly little resemblance to their predecessors. Many of the old provisions have simply disappeared. Many new provisions have no counterpart in the older code.[9]

My examination of the Center's collection of professional codes leads me to conclude that, in American history, the only period comparable to the years 1970–95 in number and importance of professional codes adopted are the first two decades of this century. So, here is more evidence of a boom.

Courses in ethics should also provide evidence of the boom. What has changed in the last twenty-five years? Let me begin with my own experience. When I was an undergraduate in the early 1960s, the philosophy department in which I majored had only one undergraduate course in ethics, what we would now describe as an advanced course in moral theory.[10] The graduate school I attended had two, one in contemporary moral theory and one in the history of moral theory. There was no course in applied (or practical) or professional ethics. Indeed, I'm sure I never heard any of those terms until I left graduate school.

Neither my college nor my graduate school was unusual in its course offerings. Their offerings had been typical of American universities since at least the late 1940s. Yet, ten years after I received my Ph.D., most of the courses I was teaching were new. The most popular introduction to philosophy was Moral and Social Values. A course in (what we now call) applied (or practical) ethics, it was organized around topics like abortion, euthanasia, war, poverty, and suicide. The advanced undergraduate courses included Legal Ethics, Medical Ethics, and Business Ethics as well as a course called "Ethical Theory" (which focused on normative theories, not meta-ethics). True, I had changed institutions during the 1970s. But that change does not explain the change in what I taught. All those courses except Ethical Theory had been added during the 1970s. Much the same happened at many other institutions during the same period.[11]

Here then is evidence of a boom in teaching ethics. There is more. For example, a significant number of philosophers now have their primary appointment in a medical school (often in a department of medical humanities). Not only do these philosophers teach ethics to medical students, many also sit on hospital ethics committees or make rounds with physicians. None of this even seemed possible in 1970.

Something similar has happened in business and government. Twenty-five years ago no one even talked seriously about ethics training for "practitioners." Today ethics training is common. My own center has done ethics training for government as well as for trade associations and businesses. Other ethics centers, including the Ethics Resource Center in Washington, D.C. and the Josephson

Institute in California, have also done ethics training in business and government. My center's list of professional societies even includes an International Society of Ethicists (ISE) for "consultants in the application of Ethics." The ISE was founded in 1985.

Publications are another possible source of evidence for a boom. What do we find? Again, let me begin close to home. In 1980, my center published a selective annotated bibliography of work in engineering ethics.[12] It listed 536 items, including Congressional hearings, court cases, and general works in professional ethics. In 1990, we were asked to update the bibliography. After a preliminary search of the literature, we concluded we could not. So much had been published on engineering ethics in the intervening decade that we could not do a useful update without adding staff.

Engineering ethics is, I should add, a relatively small part of professional ethics. How small may be gauged by considering that engineering still does not have its own journal of professional ethics.[13] Among disciplines having at least one such journal already are: agriculture, criminal justice, ecology, journalism, international affairs, and law. Business ethics already had two in 1980 (and now has at least four). And medical ethics not only has at least four journals but its own four-volume encyclopedia.[14]

Since we are now looking for evidence of a boom in ethics publications, I should point out that none of today's many journals of applied or professional ethics is more than twenty years old.[15] So, here is more evidence of a boom.

What about ethics centers as a measure of the boom? Here the evidence is just as impressive. The Hastings Center seems to have been the first ethics think tank in the world. IIT's center, Maryland's, and Bentley College's Center for Business Ethics seem to be among those tied for first ethics center not primarily concerned with medical ethics. We keep a registry of ethics centers. As of August 1989, it listed 308 in the United States, 25 in Canada, and 8 elsewhere in the world. By 1997, the number in the U.S. had grown to 347. Though the number in Canada had actually dropped to 10, the number elsewhere had more than tripled to 26. England alone had 14 by then.[16]

Some explanations of the ethics boom rejected

Taken together, this evidence seems to establish that the boom in ethics is real. So, the question becomes: Why now?

One possible answer is that a particular scandal, Watergate, caused the boom. If Watergate had not happened, there would have been no boom. We must reject this explanation. As I have described the boom, it began before Watergate, with medical ethics in the early 1960s. Medical ethics cannot be dismissed as "the exception that proves the rule." There are at least two reasons: First, we can point to boom-related activity in other fields before Watergate. For example, the ABA rewrote its code of ethics (the first time) in the late 1960s. Second, medical ethics by itself is just too important to be treated as a "mere exception." Physicians were the first to draw philosophers into applied ethics. From then on, medical ethics has been the model for most other fields. Today, medical ethics remains by far the largest field of applied or professional ethics.

While we can't attribute the ethics boom to Watergate (or to any other particular scandal), we can none the less see that Watergate and similar scandals have had a part in generating the boom. Perhaps, then, we should attribute the boom to a pervasive climate of scandal. Perhaps our society is especially corrupt and so especially in need of ethics.

Though this explanation has a certain appeal, we should, I think, put it aside. Like the previous explanation, this one does not fit medical ethics. Though medicine has had its scandals (for example, overcharging Medicaid), these do not seem to have had much to do with how medical *ethics* has developed. Technology, not scandal, seems to direct that field.

The pervasive climate of scandal has another disadvantage as explanation. Explaining the ethics boom by such a climate would require claiming that our time is worse ethically than the times preceding in which there was no boom. We would be in danger of joining the "noisy authorities" Dickens rebuked. We could avoid that rebuke only by presenting good evidence that our time is indeed worse ethically than its predecessors. What evidence do we have of that? The answer seems to be, none.

Counting scandals may seem a promising way to show that our time is particularly corrupt. The result is likely to be disappointing. Few years are without a major scandal. The number does not seem to change much from decade to decade (perhaps because news media must limit the number of scandals they report). That, anyway, is the impression I derived from a morning's unscientific browsing through old newspapers. Perhaps the more refined methods of a sociologist or historian could produce more interesting results. But, for now, counting scandals does not seem likely to prove that our age is worse than others.

What about the crime rate as a measure of corruption? Here there certainly are differences between decades. The U.S. crime rate reached a peak about 1890, declined more or less steadily until about 1930, remained unchanged until after the Second World War, then rose steeply until 1980, after which it has remained more or less unchanged. The pattern seems much the same for "white-collar crime" as for "street crime" (though records are not kept in that way).[17]

So, our society *is* today much less law abiding than in 1950 or even 1970. The difficulty is in showing a connection between this rise in crime and the alleged decline in ethics. We do not know how to calculate the rate of unethical conduct from the rate of crime. Since much unethical conduct is not illegal, differences in crime rate from one decade to another may, for all we know, have little or no connection with changes in the rate of unethical conduct. Lack of evidence seems to doom any explanation of the current ethics boom dependent on claims about the special corruption of our time.[18]

What's left? One possibility is that today's ethics boom is explained by an earlier "ethics bust." Ethics, like business, has its ups and downs. We are up now because we were down before. Interestingly, there *is* evidence for this simple explanation. Let me start with an experience I had while preparing to teach legal ethics for the first time.

I began by interviewing the law faculty to find out what they thought should be included in the course. I soon learned that my course had a predecessor. The former dean, now a respected senior member of the faculty, had taught such a course in the 1940s and 1950s, finally giving it up in the early 1960s because both he and his students had found it increasingly "irrelevant." When asked about reviving the course, he had responded emphatically, "I would rather resign." His only advice to me was, "Do something else."

Today we would probably describe his course as concerned with "professional etiquette."[19] One lawyer recalled the course as mainly concerned with topics like how large a sign you could hang over your office and when you could give someone your business card. Yet, in fact, it was a good deal more than that. The course discussed the Canons section by section, relating each provision to the problems a lawyer might face in setting up or maintaining a practice. The course also devoted substantial time to lawyers and their history, with emphasis on the good that lawyers have done and the virtues that particular lawyers have shown. The history was supposed to help law students see themselves as part of an ancient and honorable enterprise, to make them proud to be lawyers and willing to do what their code required.[20]

The course seemed increasingly irrelevant in part, I think, because the old Canons of Ethics had been written for a different age, the age of solo practitioners and individual clients. The students saw legal work increasingly concentrated in government agencies and large firms with corporate clients. These changes in the practice of law were one reason the ABA had decided to replace the old Canons.

The Canons were, however, not all that was wrong with the course. Legal ethics could never be an ordinary law course. There was not enough "law" in it. Relevant legal cases were few and increasingly remote from contemporary practice. Other sources of authority, primarily the opinions of bar ethics committees, seldom made sophisticated legal arguments. The course therefore tended to degenerate into a series of sermons and "war stories." It could neither engage students personally nor challenge them intellectually.

So the course had disappeared, not only from the law school where I was to teach a different course, but from most other law schools. And, if the reminiscences of old practitioners of other professions can be trusted, something similar had happened in their professions' schools as well. Many of the professions, including medicine, seem at one time to have had their own course in "professional etiquette."[21] How widespread they actually were is hard to say. What seems clear is that those courses disappeared earlier than their legal counterpart.[22]

There was, then, a "bust" in teaching professional ethics. But the bust included more than teaching. For example, when the IEEE undertook to write its new ethics code in the early 1970s, no one directly involved in the project seems to have been aware that the IEEE already had a code adopted in 1912. The old code had been forgotten. This is hard to explain. The IEEE was not a small organization in 1912.[23] With 15,000 members, it was already among the larger professional societies in the United States. By 1975, it had over 100,000 members, maintained an ample paid staff at its offices in New York City, and involved members in a wide range of activities through hundreds of volunteer committees. That such an organization could forget its ethics code testifies to a startling discontinuity in the attention given ethics.

Looking over this century, we can, I think, see other evidence of discontinuity in the attention given ethics, a period of increasing disinterest in ethics beginning in the 1920s and stretching into the

1960s. The bust affected different institutions in different ways. The public schools, for example, slowly gave up "moral education." Philosophers became increasingly preoccupied with questions about the very possibility of deciding moral questions by rational means. The social sciences not only became increasingly "value neutral," they also lost interest in studying values.[24]

Before this ethics bust, there was another boom – the first two decades of this century, the period during which many professions organized or adopted their first code of ethics. Further back, we can see yet another bust, the last decades of the nineteenth century, and before that, yet another boom.

Throughout much of the nineteenth century, college education aimed at building character more than transmitting objective knowledge. The final stage of education was generally a course, given by the college president, usually a minister, on "moral philosophy" or "ethics" – *not* professional ethics but on the way a "Christian gentleman" should conduct himself in a sinful world.[25] The course disappeared as colleges grew into universities after the Civil War, and universities more and more became institutions divided by discipline and united only by a commitment to discover and transmit knowledge. The last text for such a course, written by a former president of Princeton, was published in 1892.[26]

The first courses in professional ethics may have been an attempt to find a secular substitute for the old course in Christian ethics.[27] The appeal to honor in many of the early codes certainly suggests such a connection (honor being among the chief virtues of a gentleman).

The definitive history of these earlier booms and busts has yet to be written. Perhaps nothing is as it seems. But if the story I have told is basically right, what is striking is not the similarities between the present boom and past booms but the differences. Let me point out three of the more important.[28]

First, neither of the previous booms produced an institution like the ethics center. No doubt this is in part because think tanks are themselves a relatively recent phenomenon; so, think tanks for ethics would be too. But there is more to it than that. The other two booms seem to have supposed that very little about ethics was controversial. Ethics was largely a domain of settled standards. The chief problem was not to resolve controversies but to inculcate traditional standards in the rising generation. Not think tanks but "education committees" were what was needed.[29]

Related to this difference is a difference in approach. Courses in applied or professional ethics today tend to look like ordinary philosophy courses. Many in fact include some moral theory.[30] Even when they do not, they are none the less likely to be organized around "problems" and to include much Socratic give-and-take.[31] Ethics is treated as a subject in which controversy is normal, argument is appropriate, and answers are to be worked out in a shared search for the best reasons. Even in a course in professional ethics, sermons are rare. The profession's code is not just handed down. It is treated as a historical artifact to be examined, appraised, defended, or condemned. In my own experience, that is true as well, though to a lesser degree, even of the ethics training that goes on in business and government. That was not, I believe, true either of the first generation of professional ethics courses or of their predecessor, the course in Christian ethics.[32]

Related to this difference in approach is a difference in those "doing ethics." Though some of the earliest work in medical ethics, business ethics, and certain other fields was done by theologians (or, rather, people in "religious ethics"), philosophers have in fact dominated the present boom. In many professions, many of those teaching professional ethics have a degree in philosophy (whether or not they are also members of the profession whose ethics they teach). Medical ethics is a good example of this. The contrast with the other two ethics booms is stark. In the first boom, ministers dominated; in the second, the professionals themselves. Philosophers had little part in either.[33]

One more difference between the present boom and past ones is worth pointing out. Neither previous boom seems to have produced anything like the present boom's on-the-job training in ethics. For the other two booms, ethics training was something that ended with college or one's professional degree. If anything more was needed, it was for church, disciplinary committee, or prison to do.

These differences between previous ethics booms and this one suggest that we are not dealing with a mere cycle of boom and bust. We must then look for a deeper explanation of the present boom. We must look for fundamental changes in society.

Ethics as an alternative to law

Much has happened during the last century and a half that might help to explain the difference between this ethics boom and the other two. The most obvious is the increasing importance of large cities. In 1850, only 15 percent of Americans lived in a town with

2,500 or more inhabitants.[34] New York, by far the largest U.S. city, had just under 700,000.[35] By 1900, three U.S. cities had a population over one million,[36] and nearly 40 percent of Americans lived in a town of 2,500 or more.[37] Today, we no longer think in terms of cities but "metropolitan areas," vast concentrations of people in which municipal boundaries have become mere technicalities. More than half of all Americans now live in a metropolitan area of more than a *million*.[38] Very few live in a town under 2,500. The United States long ago became an urban society.

In a town of 2,500, everyone knows everyone else's business. Gossip is enough to maintain order among inhabitants and allow them to work together effectively. In a large city, no one knows more than a few others. Order cannot be maintained by conscience, family, church, and neighborhood alone. Cities must work through such formal organizations as police, zoning commissions, charities, unions, and large corporations. Like these other organizations, professions are primarily urban creatures.

The period between 1850 and today has also been a period in which religion became less important in public life (even as Americans seem to have become more attached to religious symbols like the slogan "In God We Trust"). Perhaps part of what explains this decline is a corresponding decline in the religious commitment of individuals. But more important, I think, is that religion itself can no longer provide a *common* vocabulary for evaluation of conduct.

In 1850, the United States could accurately be described as a "Protestant nation." Unitarians, Jews, and even Catholics were quite marginal. Differences between Episcopal, Presbyterian, Methodist, Baptist, and the like were relatively small. As Protestants, all were united by a tradition emphasizing the divinity of Jesus, the authority of individual conscience, and hostility to the claims of Catholicism. But by 1900, one would have had to say "Christian nation" to include the many Catholics already important in public life. The common ground between Protestants and Catholics is much narrower than that between Protestants.

By 1950, the common ground had become even narrower. Americans were then talking about a common "Judeo-Christian" tradition. Today, it is hard to find a term inclusive enough for the religious diversity of American society. The substantial number of Muslims among us can perhaps be included by appeal to the "Abrahamic tradition." Islam belongs to the same family of desert religions as Judaism and Christianity. All three share a belief in one god and certain very general moral teachings historically connected with that belief. The same cannot be said of Hinduism and Buddhism. Hinduism has many gods; Buddhism, none. These religions challenge the very foundation of the Abrahamic tradition. Yet, American cities now include significant numbers of Hindus and Buddhists – as well as many people who have no religion at all.

Without a common religious tradition, we cannot depend on religion to provide *common* standards of conduct. The major religions of the world do, of course, agree on some general standards. All, for example, condemn murder, perjury, and theft. This agreement is, however, too general to decide most disputes. And it is not itself a *common* standard. The agreement is contingent and must be discovered case by case. If the resolution of a particular case is disputed, the different religions provide different, and perhaps conflicting, procedures for settling the dispute (for example, appeal to different holy books). Particular cases will have to be discussed in terms more or less independent of religion (though, in general at least, in a way consistent with what the various religions teach). So, in a society like ours, religious vocabulary is inherently divisive.

If we cannot depend on a common religious tradition for common standards of conduct, what can we depend on? For most of this century at least, I think the dominant answer was: law. By "law," I mean centralized decision making, especially decision by government, a command backed by force rather than an appeal to faith or reason. Whether the great contest of the twentieth century was between communism, fascism, and democracy, or between dictatorship and freedom, it was largely a contest for control of centralized power. For most of the twentieth century, the law's ability to regulate most conduct was not in dispute. Centralized decision seemed to provide the common standard society needed. So, for example, the New Deal was so successful an experiment in central planning that it was still offered as a model well into the 1970s.

Yet, today, we doubt the law's ability to govern well very much of life. We try to decentralize decisions we once tried to centralize. We substitute "the market" for central planning. We "deregulate," "privatize," and "contract out."

Though this tendency is more obvious in government, it is not limited to government. The last two decades have also seen something similar in private business. Large corporations have been contracting out many services formerly performed "in house." They have decentralized much decision making, treating units almost as separate companies, assigning profit targets but leaving most matters to the discretion of the unit's management. The management pyramid is being "flattened out." Even management style seems to be changing. Commanding subordinates is out, "reasoning together" and "facilitating" are in.

I should perhaps point out that this decentralizing tendency is not peculiarly American. Thatcher's England also experimented with deregulation, privatization, and contracting out. The Russians and Eastern Europeans seem to be embarked on a similar undertaking – as were the Chinese until the events of May and June 1989. Even some countries in Latin America, Africa, and Asia have begun to "decontrol" their economies. Only Japan and the most prosperous states of Western Europe seem to be holding back.

Much of the world seems to have decided that law can usefully provide only limited guidance in a large and diverse society. Beyond those limits, law can be quite inefficient, burdening central agencies with more information than they can use, forcing individuals to ignore important information they have, and dissipating the energy of many people in bureaucracy's sterile dance. Why much of the world has lost faith in the ability of law alone to provide common standards of conduct, I shall not inquire. Perhaps the explanation is simply that we have learned something from the experiments of this century. Or perhaps our society has become too complex for much to be decided centrally any longer.

Whatever the explanation, we seem to have entered a period when more will be left to the voluntary decision of individuals. We must find means other than law by which to organize our common life. We might state the problem in this way: *How can large numbers of people without strict regulation by law, without personal knowledge of one another, and without a common religious tradition coordinate conduct in the complex ways necessary to make life in this society good or, at least, bearable?*

"The market" is today the most popular answer. A market allows individuals to coordinate their conduct by contract. Ideally, each contract maximizes the advantage of the parties while leaving everyone else as free as before. Ideally, everyone benefits from the incentive that each person has to make as much as he can.

Unfortunately, the reality of the market is less appealing than the ideal. Experiments in centralization like the New Deal were in large part responses to major market failures like the Great Depression. Much of today's most burdensome regulations – those governing pollution, land use, safety, food, and drugs – also owe their existence in part at least to market failure. Markets do not automatically exclude force and fraud. They have difficulty protecting economic interests that lack sufficient cash, non-economic interests generally, and any interest of third-parties. Markets work well only within an environment of restraint protecting the less well informed, the relatively powerless, and third parties. For most of this century, the law provided most of that restraint. The problem now is finding alternatives to law.

Ethics is such an alternative. The ethics boom consists of a variety of institutions likely to generate common standards by a highly decentralized process. Ethics centers, ethics journals, ethics courses, and ethics training provide ways to think through particular problems and develop particular standards of conduct resolving them. The same institutions provide a way of helping "society" adopt the proposed standards without central decision. The very discussions by which a particular profession, corporation, or other social group comes to agree on a standard of conduct is a means of turning the standard into a social practice. So, for example, insofar as discussing pollution helps me to see that we will all be better off if we all stop polluting, I will be less inclined to pollute than before. And insofar as I see others showing the necessary restraint, I will tend to do the same.

Philosophers have been important in the ethics boom because they have traditionally specialized in arguments that appeal to rational persons as such rather than, like ministers, in arguments that appeal to those who share a common religious tradition or, like government officials, in other means of getting people to do as they should. Philosophers represent an organizing power relatively neglected until recently, the power of secular reason.

Ethics doubtless has disadvantages as a means of social organization (most of which won't be clear until we have had more experience with it). For our purposes, however, what is important is the way ethics, whatever its disadvantages, avoids the disadvantages of law. Ethical standards are not, like law, imposed. They must be worked out by those to whom they are to apply. They must appeal to the reason of those to whom they apply, usually by benefiting them or those they care about. Responsibility for obtaining obedience does not, as in law, fall primarily upon functionaries but instead upon the individuals directly concerned. The conscience of each individual is the primary source of control. Supporting conscience are all those informal pressures basically honest people can bring to bear on one another when they share a common enterprise. Since all those subject to an ethical standard necessarily have an interest in maintaining it (even when they also have an interest in getting around it themselves), there is little need for the complex machinery of central control.[39]

Conclusion: an aside on the "ethics" in "ethics boom"

Philosophers have traditionally used "ethics" in one of three senses. In the first, "ethics" is a synonym for "morals" or "morality" (as in expressions like "the decline of American ethics"). In the second sense, "ethics" refers to the critical study of morals ("the science of morals") or to a particular philosopher's systematic views on morals or moral theory (as in "an expert on Kant's ethics"). In the third sense, it refers to that study of morals concerned with aspiration (should's rather than shall's). The "ethics" in "ethics boom" fits none of these three uses. The ethics boom is not a "morals boom" (whatever that would be). Nor is it a boom in the study of morality as such, that is, a boom in the study of those general standards of conduct that would have been the natural subject of the nineteenth century's course in "moral philosophy" or a contemporary course in "ethical theory." The ethics boom is primarily a boom in "professional ethics" and other forms of "applied" (or "practical") ethics. Though the boom does aspire to raise standards of conduct, the effort generally takes the form of mandatory rules (shall's rather than should's).

Professional ethics are standards that apply to members of a profession because of that membership, standards they must work out for themselves. A profession's ethics do not govern everyone. They vary from one profession to another. They do not necessarily cross a national border unless the profession's organization crosses too. The "professional" in "professional ethics" means that the ethics referred to cannot be ordinary morality (though it must be consistent with it).[40] Ordinary morality applies equally to all moral agents. Since "professional morality" seems to be a term without a use, "professional ethics" also cannot refer to the study of professional morality. "Professional ethics" seems to use "ethics" in a fourth sense.

The same is true of "applied ethics." If "ethics" were simply a synonym for "morality," then "applied ethics" should mean the same as "applied morality" – a term which, if it had a use, would, it seems, simply refer to ordinary morality or putting one's beliefs about morality into practice. But that is not what "applied ethics" refers to. Applied ethics is the *study* of a range of social issues like abortion, war, euthanasia, pollution, and so on. But, unlike ethics in the second traditional sense, it is not merely the study of how ordinary morality resolves such issues or even the study of how particular moral theories (the ethics of particular philosophers or schools) resolve them. Applied ethics actually tries to work out special standards even when ordinary morality or moral theory leaves an issue unresolved. That is obvious for *professional* ethics, since professional ethics typically consists of special standards embodied in a formal code. But it is true as well for the evolving standards governing an ordinary social issue like abortion or pollution. Such issues are not necessarily settled by ordinary morality or moral theory. They may yield only to agreement on a new standard.

We need to recognize this fourth sense of "ethics" quite explicitly, since the very terms we use to describe the ethics boom require it.[41] Since this fourth sense of "ethics" is at most two centuries old, and not widely used until this century, even the terms characteristic of the ethics boom testify to its relative novelty.[42] The ethics boom seems to be a new response to new circumstances. We must now consider in more detail the university's place in that response.

2

ACADEMIC FREEDOM, ACADEMIC ETHICS, AND PROFESSORIAL ETHICS

Academic ethics may be thought of either as a form of institutional ethics (on analogy with business ethics) or as a form of professional ethics (on analogy with legal ethics). The form in which we cast academic ethics has significant substantive consequences. Appreciating the difference between the two forms will also prevent a good deal of confusion. So, we must begin with that distinction. We may best approach that distinction, as so often in practical ethics, by examining some cases recognized as "hard." Here are two cases I hope you'll find as hard as I do:

Case One: Professor A publishes several articles in newspapers and popular magazines arguing that the average black is significantly less intelligent than the average white and that therefore affirmative action is mistaken in its fundamental assumption of racial equality. Professor A's purpose is to refute what he believes to be fallacious reasoning. While his own reasoning puts great weight on IQ tests as a measure of intelligence, A is a philosopher with no special knowledge of intelligence testing. Those with such knowledge describe his views as "academic dishonesty" because (they say) research long ago discredited any link between race and intelligence. Most black students, a substantial part of the student body, refuse to take his classes when given the choice. Organizations inside and outside the university demand that he be fired. While the few black students who have taken a course from him say that he treated them fairly and never discussed race, they add that they none the less felt uncomfortable in class just knowing what he thought. His department responds by assigning him to teach only courses students are not required to take.[1]

Case Two. Professor B turns to the lone black student in class and says, "We have a nigger student here." Professor B does this to help students understand the power of racist language to harm even when no harm is intended. Though this purpose is appropriate to the course (Business Ethics), the black student takes offense and later demands that Professor B be disciplined. "I couldn't move," she recalls, "I wanted to run but was afraid I didn't have the strength to make it to the door."[2]

These cases differ in some ways. For example, in the first, the objection is to what the professor thinks, as indicated by his participation in debate outside the institution; in the second, to what he did in class, not at all to what he thinks. Yet, what concerns me here is something these cases share.

One feature they share is the newsworthiness of their subject, racial harassment. Racial harassment on campus (even more than sexual harassment) makes news today. I don't know whether that is because such harassment is increasing, because the victims no longer fear to speak up, because our conception of what counts as harassment has changed, or because of some combination of these or other factors. But, for my purpose, it does not matter. Nothing I say will require that these cases concern racial harassment or any particular explanation of the current newsworthiness of that subject. All I require is that these two cases be hard to resolve to everyone's satisfaction; indeed, and more to the point, that they be hard to resolve to anyone's satisfaction. If they are hard to resolve, they are so because they pull us in opposite directions.

We can, for example, readily understand why Professor A's department relieved him of responsibility for required courses. We may even judge that action as, all things considered, worthy of Solomon. And we – or, at least, those of us who have ourselves faced prejudice – can also understand why black students would feel uncomfortable sitting in Professor A's class knowing what he thinks of their race. ("How can he treat us fairly?") Yet, the professor in many of us is also likely to think that both the department and the black students may have lost more than they gained. The skills black students could develop confronting Professor A would almost certainly prove useful later; and Professor A might learn something too. From this perspective, it is unfortunate that Professor A does not discuss his views on race in class.

Something similar is true of our second case. Professor B probably could not have made his point as effectively had he used a word less charged with history. His purpose was the wholly proper one of bringing home a significant fact. He seems to have succeeded. His student's pain provides a measure of his success in that. So, from this perspective, he seems to have been doing exactly what a professor should do. And, yet we can also understand the altogether human reaction of the black student. By some standard we all recognize, Professor B seems to have gone too far. Discipline may not be the right response to what Professor B did, but praise of Professor B's technique, or even indifference, does not seem right either.

That is enough about our cases for now. We can, I hope, agree that they are hard cases. But hard cases of what? They might, for example, be hard cases all things considered. That would do us no good. They must be hard cases for academic ethics, for that is now our subject. Are they hard cases of that? That depends on what we mean by "academic ethics." What do we mean? The answer is not self-evident. The term seems to have gained currency only recently. Like any new coinage, it is likely to cause confusion even if its value is clearly stamped upon its face. So, to avoid confusion, let me explain what I mean by "academic ethics."

Academic ethics, professional ethics, and morality

The professorate is commonly thought to be a profession, as old and honored as law, medicine, or the clergy. Until recently, however, the professorate has differed from the first two of these, law and medicine, in at least one significant way. Lawyers and physicians have generally not been employees of large organizations. They have been independent contractors, each with many clients or patients. They have formed "liberal" or "free" professions. The professorate, in contrast, is the other kind, what we might call an "employed" or "institutionalized" profession. Professors have worked in institutions since certain teachers first carried the title. Professors are either part of a faculty or not professors at all. The single teacher sitting at one end of a log, with a single learner at the other, is a private tutor, not a member of the professorate. Kant was a professor; Hume was not.

Any discussion of the ethics of the professorate is, then, necessarily connected with a wider subject, what (for lack of a better name) we now call "academic ethics," "academic" being the adjectival form of "academe," "academia," or (as I prefer) "the academy." What is the academy? We may distinguish two related senses of the term.

In one sense, the academy is the set of all American institutions employing professors of whatever rank. The academy includes colleges, universities, certain technical institutes, and perhaps a few institutions with "academy" in their name, for example, the United States Military Academy at West Point. The academy does not, however, include trade schools like the Academy of Allied Health Careers (in Chicago) or secondary schools like Phillip's Academy (in Andover). "Academy" in this sense serves to distinguish professors from other teachers. Not all teachers are academics.

In another sense, however, "academy" refers to an enterprise in which professors are only a part. The academy then includes students, administrators, researchers, and some other of the enterprise's auxiliaries – but not all. For example, I don't think an engineer in charge of the heating plant is part of the academy, though she works for it and is important to its operation. Employment by the academy is not sufficient for membership. Indeed, even employment combined with higher education is not. The heating plant's engineer could hold an advanced degree. She would still not be an academic, only a member of the "university community," that suburb of the academy beyond which lies an ill-defined province, "the community," that the academy is supposed to serve.

The academy exists within corporations, each governed by a board of regents, trustees, or the like. These "lay boards" seem to lie at the border between the university community and the community the university serves. They are outside the academy.

The academy, in either sense, necessarily differs from the professorate in inclusiveness. Besides professors, the academy includes students, administrators, and so on. That, however, is not the only way the academy differs from the professorate. The academy is an institution, that is, an organization with determinate locations. For example, one part of the academy, IIT, has several addresses in Chicago. The professorate is not like that. While IIT's professors teach or do research at determinate locations, both in Chicago and elsewhere, IIT's faculty cannot be said to be located even at the sum of those locations. The faculty is wherever its members happen to be – or, perhaps, nowhere in particular. Like the republic of letters (and other professions), the professorate is, in this sense, "invisible." The academy is not.

So, while the ethics of the professorate is a species of

professional ethics, academic ethics must be a species of something else, what we might call "institutional ethics." In this respect, academic ethics stands in much the same relation to professional ethics as business ethics does. It is a different subject. We must, then, explain the connection between the ethics of the professorate, a kind of professional ethics, and academic ethics, a kind of institutional ethics. Let's begin by considering what the relation is between ethics and professions.

Ethics – as used here – refers to those special standards of conduct governing members of a group simply because they are moral agents belonging to that group. Ethics is a "special morality." Hopi ethics applies only to the Hopi; religious ethics, only to the religious; and business ethics, only to those in business.

Professional ethics is a species of ethics (in this sense). A profession's ethics consists of those standards of conduct governing participation in a certain cooperative practice. A profession's ethics is morally binding insofar as most members of the profession do their part and each voluntarily shares in the benefits of the (morally permissible) practice defining the profession. Those who voluntarily take the benefits of a cooperative practice while failing to do their share cheat other participants of benefits they would otherwise receive. That is morally wrong, a violation of the principle of fairness. Professional ethics is a part of morality because professional obligations are ultimately moral obligations, but distinct from ordinary morality insofar as professional obligations presuppose a specific (and local) practice.

Though professional ethics is a part of morality, it does not stand in any interesting *deductive* relation to the rest of morality. The connection between the rest of morality and professional ethics is no closer than that between the moral rule "Keep your promises" and the content of a particular morally-permissible promise. A profession's ethics are the continuously unfolding conclusions of a more or less conscious discussion of how "we" (the members of the profession) should work together to achieve the good we jointly aim at. It is the product of a "social contract" of sorts, the parties to which are all those sharing a common profession. So, while the ethics of the professorate might resemble the ethics of, say, administrators – or, indeed, even those of nurses or lawyers – the resemblance, while not precisely coincidental, must be contingent. It must result from the congruence of choices different groups have made, each for its own reasons.

Each profession is defined, in part, by the moral ideal it seeks to serve (public service, for example). Each serves such an ideal insofar as what it aims at (and achieves) is more than what morality, law, and market require. The ideal is moral insofar as those to be served are not the members of the profession itself. An organization that does not aim at a moral ideal is (by definition) a business, trade association, social club, or other organization of self-interest, not a profession, however much good it in fact does.

So, for example, lawyers form a profession. They claim to aim at justice for all under law, are organized more or less accordingly, and seem to have had some success. They have done more than morality, law, and market require. The market merely requires them to take enough paying clients to make a living. The law requires only that they provide legal help under certain special circumstance (that is, when a judge orders it). Morality requires only that, in addition, they sell legal help the way an honest grocer sells cheese; it does not require lawyers to organize to serve legal justice.

Few lawyers are public servants, that is, government employees. Most serve private clients under arrangements privately made. Yet, insofar as what each lawyer does satisfies a common standard designed to contribute to justice for all under law (beyond what morality, law, and market require), each has part in a public service. Each contributes a share to achieving a moral ideal.[3]

Though each profession is defined (in part) by the moral ideal it serves, professions as such are defined (in part) as a way to make a living. A profession is an occupation, not a hobby. Though professionals should love their work, there can be no profession of amateurs. An organization that does not serve a moral ideal in a way calculated to earn its members a living is not a profession but a charity, government, or other organization of public service. So, students, however public spirited, cannot form a profession. They must first become practitioners of a paying art.

We already had one reason to distinguish academic ethics from professional ethics – the academy is an institution and institutions are not professions. That reason may have seemed so slight as to be Pickwickian. We now have two more substantial reasons. First, a profession is an organization of professionals. So, insofar as students are more than honorary members, any organization of academics including students cannot be a profession. Second, an organization cannot be a profession unless its chief purpose is to benefit nonmembers. While the purpose of the academy remains to be worked out, this much seems safe: Whatever else we think it should be, the academy must be an educational institution. Without students, there could be no professors, only researchers in a think-tank. Education seems to aim at benefiting those being educated, whoever else may benefit in consequence or beside. So, insofar as the academy seeks to benefit its students, and they are not merely honorary members, the academy cannot be a profession.

What I have said about professions so far is true more or less by definition. What I shall now say, though a contingent truth (if true at all), is equally important: Professions need to take seriously the welfare of their members. A profession that does not may soon have too few members to do much good. Think, for example, of the Catholic clergy today, the absolute number sharply down even though the number of practicing Catholics is up. Too few potential priests find the required celibacy compatible with a decent life.

We must, however, take care not to understand the welfare of professionals too narrowly, that is, as merely selfish, self-centered, or otherwise largely independent of the welfare of those they serve. For most teachers, for example, their welfare is bound up with that of their students. A student's success helps make the teacher's life worth living. While the moral ideal a profession serves and the good of each professional are necessarily in tension, they are not necessarily in conflict.

Virtually all professions have a written code of ethics. Indeed, for most professions, the writing of such a code was part of becoming a profession. Why this connection between professions and codes of ethics? The answer, I think, is to be found in the tension between the definitional requirement of a moral ideal and the practical requirement that professionals do reasonably well for themselves. There is no natural resolution of that tension, no unique point at which all considerations balance. There may be many points of balance, each justifiable for somewhat different reasons (and all consistent with ordinary morality). A profession must choose. For this reason, organizing a profession requires formulating conventions of cooperation. These conventions can be quite vague, mere slogans, or quite detailed. They will, however, always include special standards of conduct each member wants every other member to follow even if their following them means she must do the same. These standard are the profession's code of ethics.

Professions are, or at least should be, interpretative communities.[4] That is, members should try to understand their profession as a coherent undertaking aimed at a good every member wants to achieve, an undertaking guided by standards of conduct each can endorse because they serve that good in the best way possible. While recognizing that their standards are open to widely different read-ings, members of a profession should suppose that there is (generally) a best reading and that the profession itself determines which that is. "Lay people" may participate in the discussions, but their participation, however valuable, is contingent and merely advi-sory.

Lawyers form an interpretative community. They have, for example, long debated among themselves whether the ideal they aim at, "justice under law for all," is mere legal justice (what the law happens to give) or justice more broadly understood (what the law should give).

Professions are, however, more than interpretative communities – they are legislative communities. Not only can they reinterpret their standard of conduct; they can also rewrite it. Even their ultimate purpose, the moral ideal they aim at, is subject to change. For example, physicians now seem to be giving up the preservation of life as an end for their profession for some combination of protecting the healthy from disease, curing the sick, and comforting the dying.

I say "seem" only because some doctors claim this is "really" what they meant all along, only now technology has forced them to be more explicit. Perhaps they are right. The distinction between reinterpreting a standard and rewriting it is sometimes hard to draw in practice. Nonetheless, it is a distinction worth keeping in mind. Most interpretative communities, including professions, are free to break with the past by legislation should interpretation lead to an impasse.

Those professions that are interpretative communities develop an ethics literature (or, at least, an ethics lore), that is to say, a body of interpretations together with supporting reasons and alternatives rejected. Many professions, especially law and medicine, now have such a literature; the professorate does not. Why? Have we just been too busy doing professional ethics for others? Or is there something about our profession discouraging discussion of its ethics? Does a rich literature require a crisis in the profession which, happily, the professorate has not yet suffered?[5] These are questions I hope histo-rians and social scientists will investigate. The few hypotheses I shall offer below I offer only as a way of trying to understand academic ethics.

Most of what I have said about professional ethics would be true of institutional ethics as well. Like professions, institutions can be organized to provide a public service, can adopt special standards of conduct, and can become an interpretative community. Indeed, for any institution that, like a hospital, is dominated by a particular profession, the line between the ethics of the profession and the ethics of the institution may be so blurred as to be almost useless. In practice, for example, "medical ethics" now seems to be primarily concerned with what doctors, nurses, and other health-care workers do in hospitals. As medicine moved into the hospital, the professional ethics of yesterday's doctors became the institutional ethics of today's health-care workers.

The analogy with academic ethics, though suggestive, is far from perfect. Academic ethics is, of course, necessarily institutional while medical ethics is not. More troubling, the clientele of the two institutions differ in a morally important way. Those the hospital seeks to benefit inside, its patients, are conceived primarily as, well, patients, people too passive to have obligations. Most patients stay only a few busy days; those staying much longer are seldom in condition to take much part in hospital affairs. Medical ethics is therefore primarily about the rights of patients and the responsibilities of health-care workers.

Those the academy tries to benefit inside, primarily students, are not like that. Students have the numbers, energy, and skills to do the enterprise great good or harm; and they have the time to do it. Their cooperation, both active and intelligent, is essential to the enterprise. Students are also full-fledged moral agents, capable of taking on responsibilities. So, students cannot safely or justly be treated as mere honorary academics. Any code of academic ethics must address them as partners in the enterprise (though, of course, partners with distinct powers, vulnerabilities, and purposes).

If students are to be partners in the academic enterprise, they must have sufficient reason to cooperate in the way partners do. They will probably not have that unless, like other partners, they participate in defining the enterprise. Students, then, should join both in formulating any code of academic ethics and in interpreting it (even though such participation – as partners – would make no sense for the professorate's code of ethics). Insofar as students participate in formulating and interpreting a code of academic ethics, academic ethics may differ from professional ethics in ways hospital ethics could not differ from medical ethics. (Is this an argument for or against doing academic ethics rather than professorial ethics?)

Though the academy, like the hospital, may also seek to benefit people outside ("the community"), the participation of such outsiders in the shaping of the academy's ethics is necessarily unlike that of academics. There are at least three reasons. First, since outsiders do not live the academic life, they generally lack the knowledge of that life academics generally have. Second, outsiders do not have the stake academics necessarily have. They do not have to live under the code of academic ethics (though they may have to live with some of its consequences). And third, outsiders lack the commitments academics necessarily have. Outsiders have not joined their career to that of the academy. First-year students, knowing little of what the academy offers, have still committed a part of their life to the academy. Even a recent graduate, now "out in the world," can no longer claim that. Graduates are no longer academics and will never be again, unless they seek another degree, or join the faculty or administration. They have cashed in their stake.

Academic ethics: the literatures and its substitutes

I earlier noted two uses of "academic," one distinguishing the place professors teach from the places non-academics teach, the other recognizing that professors are partners in an enterprise in which some partners are non-professors. Whichever use of academic one prefers, the fact remains that instead of a literature of academic ethics, we have two substitutes.

One is a "literature" of homily, that is, of denunciation and exhortation, to which Steven Cahn's *Saints and Scamps* is a recent addition.[6] Characteristic of this "literature" is the division of the academy into good guys and bad guys, saints and scamps. The good guys are praised, the bad guys condemned. The unstated assumption is that choices between right and wrong are easy in the academy – if only one has the moral courage to do what is right. Virtually absent is any sense of moral perplexity. The homily leaves little room for honest disagreement among rational people. The academy is understood as a machine in need of repair rather than as an interpretative community.

The other substitute for an ethics literature is the literature of freedom. It has two branches. One is a literature of civil freedom (that is, of civil liberties and civil rights). Some of this literature is philosophical, with Mill's *On Liberty* the dominant influence. The rest is legal. In the United States, the Supreme Court is the dominant influence.[7] The assumption of this literature is that the academy is continuous with the rest of society, not a distinct interpretative community. Ordinary principles of civil freedom apply to the academy more or less as they do to society as a whole. That assumption obscures the possibility of a distinct academic ethics.

The other branch of the literature of freedom does distinguish between the academy and the larger society. Indeed, it explicitly rests on the assumption that the academy has a special function, purpose, or nature, making it a place unlike any other, and that the academic therefore has (or, at least, should have) special rights. Edward Shils' recent *The Academic Ethic* is a strong but orthodox addition to this literature.[8]

The literature of academic freedom, the second literature of freedom distinguished here, is certainly an advance over the "literature" of homily. Disagreement is generally not treated as evidence of corruption. There is a recognition that certain questions require careful analysis. Particular standards of conduct are not only explicitly stated, they are often also defended with considerable subtlety. Even underlying claims about the function, purpose, or nature of the academy are open to reinterpretation. Later writers build on earlier work.

Though an advance over the "literature" of homily, the literature of academic freedom still discourages a genuine literature of academic ethics. In this respect, it resembles the literature of civil freedom. It differs only in the way that it discourages. The literature of academic freedom assumes that the function, purpose, or nature of the academy is, or at least should be, uncontroversial. The academy is not thought of as an institution defined – and redefined – through its own deliberations. Instead, it is thought of as a Platonic form the function, purpose, or nature of which can be discovered once and for all. Anyone can bring the academy into the world simply by following a set plan. Consider, for example, Shils' brief history of "the academic ethic":

> [Its] origins [were] in the time when there were no universities, but only learned men seeking reliable and fundamental knowledge. It goes far back into the long period before the formation of modern science. It was practiced by devoted university teachers and by scientists long before it began to appear in very rudimentary formulations in connection with the reform of the German universities in the first decade of the nineteenth century. Even at the height of the

glory of the German universities,…the promulgation of an academic ethic was not taken in hand.[9]

We are so used to this second literature of freedom that it is easy to overlook how controversial it should be. Let me then briefly point out some of what should be controversial. Much of what Shils lays out in several chapters is nicely summarized in the first paragraph of the 1966 "Statement on Professional Ethics" of the American Association of University Professors (AAUP). That paragraph concerns scholarship:

> The professor, guided by a deep conviction of the worth and dignity of the advancement of knowledge, recognizes the special responsibilities placed upon him. His primary responsibility to his subject is to seek and to state the truth as he sees it. To this end he devotes his energies to developing and improving his scholarly competence. He accepts the obligation to exercise critical self-discipline and judgment in using, extending, and transmitting knowledge. He practices intellectual honesty. Although he may follow subsidiary interests, these interests must never seriously hamper or compromise his freedom of inquiry.[10]

As a philosopher, I have no difficulty accepting this characterization of what I should be doing (subject, of course, to a liberal reading of "knowledge" and to ordinary moral constraints). I imagine few scientists, mathematicians, or other scholars would have much more difficulty. Their respective disciplines, like mine, belong to the tradition of Plato and Aristotle. They too think of their work as seeking to learn the truth, to state what they learn, and to make those statements available to anyone who cares. This tradition is, however, not the only one harbored under the roof of the American academy. Almost every college and university in the United States has at its center the "arts" as well as the "sciences." The arts always include expositive writing, public speaking, and foreign languages, and may include as well acting, painting, physical education, dance, and the like. The departments teaching the arts may, of course, have a majority of scholars – editors of literary works, historians of painting, and so on. But such departments commonly include many whose work is not "merely academic," for example, poets, novelists, actors, musicians, weavers, or speech therapists. These are practitioners, not scholars (though all are teachers in an institution of higher learning).

Practitioners as such are committed to doing rather than knowing. They are not simply committed to knowing-how rather than knowing-that. Their knowing how is itself only a means to doing. Rather than state their discoveries, they perform them. For them, beauty, delight, utility, or service have the place truth has for a scientist, mathematician, philosopher, or other scholar.

Outside its center (the college of arts and sciences), the academy has many more practitioners – in schools of business, architecture, education, nursing, and so on. Of course, even professional schools do research. But they have not always done that and, even now, their research may not combine easily with the professional education that is their chief mission. Some professions, like architecture, still rely heavily on adjunct professors to teach courses. For such professions, professional education is openly practical. Other professions, especially law and engineering, often have faculties most of the members of which have little experience outside the academy. Such professions must either leave practical training to "the world" (as engineering generally does) or bring the world into the academy through clinics (as law has recently been trying to do). If a profession adopts the clinical approach, it must find a way to evaluate professors whose work is clinical rather than scholarly.

Not only can the AAUP's "Statement on Professional Ethics" not help in guiding such evaluations, it positively hurts. Among it implication is that a clinician who puts the welfare of a client ahead of seeking and stating the truth may be unethical. The academy is treated as a place in which the pursuit of knowledge takes precedence over other professional commitments and perhaps even over ordinary human decency. For an academic, the welfare of a client is (the AAUP statement implies) an interest subsidiary to freedom of inquiry.

I doubt that anyone in the AAUP intended that implication. The implication is none the less there, suggesting that we should long ago have begun to think more carefully about what the academy is or should be. Why assume, as the AAUP seems to have for its whole history, that the primary responsibility of a *professor* is to seek the truth and state it?

That assumption may be, as Shils' work suggests, the consequence of the American academy taking over the German model of the university without realizing how different an institution its American cognate was. But that seems unlikely. The two institutions differed too much for that. German universities did not sponsor sports teams, own dormitories, or provide counseling. They did not teach exposition, agriculture, engineering, or the fine arts. Instead, they graduated scholars and produced scholarly work of such quality and on such a scale that Americans a century ago could only describe the German university with a mixture of awe and envy.

What then explains our taking over the German model (and the equation of the academy with scholarship)? The answer is obvious: American academics saw how the German model differed from the American and liked what they saw. From late in the nineteenth century until quite recently, we have been trying to make the American university into the German. So, for example, under John Maynard Hutchins, the University of Chicago won the praise of many academics by abolishing intercollegiate sports. American academics wanted a new institution, the academy, to replace the old college of liberal arts (with its collaterals, the normal school, the polytechnic, the conservatory, and the like free-standing schools for training in practical arts). Why?

The liberal arts college was – as noted in Chapter 1 – an institution for which character, not knowledge, was the primary object. With that single object pursued through a single course of study (originally without electives), the liberal arts college was more like a professional school than today's college of arts and sciences – even though it made no pretense of preparing its graduates to make a living. Given the choice between this older tradition of higher education and the German, most of us would, I think, still choose the German, however inadequate we may find it in detail.[11]

That may seem enough to explain the attraction of the German model, but there is more. The German model came with a work-out theory of academic freedom. The liberal arts college did not. Indeed, its purpose and program made the old liberal arts college positively hostile to academic freedom. The single course of study required a coordination among teachers that worked powerfully against freedom to teach. The emphasis on building character made scholarship of any sort seem peripheral. In the classroom, the teacher carried out a well-defined mission; outside, they were bound to do nothing to undo what they had done in class. The teacher had no more right to a private life than did a member of the clergy. Indeed, throughout most of the nineteenth century, the most common preparation for college teaching in the United States was a degree in divinity. The professorate was virtually an arm of the clergy.

The old liberal arts college would, of course, have been just as unfriendly to artistic as to scholarly freedom. But, at the beginning of the century, there were not, it seems, many poets, composers, or other artists in the academy. They seem to have begun arriving in large numbers only after the Second World War, that is, after the first great battles for academic freedom had been won. They arrived after the German model had proved itself. They then had no alternative but to try to accommodate to it and, being reasonably well treated thereafter, little reason to look for alternatives.

The German model is, however, not without disadvantages. Its origin in a relatively closed society and centralized state shows in the limited freedom it grants academics. Its defense of academic freedom is that the academy can only be useful if academics are free to study their subject and teach what they learn: Restrict academic freedom and society will not get the scientific knowledge and educated functionaries it wants. Because of its origin, the German conception of academic freedom does not fit well with a principled defense of speech which, like Professor A's, is outside his subject. Civil freedom does.

That disadvantage would not concern us now, were it not related to one that does. Because it treats academic freedom as a privilege that society grants, the German model must either suppose no special academic ethics whatever or find a specifically academic ethics in society's grant. Society must decide what is due from academics just as it decides what is due to them. Society is the sole rule-maker and the ultimate interpreter of its own rules. The academy cannot be a distinct interpretative community, even if it is a distinct community of rights. The academy can only advise society on how society should interpret its own rules. Understood this way, the literature of academic freedom can no more disengage from social philosophy or constitutional jurisprudence than the literature of civil freedom can.

Academics occasionally note the absence of a significant literature explicitly discussing academic ethics. They generally respond by trying to explain that absence away. The principles of academic freedom are, they say, *implicitly* principles of responsibility as well. The academy really has an ethics literature, but one written in terms of freedom rather than obligation.

That explanation is not entirely wrong. The freedom of each academic is possible only if academics generally observe certain standards of conduct. So, all else equal, each should respect the academic freedom of every other academic because each voluntarily benefits from the others doing the same. Academic freedom does imply something like ethical standards. But there is more to academic ethics than that. What? We must return to the two cases with which we begin.

The two cases revisited

Traditional principles of academic freedom are quite capable of resolving our two cases. The cases are not hard from that perspective. Academic freedom includes a right of professors to teach and publish what they know about their subject, not a right to publish anything, however incompetent. Professor A did not publish in a field in which he was expert. He was outside his subject. Those who were expert judged his work incompetent. The publications in question were, then, not academic. If some non-academic activity interferes substantially with a professor's ability to do his academic job, he has two professionally proper options: to give up the non-academic activity, or to give up the job. He has no right to do his job badly. So, the only hard question for Professor A's institution is whether the discomfort of black students impedes his teaching enough to justify dismissing him. The answer seems to be no – or, at least, no while his colleagues are willing to pick up the required courses he would otherwise be teaching.

Professor B's case is even easier. The principles of academic freedom tell us that, while he may have made a pedagogical mistake, alienating one of his students, he made it honorably, that is to say, seeking to teach what he was supposed to teach.[12] If teachers are not free to make such mistakes, they will take fewer risks and teaching will be impoverished. That is just the evil academic freedom is supposed to fend off.

If these two cases seem harder than that, the reason is not, I think, that I have misinterpreted traditional principles of academic freedom. Of the many universities that have recently had cases of racial harassment, a few have adopted a formal policy in response. These draw the line between permitted and forbidden conduct about where I suggested the traditional principles of academic freedom do.

Consider, for example, the policy the University of Wisconsin-Milwaukee adopted in 1990. It forbids:

> (1) Intentional conduct, either verbal or physical, by any member of the faculty, staff, or student body, which (2) occurs on property under the jurisdiction of the Regents or where an affiliation with UWM is significant in the occurrence; and (3) is predicated on considerations of any of the following: race, color, national origin, creed, ancestry, sex, sexual orientation, age, religion, disability, or other status protected under law; and (4) which has the purpose and effect of adversely affecting any aspect or condition of any individual's education, employment, housing, or participation in a university activity.[13]

What is the consequence of applying this policy to our two wild professors? The conduct must have as its "purpose and effect" adversely affecting an individual's education, (university) employment, or the like. Neither of our professors had such a purpose. The discomfort Professor A caused in class was not intentional at all; and even his conduct off campus was intended to refute what he believed a fallacious argument, not to affect any student adversely. Professor B actually intended to benefit all the students, including the one he offended, by bringing home what he believed an important truth.

This may seem a strained reading of relatively vague language. I don't think it is. The policy includes a section on "Protected Expressive Behavior." The following is the only provision relevant here:

> If an instructor claims that expressive behavior constituted an opinion or statement germane to the subject matter of the course in which the behavior occurred, the behavior shall not be a basis for disciplinary action unless an authorized hearing body finds the instructor's claim clearly unreasonable.[14]

While the policy seems not to have contemplated the problem posed by Professor A, it explicitly protects Professor B. His words were, it seems, germane enough to meet any reasonable standard of reasonableness.

This resolution of the two cases protects academic freedom, but at some cost. The principles invoked are silent concerning ordinary morality, the non-academic interests of students, and any interest academics may hold in common except using, extending, and transmitting knowledge. In this respect, the principles seem open to the taunt Shaw directed at vivisectionists in *The Doctor's Dilemma*:

> No man is allowed to put his mother into the stove because he desires to know how long an adult woman will survive at a temperature of 500 Fahrenheit, no matter how important or interesting that particular addition to the store of human knowledge may be.[15]

Anyone giving the matter a moment's thought would, I hope, admit that academic freedom can only be one factor in judging the conduct of our two wild professor, and only one factor too in determining how we (and they) should respond to what they did (and others may do). That admission opens the way for an academic ethics that is more than academic freedom in different words. Whatever their purpose and context, both Professors A and B caused harm. Professor A made his black students uncomfortable. Professor B subjected a black student to verbal attack. Such harms require some response for reasons having nothing to do with academic freedom.

This last claim may seem an appeal to ordinary morality rather than any specific academic ethics. It is not – even though an appeal to ordinary morality is always in place (academics always being moral agents subject to ordinary morality whatever additional responsibilities they have). The appeal is, instead, to interests internal to the academy as it is, though not to the academy as it must be; to interests of academics as particular human beings voluntarily committed to a common venture, not to their interests as abstractions capable of existing nowhere else; to historical persons who must continually work out the terms of their cooperation, not to subjects of a timeless ideal. Searchers after knowledge, whether professors or students, are, as such, not sensitive in the way the black students in our two cases were. Searchers after knowledge have no history and care only for knowledge. But ordinary human beings, even academics, are not like that. They can therefore be harmed in ways mere searchers after knowledge cannot. What the academy lacks is a recognized way to talk about its standards of conduct in such terms, a distinct "forum" or "discourse" for that. That is what the literature of academic ethics would be.

Conclusion: the next step

Academic ethics is, then, best understood as concerned with how academics – professors, students, and others – should conduct their common institutional life. Academic freedom, though a relevant consideration, need not be the only relevant one, the one that pre-empts all others, or even the weightiest. The responsibility of academics may require a restriction of what they do for considerations that *dis*serve knowledge. Whether their responsibility is in fact ever inconsistent with serving knowledge is another question, one ultimately to be decided by the academy itself. The academy must deliberate. Philosophy can contribute to the deliberations by formulating and analyzing arguments – which is what I shall be doing in the chapters to follow.

What will those deliberations yield? That cannot be known in advance. Certainly, one possibility is new penal rules, or interpretations of old ones, that further restrict the freedom of academics. That, however, is not the only possibility. Suppose, for example, as I now believe, that free speech, whether civil or academic, is important enough, all things considered, to bar the use of dismissal, suspension, or other ordinary penalties for conduct such as Professors A and B engaged in. Does that necessarily end deliberations? No. We can still consider formally censuring or rebuking our wild professors; formally apologizing for them; formally condemning their views; formally inviting them to justify what they have done in open debate; and so on. We can still engage them, the injured students, and the rest of the academy in discussion of how we are to get through a time when students seem a bit more sensitive than usual or professors a bit more wild.[16] Ethics differs from law precisely in emphasizing non-penal means of guiding conduct, especially giving reasons that show that the standards of conduct in question are ones everyone has reasons to want followed. Ethics is not so much about restricting freedom as guiding free choices.

What, if anything, has this to do with reality? Much, I think. Many of the universities at which incidents of racial, sexual, or other harassment occurred responded in one or more of the less restrictive ways I mentioned, whether or not, like the University of Wisconsin-Milwaukee, they adopted a new penal rule. They have, however, had considerable difficulty explaining their actions in terms of academic freedom – which is what they generally tried to do. That they could think of no other way to explain what they were doing testifies to the need for academic ethics as a distinct way to talk about such matters.

What then of our two wild professors? To those expecting a final answer here, I offer two reasons for not providing the desired "closure." First, I do not yet have an answer I want to defend. Second, and more important, even if I did, giving it here would suggest the opposite of what I want to suggest. The purpose of this book is to begin a discussion that should take many years, much careful thought, and more honesty about what we do than I find in the literature so far. The demand for a resolution of the hard cases *now* amounts to a refusal to admit the need for that long discussion. Those who think that they can do without it are, of course, free to try. Indeed, I urge them to try. They will, I hope, learn much from the silence or confusion that ensues.

Part II

RESEARCH ETHICS

3

THE NEW WORLD OF
RESEARCH ETHICS: A
PRELIMINARY MAP

This chapter's title promises a preliminary map of a new world. What's new about research ethics? Consider the *Chicago Tribune* of Sunday 19 March 1989, Section 4, the section that is supposed to provide a thoughtful perspective on the week's news: The front-page headline reads "Cheating in the lab"; the subhead, "Under pressure, some researchers break the law." The accompanying article begins by reporting that one Stephen E. Breuning, Ph.D., had been sentenced to a term of imprisonment for fabricating research data and using the results to support his application for federal funding. After discussing a number of other cases of questionable research, the article notes that Rep. John Conyers suggested making it a federal crime to falsify any scientific research, no matter where it is done or by whom. Next to the headline is a cartoon showing a serpent in a chemical laboratory. For most researchers, the idea that wrongdoing among them could be widespread enough to provoke Congress into such legislation is as unfamiliar as it is frightening. The cartoon's serpent seems to represent both the scientists' loss of innocence and the intrusion of the world into the laboratory. That is the new world of my title.

Defining the subject

My title also speaks of "research ethics." What do I mean by that? "Ethics" means here what it has meant in the preceding chapters: those morally-permissible standards of conduct every member of a particular group wants every other to follow even if everyone else's doing so would mean he would have to follow them too. Ethics (as I use the term) is only a part of morality, the part relative to a particular group's practice. Legal ethics applies only to lawyering; medical ethics, only to providing health care; and so on.

Given that definition of ethics, one might suppose that "research ethics" refers to standards of conduct that do, or at least should, govern those engaged in research. Unfortunately, that is not quite so. "Research," while a conveniently short term, is somewhat misleading. Lawyers, journalists, scholars, philosophers, theologians, and even astrologers engage in research. Yet their research lies beyond my subject. I must admit to having no explanation of why that is. Lawyering, journalism, philosophy, theology, and humane letters each have standards for conducting and reporting research, standards we might properly describe as their respective research ethics. And individual lawyers, journalists, and so on certainly violate those standards now and then. Yet, as far as I know, such researchers have never appeared in any discussion of research ethics. (Note, for example, that Rep. Conyers would limit his legislation to "*scientific* research.") Why? Are the present borders of research ethics determined merely by historical accident or, in part at least, by important practical or theoretical differences between research in the sciences and research in other disciplines? I raise that question only to put it aside.

My subject, then, might better be described as "the ethics of scientific research." But even that description has difficulties. What is "science" here? Does it include medicine, engineering, mathematics, and logic? What about "library science" or history?

Medical research has been at the center of discussions of research ethics from the beginning. Yet we might well wonder why. Much medical research is done by physicians, not people with a research degree in any science. In this respect, medical research resembles legal research rather than scientific research. Medical research is also often highly practical, the purpose being to find cures for disease rather than to increase knowledge for its own sake. Medical research will seem to be scientific research only if we define scientific research by method rather than purpose. When engaged in research, physicians use methods common elsewhere in the life sciences.

If medical research is scientific research, then so is engineering research. Engineering research both resembles other research in the physical sciences in method, and receives much of its funding from the same sources. Many engineers have a research degree. Engineering research is even occasionally explicitly mentioned in official documents concerned with the ethics of scientific research. For example, in 1987, the National Science Foundation (NSF) issued regulations for handling research misconduct under the title,

"Misconduct in Science *and Engineering* Research."[1] Yet, so far as I know, no recent discussion of research ethics has included examples from engineering. Unlike physicians, engineers have had to carry on a separate discussion.[2] What explains that? This is another question I raise only to put aside.

Here's a third. Like engineering research, much research in mathematics and logic is closely linked to scientific research generally. And like engineering research, research in logic and mathematics seems to have been left out of discussions of research ethics. Of course, research in mathematics or logic is not generally laboratory research, but we have no reason to limit research in that way (even though the *Tribune*'s headline writer did). The research of concern to us clearly includes more than laboratory research. Breuning, for example, fabricated data concerning observations of patients in a clinic, not a laboratory.

Such considerations seem to provide reasons to include mathematical and logical research within research ethics. There is, however, at least one good reason not to. Unlike engineering (and clinical) research, research in mathematics or logic is rarely empirical; and discussion of research ethics has so far been limited to empirical research. Is non-empirical research of the sort mathematicians and logicians do therefore *not* scientific in the relevant sense? What then of the equally non-empirical work of computer scientists or theoretical physicists? Here is another question I raise only to put aside.

I have one more such question. There are a number of empirical disciplines that lie on the boundary between (what we call) science and (what we call) scholarship. I have in mind such diverse fields as lexicography, etymology, and history. Some of these disciplines have in fact had cases of alleged misconduct not too different from those in the sciences. History, for example, recently had a heated controversy concerning a well-known scholar's "fabrication of data" (radical mistranslation of archival material).[3] A decade before, history had a scandal in which a university president was discovered to have plagiarized his dissertation. He lost both his job and the doctorate he had received fifteen years earlier.[4] Such misconduct, though it clearly exists, is rarely mentioned in discussions of research ethics, never as an example of scientific misconduct. Apparently, disciplines like history are not sciences. Why not? Where does science end and scholarship begin?

I should, I think, point out that such questions are of practical as well as theoretical interest. The theoretical interest is obvious.

Trying to define research ethics seems to reveal vast blank areas in our conception of science. The practical interest may be less obvious. Consider then what a university committee appointed to hear cases of scientific misconduct should do when a complaint is brought concerning misconduct in historical, literary, or philosophical research (for example, the case described in Chapter 6).[5]

That, I think, is enough about the extent of my subject. In this chapter (and the next), we shall be talking only about the ethics of scientific research, with "science" having a relatively narrow interpretation.[6] This, I think, is a wise strategy. Narrowing our field of study now does not preclude broadening it later. But it will put us in a better position to decide where the field's natural borders are. We shall be in less danger of being overwhelmed by the enormous diversity in research.

This chapter has three parts. The first briefly describes the history of research ethics as a field and the topics it today includes. The second part summarizes what little we know about the apparent crisis in scientific research. The third part outlines the practical responses to that crisis.

Survey of history and topics

Work on the ethics of scientific research has a relatively short history. We can identify certain precursors concerned with the "norms of science," especially the sociologists Max Weber, Talcott Parsons, and Robert Merton.[7] We can also identify certain plaintive essays by natural scientists of the nineteenth or early twentieth century condemning trimming, cooking, forging, and similar misconduct in research. The earliest such work seems to be Charles Babbage's *Reflections on the Decline of Science in England*, which appeared in 1830.[8]

We can also identify more recent debates that, in retrospect, seem to be about the ethics of scientific research. Two deserve mention. One was a debate that began just after the Second World War, primarily among physicists, concerning the responsibility of scientists for the use to which their discoveries would be put. The other concerned the treatment of research subjects, both human and animal. In the United States, this latter debate led surprisingly quickly to federal regulation, to the establishment of internal review boards within research institutions, and to substantial changes in the way research is conducted. But the debate over the use of animals in research continues.

While all this activity is, in retrospect, relevant to research ethics, it is only now being integrated. The field itself is really much newer than such precursors suggest. Though saying when a new field of study was born requires some poetic license, I think we may usefully date research ethics from 1982. Not much was written about the ethics of scientific research until a series of scandals in the 1970s aroused interest in the faking of research. Some of the scandals involved contemporary researchers. You may, for example, remember white mice with black spots painted on them where black fur should have been.[9] Some of the scandals involved older research, for example, a famous series of studies of intelligence in identical twins discovered to have been entirely fabricated.[10] These scandals produced what (in retrospect) was a trickle of publications, popular as well as scholarly.

Then, in 1982, two journalists, William Broad and Nicholas Wade, published *Betrayers of the Truth*.[11] *Betrayers* is a work of journalism, not scholarship, with most of the virtues and vices that that suggests. Let's begin with the vices.

Betrayers relies entirely on secondary sources for its stories of faked research going back to Millikan's oil-drop experiments (1913) and before. The book would have added nothing to the knowledge of anyone familiar with the history of science. Indeed, it would have subtracted a bit, since it relies on outdated sources for some of its stories. By 1982, for example, some scholars had begun to think that certain of Mendel's research practices, though they would now be improper, were at the time acceptable substitutes for statistical techniques not yet available.[12] Broad and Wade none the less list Mendel among those who betrayed the truth.

So much for vices. One virtue of *Betrayers* is its Watergate-style reporting, an excitement and indignation certain to get the attention of people till then unfamiliar with the history of science. Another virtue of *Betrayers* is that it combines this reporting with three theses certain to get the attention of people already familiar with the history of science: first, that fraud in science is common; second, that the belief of scientists that fraud is uncommon is the consequence of self-deception, not evidence; and third, that the much-vaunted guarantees of scientific probity – especially, quick replication of research – are myths. That there is a huge gap between these theses and the evidence *Betrayers* actually provides only enhances the provocation.

Betrayers of the Truth provoked an enormous response, much of it from outraged scientists, but a surprising amount from scientists who had till then worried privately about what they saw around them. *Betrayers* also created a common vocabulary for scientists, scholars, and government officials interested in the problems *Betrayers* identified. Suddenly there was a field defined by the topics *Betrayers* discussed.

This way of defining the field was not without disadvantages. *Betrayers* was in fact almost entirely about empirical research in physics, biology, and medicine. While it managed to touch on a great many other issues, its focus was fraud. Early response to *Betrayers* was largely concerned with "fraud in science," so-called. Very soon, however, we find somewhat more general terms as well, especially "misconduct in research" and "cheating in science." The positive terms "research ethics" and "ethics of scientific research" seem only now to be catching on.[13]

We may identify six topics central to research ethics, all related to fraud and all discussed extensively in *Betrayers*:

1 "Smoothing out" reported data, for example, quietly dropping certain experimental results because of unreported inferences concerning weaknesses in research design or implementation ("trimming").
2 Suppressing data clearly inconsistent with one's conclusions ("cooking").
3 The outright fabrication of data ("forging").
4 Plagiarizing the work of others, for example, by publishing as your own in one obscure journal work another published in another obscure journal. *Betrayers* was concerned with plagiarism of this sort because it seemed to reveal a weakness of peer review. Neither the journal editors nor the journal readers knew the literature of their field well enough to recognize that what they were reading did not add to knowledge but merely repeated what had already been published. Was anyone reading those articles?
5 Claiming credit for work you did not do, for example, by allowing yourself to be listed as co-author of a paper to which you contributed little or nothing. *Betrayers* was particularly hard on senior researchers who took credit for the work of those under them but neither supervised it closely nor accepted responsibility when fraud was discovered.
6 Turning "a blind eye" to the misconduct of others, whether from fear of reprisal, personal friendship, or concern for the

welfare of the institution. Why did researchers not put the truth first?

Betrayers also touched on most of the following topics which, in any case, soon became important because they seemed relevant to understanding what might lead scientists to commit fraud:

1 Keeping incomplete records of research, discarding records after research is complete, or denying others access to data on which published research relied.

2 An overemphasis on new discoveries among laboratory directors, academic institutions, and funding agencies, for example, by rewarding researchers for new work but not for checking the work of others.

3 Judging a researcher's productivity. Why the emphasis on *number* of publications? Why not more emphasis on *quality*? How is quality measured? How should it be measured?

4 Mistreatment of graduate students, post-doctoral fellows, and junior faculty. What happens, for example, if a post-doc expresses doubt about the research of another post-doc? What happens if they object to giving the laboratory supervisors credit for work they did not do? How can such underlings be protected if they become whistleblowers?

5 What journals demand of those who submit papers. Should co-authors be required to indicate what each is responsible for? Should journals check the research plan, records, or raw data? Should each journal try to replicate the research itself?

6 The competitiveness of contemporary science, especially such "research strategies" as reporting results in such a way as to mislead competing researchers, holding back research results long enough to make sure they will not be of use to competitors (or interfere with getting a patent), and denying competitors access to one's lab.

7 Unauthorized use of privileged information, for example, using information gained as a reviewer to redirect one's own research without receiving permission from the person whose work was reviewed and without giving credit.

8 Honest but reckless or negligent error in conducting or reporting research ("sloppy science"). What is science-as-usual and what is misconduct?

Once the discussion spread from fraud in science to questions such as these – many concerned with the general environment of research – research ethics might easily be thought to include other topics as well. The treatment of research subjects is an obvious example. The scientist's responsibility for the use to which their research is put is somewhat less so; sexual harassment of fellow researchers perhaps even less so. One topic that may not seem obvious at all deserves special mention, *conflict of interest*.

By "conflict of interest" I mean any factor that might tend to undermine a competent researcher's ability to make scientifically reliable judgments concerning research strategy, evidence, or conclusions. Conflict of interest now seems to be a recognized part of research ethics. So, for example, the *Tribune* article with which I began spends several paragraphs on the effect the boom in biotechnology has had on the ability of biologists to trust the reports of others in their field. The concern is less possible fraud than the bad effect a large financial interest in the results of research can have on a researcher's scientific judgment.[14]

That completes this incomplete survey of topics included under the rubric "research ethics." Now let's see what we know about them.

What we know about research ethics

Evidence of misconduct in scientific research is of at least six kinds:

First are the few spectacular cases widely discussed in print. Most of these concern biomedical research.

A second source of evidence are the new centralized procedures for handling charges of research misconduct that the large research universities have begun to adopt. Though these procedures guarantee confidentiality, their centralization assures that a few people in each university will have a much better sense of the minimum extent of the problems there than they could have had before. We have yet to hear much about what has been learned, but my informal soundings suggest that many administrators responsible for receiving charges of research misconduct have been surprised by the number of charges received (even though only a small percentage turn out to involve significant wrongdoing).

A third source of evidence are the reports on the basis of which governmental agencies such as the Food and Drug Administration may disqualify a particular researcher or undertake their criminal prosecution. Most of these reports are about biomedical research (as is most of the research these agencies fund).

A fourth source of evidence are the retractions scientific journals seem to be printing with increasing frequency. These retractions do not seem to be limited to biomedical research.

A fifth source of evidence are the anecdotes scientists tell one another. Among scientists, journal editors form a special sub-category. Most editors have an informal blacklist, each name on it having its own story. Few disciplines seem to be without these.

The sixth source of evidence is the vague sense of many scientists that research misconduct is now common enough to threaten the well-being of science. This sense of trouble seems to vary considerably from field to field. Physicists, for example, seem much less likely to report it than biomedical researchers.

What can we conclude from this evidence? As in most other areas of human activity, reported cases of misconduct are likely to constitute only a fraction of actual cases. For comparison, consider that less than half of all burglaries in the United States in 1980 were reported to the police.[15] Few of the burglaries reported to the police will be reported in the press even though burglary usually leaves a victim ready to talk to anyone willing to listen. Most research misconduct either does no harm (since most research has little effect even on other research), or harms only indirectly (for example, by contributing to a general decline in trust), or harms in ways likely to go unnoticed (for example, Breuning's research affected the medication of the severely retarded in institutions, a group whose suffering is easily overlooked).

We must then suppose that the cases of misconduct we know about are only a small sample of those that actually occur. That, of course, is reason enough for caution. But there is another reason. That sample probably does not fairly represent the underlying population. Again for comparison, consider that most murders are reported to the police while most embezzlements are not.[16] Some embezzlement goes undiscovered. Much embezzlement that is discovered may be handled informally, for example, by firing the embezzler without notifying anyone else. Our present knowledge of research misconduct is subject to similar distortions.

For now, then, all we can conclude about misconduct in research is that it is probably more extensive than it appears to be. The evidence certainly does *not* entitle us to conclude that it is worse than it used to be. So, since none of the forms of misconduct seems new, our new interest in research ethics is itself in need of explanation: Why this interest now? One possible explanation is that *Betrayers* is all that is new. Had that book been published twenty-five or even fifty years ago, we would have had the impression back then that there was too much misconduct in research. While admitting the evidence does not now rule out that possibility, I find two other explanations much more plausible, especially since they are consistent with each other. One is that the rate of research misconduct actually has increased recently; the other is that science today can no longer tolerate even the traditional rate of misconduct. What might be said in support of these two explanations for the new interest in research ethics?

Reasons for thinking that the rate of research misconduct might actually have increased include:

1   The greater cost of research today – and the greater dependence on outside (especially, governmental) sources to pay for it – creates pressures beyond those traditionally associated with "publish or perish."
2   The greater cost of research today makes any unsatisfactory result a threat to the scientist's ability to continue research, reducing the relative importance of truth.
3   The increasing availability of research grants in certain fields (especially, biomedical) tends to attract researchers with the "wrong motives," that is, those more concerned to make money than to win recognition of peers or discover something important.
4   The increasing number of university researchers without tenure or academic standing increases pressure to make a good showing on every project.
5   The increasing expense of particular sorts of research makes replication less likely (thereby weakening one check on a researcher's ability to deceive themselves or others).
6   The increasing tendency to list as authors of an article all those in a particular laboratory rather than those who actually did the crucial work tends to dilute individual responsibility.
7   The increasing complexity of research, especially the need to cooperate with people from quite different disciplines, also tends to dilute individual responsibility for the project as a whole.
8   The increasing tendency of researchers to deny others access to research notes and raw data further discourages replication.
9   Scientists increasingly feel that they are competitors in a rough business rather than cooperators in a noble enterprise and therefore feel less responsible for the misconduct of others in their field.

That is my list of possible reasons for thinking the rate of misconduct may have increased. I do not necessarily accept any of them. They are simply what I have heard others say at one time or another and not yet seen refuted. Now for some reasons people might find research misconduct increasingly difficult to tolerate even at the traditional rate:

1 The increasing expense and difficulty of replication is making individual scientists more dependent than ever on the probity of others.
2 The increasing complexity of much research makes it harder than ever to identify where a certain experiment has gone wrong (when it has gone wrong) making each research project more vulnerable to misinformation in the literature.
3 The increasing tendency of journals to print less than a full description of research design makes informal cooperation among scientists more important.
4 The money involved in research is increasingly public money subject to unprecedented media scrutiny in an increasingly tight budget.
5 Conscientious researchers feel that as money for research becomes scarce, the misconduct of other puts them at a serious disadvantage in the competition for support.
6 The shortening of time between discovery and application increases the likelihood that third-parties may be injured because of research misconduct.

You will have noticed a close relation between these reasons for thinking misconduct more common or less tolerable than in the past and the list of topics under discussion in research ethics. I assume the reason for that close relation is obvious. One question for the new field of research ethics is whether we really have a problem of research misconduct or only the impression of one. Another is: if we have a problem, what is its extent and cause?

The sciences as nascent professions

That brings me at last to practical responses to misconduct in research. There are at least five: (1) study, (2) regulation, (3) punishment, (4) education, and (5) environmental change. They should seem familiar after our discussion of professorial ethics in Chapter 2.

I have, I think, already said enough about what there is to study.

I should only add that the federal government, especially the NSF, has been actively encouraging study. There have been both individual research projects (for example, one to determine how research ethics is now being taught in graduate school) and research conferences. There have even been conferences bringing together those studying research ethics with those holding the levers of power in science. One of these conferences recommended changes in the way scientific journals review submissions.[17]

By regulation, I mean adopting standards explicitly defining misconduct in research. The agency adopting the standard may be a professional society, a research institution, or a government. Some of the sciences had such standards well before 1982. For example, the American Psychological Association adopted a comprehensive code of ethics in 1973 (a major revision of its 1963 code). A substantial part deals with research ethics. In contrast, the American Physical Society only adopted a code of ethics in 1991. The problem today does not seem to be an absence of such standards so much as a failure to make those standards an explicit part of the research environment.[18]

By punishment, I mean setting up procedures enforcing the standards of research ethics, whatever the particular penalties might be and whatever the agency administering them. Rep. Conyers provided one example of what might be done, enforcement by the ordinary machinery of the criminal law. Several academic organizations recently provided a more interesting one, enforcement within research organizations themselves. The example, though titled "A Framework for Institutional Policies and Procedures to Deal with *Fraud* in Research," in fact deals with a wide range of research misconduct, including even "serious scientific error."[19]

The "Framework" recommends procedures for soliciting, examining, and settling complaints, provides a list of appropriate responses, and only omits to provide guidance on how to proportion punishment to misconduct. The omission is unfortunate, though understandable. What university disciplinary procedures most need today is, I think, some standards for judging the seriousness of various forms of misconduct and a corresponding scale of penalties. For example, plagiarism, whether deliberate or accidental, is "unacceptable conduct" within a university. Yet, deliberately plagiarizing someone else's research seems much more serious than deliberately plagiarizing a few paragraphs from someone else's survey of the literature. Universities (wisely, I think) do not fine for breaches of academic ethics. They cannot imprison. They are therefore left with few options between "censure" (which outsiders are likely to regard as a wrist slap) and discharge (which seems too severe for all but the most serious wrongdoing). Research institutions need to experiment with such intermediate penalties as reduction-in-rank, revocation-of-tenure, and suspension-of-research-for-a-term-of-years.[20] Here, perhaps, research ethics might benefit from contact with recent work in theory of punishment.[21]

By education, I mean just what you think, changes in the way future researchers are taught. Until recently very little was said about the ethics of research in most graduate programs. Graduate students either caught on from a few anecdotes professors or other students told or from an occasional reprimand received, overheard, or rumored. Formal instruction in research ethics was virtually unknown. In this respect, graduate education in the sciences is at least a decade behind professional education in law and medicine. But change seems to have begun. Some researchers, including the man who uncovered and reported Bruening's misconduct, Robert Sprague, now teach a course in research ethics, while others have begun to deal explicitly with research ethics in ordinary undergraduate or graduate courses.[22] (Chapters 7–8 provide some examples of what can be done.)

That brings me to the last practical response, changing the environment in which researchers actually work. Some of the other responses may change the environment as well. For example, explicitly defining research misconduct can make researchers more likely to notice misconduct and report it. Teaching research ethics can have the same effect. Insofar as researchers think about research ethics more often, and talk about it more openly, the working environment of researchers will discourage misconduct in a way it would not otherwise.[23]

But certainly more can be done. Whether it should be done is harder to say. We could, for example, try to reduce the pressure on researchers by reducing the importance of sheer quantity of publications in decisions to tenure, say, by allowing only five publications to be submitted in support of a tenure recommendation.[24] But would limiting the effect of sheer quantity in this way actually reduce overall pressure on young researchers or simply make them more dependent on the senior researchers whose letters of support will have to explain the importance of those few publications?

The last question may suggest that the response to research misconduct is already well ahead of our knowledge. While true, it is, I think, less so than it seems. After all, we have experience outside science of problems similar to many of those we have been calling "research misconduct." Each profession seems to have been formed when those engaged in the calling came to believe that the old informal constraints, whether market or religion or culture, were no longer adequate to keep abuses within tolerable limits. The response has always been some combination of study, regulation, punishment, education, and change in the working environment. Each profession has found a combination that seems a relatively satisfactory substitute for the old informal constraints – though *how satisfactory* is always in dispute.

Let me put this point another way. We will, I think, better understand what research ethics is if we think of the sciences, more or less one by one, as being forced by circumstances to become more like the traditional professions. Where once individual researchers could work in the same field, confident that the unseen hand of individual self-interest, conscience, or scientific spirit would maintain good order among them, they are now losing that confidence. Circumstances are forcing them to think of themselves more and more as engaged in a cooperative enterprise made possible in part at least by the self-discipline of other researchers, a discipline needing more than self-interest, conscience, or scientific spirit to maintain itself. The good each scientist aims at, whatever it is, depends, in part at least, on everyone else in the field taking some responsibility for the common good. This responsibility must now be defined explicitly (if only in general terms), taught vigorously, clearly embedded in scientific practice, and routinely enforced.

With that, I have passed beyond what I know and reached that much-more-interesting land of what I merely think. The promised map, though preliminary, is complete enough. So, we are ready to go on to some specific topics, beginning with the justification of standards for research ethics.

4

SCIENCE: AFTER SUCH KNOWLEDGE, WHAT RESPONSIBILITY?

Do scientists have special moral responsibilities simply because they are scientists? I shall argue that they do *not*. Though concerned with scientists, the argument has wider implications, especially for the assumption – common among academics – that professors have special moral obligations simply because they are professors.

The problem

This chapter began as a contribution to a conference, "Knowledge and Responsibility: The Moral Role of Scientists." The conference's sponsors, the Midwest Consortium for International Security Studies and the American Academy of Arts and Sciences, seemed to assume that something in the nature of scientists, their *knowledge*, imposes special moral responsibilities on them, whatever they may do, say, or wish. The assumption is, however, not limited to the organizers of that conference. For example, two researchers, one at the University of Texas at Houston and the other at the Uniformed Services University of the Health Sciences in Bethesda, Maryland, declared in a joint paper on "The Social Responsibilities of Biological Scientists":

> when a person has special knowledge about and responsibility for a particular discovery and the discovery becomes the basics for a consequential outcome, as *scientists* have when they discover and interpret phenomena, their responsibility flows not from a general commitment to serve one's fellow citizens, but from a direct commitment to take account of effects which their own actions revealed.[1]

Though mere knowledge is often the specific feature of scientists identified as the basis of their special responsibility, it is not always the specific feature identified. Consider, for example, this passage from a recent publication of the American Association for the Advancement of Science (AAAS):

> Maintaining the quality and integrity of scientific research is one of the primary responsibilities of scientists. This responsibility stems from scientists' desire for autonomy in the conduct of their work and from their unique capabilities to evaluate the work of their colleagues.[2]

Here the responsibility-imposing feature of scientists is not their knowledge but their "unique capabilities" and "desire for autonomy."

There is no indication that the responsibility in question might arise from some convention scientists have worked out among themselves over many years. The responsibility is instead presented as arising out of the very nature of scientists. The assumption of such a special moral responsibility, though apparently widespread, is deeply problematic. I will note just four problems now.

First, there is the problem of what the responsibility-imposing feature is. Knowledge? Some "unique capabilities"? Some common desire?

Second, none of the features commonly suggested as responsibility-imposing seems likely to be shared by all (or even most) scientists. For example, what knowledge do most sociologists, physicists, and zoologists have in common?

Third, there is the problem that others, non-scientists, often share the feature in question, for example, knowledge of a particular sort. Engineers know much physicists know; physicians, much zoologists know; and social workers, much sociologists know. If such non-scientists share in scientific knowledge, do they also share in the special responsibilities of scientists? If they do, how can the responsibilities in question be responsibilities of scientists *as such*?

Fourth, there is a problem of who counts as a scientist for this purpose. Clearly, not all who call themselves scientists will count. Christian Scientists do not count; nor do practitioners of the "occult sciences." But what about practitioners of library science, criminal justice science, or information science? The question cannot just be ignored. If we are to make a case for scientists having special moral responsibilities, responsibilities non-scientists do not have, we must have a relatively precise way to distinguish scientists from non-scientists.

These problems make me think that we are on the wrong track, that rather than trying to *derive* moral responsibilities from the *nature* of the agent (or activity), we should recognize that, *if* scientists are to have any special moral responsibilities, they will have to take them on just as lawyers, engineers, and professors do.[3] Any special moral responsibility of scientists will be contingent, much as are debts or the rules of chess.

Unfortunately, I cannot *prove* that claim here, not in a single chapter of reasonable length. But perhaps I can make it more attractive than the alternative. That, anyway, is what I shall try to do. If I do a good job, those who still prefer the alternative will have their work laid out for them. The rest of us may turn to other matters until they have done it.

I shall proceed in this way. First, I shall describe a case reasonably typical of those in which we may – and many scientists do – want to speak of a special moral responsibility of scientists. Next, after sharpening a few terms, I shall examine (under three headings) the main arguments purporting to derive such a responsibility from what scientists are. These arguments turn out to have little appeal when applied to our example. Last, I shall sketch my conventionalist alternative. While yielding only modest responsibilities, it is also free of the problems to which the immodesty of others leads.

A case to consider

Suppose that it is 1986, that I have a Ph.D. in physics, that I am working at an independent research laboratory such as MIT's Lincoln Laboratory or IIT's Research Institute, and that I am an expert on computer-supported radar identification of objects in space in "real time" (that is, fast enough to respond to them). I recently completed a study under contract with BIN Industries, a major defense contractor, on the possibility of such radar supporting an effective "star wars" defense (that is, a space-based defense that would destroy most or all of a large number of attacking long-range missiles after they left their protective silos). My "classified" report concluded that no computer-supported radar now available or likely to be developed in this century could hope to identify in time more than a small fraction of the attacking missiles. The report was transmitted to BIN. I believe it was read carefully because I received (and answered) several detailed inquiries from relatively senior officers at BIN. Now, suppose that I learn that BIN officers (including some who contacted me) testified before a Senate committee on behalf of building just such a system as I told them could not be built. Do I, because I am a scientist, have a moral responsibility to notify the Senate committee (or the public or someone else) that my findings are inconsistent with BIN's testimony (and that at least some of those testifying know that)?

If I chose to come forward, I probably would do so with some such justification as this: "As a scientist, I had no choice. I could not allow my findings to be kept secret when the public welfare would be harmed in consequence." Our problem is, in part, to understand what "I" could mean by "no choice."

Legally, the only choice I have is to keep quiet. I have no legal duty to report my findings to anyone but my employer, the research laboratory (which, in turn, has a legal duty under its contract with BIN, to pass the report on once satisfied it is accurate and does what the lab was contracted to do). Indeed, under the common law, I have a general duty to my employer to keep confidential what I learn in the course of employment and, in this case, the additional duty of silence created by work on a "classified" project.[4] My employer, in contrast, would be well within its common-law rights to fire me for revealing what I learned about BIN in the course of working on its project. Indeed, the research laboratory, with a few exceptions not relevant here, could fire me for any reason (or for none). The common law gives me no protection.

Some state or federal statutes do provide some protection for whistleblowers. For example, one federal statute makes it unlawful to fire an employee for revealing certain kinds of information to the EPA. But let us assume no such statute applies here. Do I, *as a scientist*, none the less have a special moral responsibility to reveal what I know about computer-supported radar to the Senate committee?

What is a special moral responsibility?

Because the words "moral," "responsibility," and even "special," have been known to run wild if left unchained, we should pause a moment to chain them.

By "morality," I mean the same as in the chapters preceding: those standards of conduct everyone – that is, every rational person at their rational best – wants everyone else to be subject to, even if that means they too must be subject to them.[5] Morality, so defined, is personal insofar as each person (at their rational best) has a veto. Nothing can be morality unless *each* person wants it to be. Morality, so defined, is, however, also objective (or, at least, inter-subjective). Nothing can be morality unless *every* person (at their rational best) wants it. Morality, though personal to each, is a common possession of all.

The twin tests of unanimity and rationality together provide a standard of practical justification. The test of unanimity assures that morality will be something that those subject to the standards will take an interest in. The test of rationality (that each – *at their rational best* – wants the standards) makes morality a rational undertaking as well. Morality must be both desired and desirable.

Morality, though justified, may still be either actual or ideal. *Actual morality* consists of those justified standards actually in place in our society; *ideal morality*, of those standards we endorse when we ignore the costs of changing current practice. Actual morality is, in part, a product of historical accident in a way ideal morality is not. Nonetheless, actual morality binds us while ideal morality merely offers terms of exhortation, grounds for criticism of existing moral rules (however justified now), and so a basis for planning the future.

Whether actual or ideal, there are at least three kinds of moral standard: rules, principles, and ideals.

A rule requires (or forbids) a course of action. "Don't kill" and "Keep your promises" are moral rules. Rules have exceptions. For example, "self-defense" is an exception to "Don't kill." To fail to do what a rule requires (or to do what a rule forbids) is wrong, unless justified under some exception. Rules lay down relatively rigid standards of conduct. Even when justified, doing what a rule forbids may leave behind liability to make good the harm one caused.

Principles, in contrast, do not concern conduct directly. They merely require certain considerations to have a certain weight in deliberations.[6] They state reasons. For example, "Help the needy" does not require us to give charity whenever we can but to give the needs of the needy significant weight when we are making alloca-tions. Principles are primarily standards of deliberation.[7]

Moral ideals do something more complex. Like rules, they are concerned with conduct; but, like principles, they do not *require* any particular conduct. Instead, they present the conduct in question as a state of affairs good to try for or approach but not bad to ignore or fall short of. The injunction, "Be a hero," is commonly thought to state a moral ideal. Moral ideals are morally important insofar as they give others a reason to help, reward, or at least praise those who try to realize a particular ideal.[8]

That is enough about morality generally. Where does responsibility fit in? By "responsibility," I mean what a rule *requires*, that is, a duty or obligation. Why understand "responsibility" in this way? Why not understand "responsibility" as indicating that a certain (moral) principle applies or even that some (moral) ideal might be realized?[9] The answer is simple. Such an understanding would not serve our purpose. To say, for example, that someone has a responsibility to report wrongdoing is, it seems, to say more than that he ought to give such-and-such weight to reporting (as a principle would) or that it would be good for him to report (as an ideal would). Rather, to say that someone has a responsibility to report wrongdoing is, all else equal, to say that not reporting would be wrong.[10]

To point out a responsibility is, of course, not to require a course of action come what may. We are not always justified in fulfilling a responsibility. Rules can have exceptions; and, even when no exceptions apply, there may still be sufficient reason to *excuse* us from doing what the rule requires (though the excuse will generally leave behind liability for costs imposed on others). In this respect, too, responsibilities do not seem to differ from obligations, duties, or requirements. This should come as no surprise. Except for "requirement," all of these terms have similar etymologies, arising from debts (things owed, due, and for which one must answer).

Talking in terms of obligation, duty, or requirement none the less seems clearer than talking in terms of responsibility. Why, then, are discussions of what scientists ought to do generally cast in terms of responsibility? I can think of only one reason, one of no importance here. "Obligation" has a legal connotation ("the obligations of contract"); "duty," a military connotation ("my station and its duties"); and "requirement," a harsh suggestion of command (as its origin fully justifies). "Responsibility" is, in contrast, a civil and civilian word, connected less with bargains than with roles and rights, words of discretion and judgment. While "responsibility" says no less than "duty," "obligation," or "requirement," it says it more gently.

What then makes a moral responsibility "special"? Let's say that a responsibility is special if, and only if, it derives (at least in part) from a rule obliging some people but not all. A moral responsibility, then, is special if it binds only some moral agents.

Is there a paradox here? How can a standard of conduct be both moral (one everyone wants everyone else to follow) and special (oblige only some)? Consider the obligation to keep a specific promise (for example, to meet my class tomorrow). "Keep your promise" is (we may assume) a moral rule, that is, a rule everyone wants everyone else bound by even if that means being bound by it oneself. Hence, the obligation derived from it, the obligation to keep this promise, is moral too. Yet, *this* promise is not a standard of conduct binding everyone, only a standard binding those who make the promise. The obligation to keep this promise, though moral, is special.

A special moral responsibility is, then, simply the consequence of a rule which, though applying only to some, derives it moral force from a rule applying to all. A special moral responsibility is a special case of a general moral responsibility. Convention, while the obvious way to create special responsibilities, may not be the only way. For example, the responsibility of parents to care for their own children, though a natural duty (if any is), seems both moral and special.[11]

So, an adequate answer to the question with which we began would offer an argument establishing: (a) that "I" (the physicist) have a *moral* duty (or obligation); (b) that all other *scientists* share that duty (or obligation); and (c) that the duty (or obligation) applies to them *because* they are scientists (rather than, say, because they are employees, citizens, or neighbors). Are there any such arguments? Let's see.

Good Samaritan arguments

The simplest argument for my having a special moral responsibility might be put this way: My knowledge of physics (and my technical judgment) have put me in position to prevent harm (a waste of public money, misleading a Senate committee, or the like). With that position comes a responsibility. I should therefore try to prevent the harm in question.

This may look like a simple act-utilitarian argument. (When we are in position to make the world better, we should do it.) So understood, it would, of course, be open to all the usual objections made to that relatively unpopular moral theory. That is one reason not to understand the argument that way. There is another. The argument does not explicitly call for an overall assessment of benefits and burdens (as an act-utilitarian argument should). There is no claim that society would benefit overall from my revealing what I know, no attempt to deduct for the costs to my employer, BIN Industries, or the BIN employees involved, only an appeal to the harm I can prevent. In effect, the argument would require me to be (what we now call) a Good Samaritan. The Good Samaritan argument, whatever its faults, is not a simple act-utilitarian argument.

How appealing is the Good Samaritan argument? Recall the parable from which its name comes. Finding a stranger by the side of the road, wounded, robbed, and left for dead, the original Good Samaritan gave first-aid, then took the stranger to an inn some distance away, cared for him that evening, and paid for his care after that. The parable is generally thought to exemplify the *ideal* of "loving thy neighbor." The original Good Samaritan is not generally thought to be someone merely fulfilling a responsibility.

Defenses of a moral, or legal, *requirement* to rescue recognize the ideal quality of what the actual Good Samaritan did. They therefore (generally) narrow the responsibility in some such way as this:

> Go out of your way to prevent great and imminent harm when, without breach of an important duty (or obligation), you can prevent the harm by some relatively safe, easy, and inexpensive act (for example, throwing a life preserver to a drowning child).[12]

Such a requirement, though still controversial, falls well short of what the original Good Samaritan did.

Nonetheless, what even the original Good Samaritan did falls well short of what we want to ask of me. On the one hand, the immediate harm "I" would prevent is relatively minor, misleading a Senate committee concerning possible space-based defenses. The more substantial harms – for example, waste of billions of dollars on research and development – are not imminent. They cannot begin for at least a year, that is, after the project is funded, contracts given, and work begun. They are also not certain. The project may be rejected for reasons – such as cost or diplomacy – having little to do with what BIN says.

On the other hand, "my" burden *will* be great whatever good I do. I will breach two significant obligations, the obligation of confidentiality every employee owes an employer and the special obligation imposed by classified research. I will risk my research classification, my job, and my ability to find other employment in my field. And, like most whistleblowers, I will probably lose many friends, become entangled in litigation, and otherwise darken my prospects for a long time.[13] Even many who accept some version of the Good Samaritan argument should find counter-intuitive a version strong enough to apply here.

To say this is, of course, not to say that we would not prefer to live in a world where people took more of an interest in the public welfare than we do here. It is, rather, to admit that at least some of us (even at our rational best) are probably unwilling to accept the burdens necessarily accompanying a rule *requiring* us to be Good Samaritans. Requirements have costs as well as benefits. The problem with a Good Samaritan rule is the cost, not the benefit.

That, however, is not the weakness of the Good Samaritan argument most relevant here. We are looking for an argument establishing a *special* responsibility of scientists as such. No ordinary Good Samaritan argument can do that. A Good Samaritan argument would apply to anyone who came to know what I know. Even a secretary typing my memo would have precisely the same responsibility for precisely the same reason. Being a scientist is, at best, contingently related to the information a particular scientist has. So, the responsibility in question would not be a responsibility of scientists as such – except in the Pickwickian sense that it happens to be my responsibility and (we are supposing) I happen to be a scientist.

Arguments from the status of scientists

One significant difference between "me" and my secretary, even supposing we share the same knowledge, is that I can speak as a scientist (or, at least, as a physicist). The secretary lacks the authority that my status as a "scientist" confers on me. In this respect, I have a power no non-scientist can have, the power to speak "as a scientist."[14] That power gives me (it might be said) a special responsibility to speak.

This is the *argument from status*. What kind of argument is it? What is its appeal? One possibility is that the argument from status is merely a special case of the Good Samaritan argument. So understood, the argument simply points out that being a scientist puts one in a better position to prevent the harm in question than not being a scientist does. The scientist, being in a better position than any non-scientist (even a non-scientist with the same knowledge), would have a duty to act that those lacking his status would not have.

The argument from status supposes a moral rule. Stating the rule supposed will, I think, make clear how unattractive the argument is (if it is to cover a case like mine). The *rule of status* must, I think, look like this:

> Go out of your way to help change public policy when: (a) you have a special competence with respect to the policy in question; (b) that competence gives you special authority or credibility (a special ability to guide deliberation on the policy); and (c) that competence also reveals to you a significant threat to the public health, safety, or welfare.[15]

The responsibility this rule imposes is both narrower and broader than that of any ordinary Good Samaritan rule. The responsibility is narrower insofar as the rule links competence to authority and authority to policy-making. Not all ability to help is covered (though much ability beyond science is, for example, legal competence). The rationale for this narrowing is hard to guess. If what motivates this rule is the public health, safety, and welfare, why single out for special burden *this* ability to help?[16] Without a good answer to that question, the rule of status looks arbitrary, an attempt to save a thesis by *fiat*.

Because the rule of status applies without an imminent danger, it is also broader (that is, more burdensome) than any ordinary Good Samaritan rule. The rule makes demands even while the threat to the public health, safety, or welfare is far off. Only someone accepting an ordinary Good Samaritan rule is likely to find this broadening attractive. All the standard objections to the Good Samaritan argument would still apply. The rule of status certainly requires more than many people (even at their rational best) are willing to give up in exchange for others giving up the same.

Another way to understand the argument from status is as an appeal to gratitude (or reciprocity).[17] Society has given scientists a special status, an (epistemic) authority others do not share. Scientists benefit from that, for example, by being paid more, or by being given a more respectful hearing, than others would in similar circumstances. Scientists therefore owe society a debt of gratitude, payable by (among other means) coming to society's aid when in a position to do so. I am a scientist. My research has put me in position to come to society's aid. Therefore (the argument runs) gratitude requires me to do it. I have a special responsibility as a scientist.

Of the many criticisms I could make of the argument from status understood in this way, I will make only three.

First, the status society accords scientists does not seem to be a "gift" (in the relevant sense), hence something for which gratitude is the appropriate response. Society does not give (epistemic) authority to scientists; scientists have earned that authority by being right more often than astrologers, mediums, and certain other would-be advisors (or, at least, so most scientists believe). So, while scientists continue to be relatively accurate, society cannot rationally deny them that authority.[18]

Something similar is true of the higher pay and status society (supposedly) accords scientists. They are not gifts. Consider "me": My pay was the product of an exchange in the marketplace, each side giving value for what it got. The other party was my employer, not society. No gratitude to society is appropriate – unless society accorded me special protection, for example, by setting a minimum wage for scientists. No such arrangement exists in this society.[19]

Similarly, status in this society is largely a function of income or of other achievements. I have said enough about income. What about other achievements? The status we accord those who do impressive things is, it seems, not a gift we are entitled to grant or withhold as we wish. The recognition of an achievement, that is, its very appreciation, is itself an admission of its status. To show gratitude for having one's achievement recognized is a kind of false modesty or servility. Why require that?

The resources that society devotes to science, both to train scientists and to pay for their research, seems to be different from both income and status. Society does devote those resources to science in expectation of benefit. Society could rationally choose to seek other benefits and is free to do so even if not free to withdraw the authority or status it accords scientists. So, this "gift" of resources does seem a good candidate for creating a "debt of gratitude."

The "debt" in question would, however, not be special to science. Anyone feeding at the public trough, even graduates of a business school, or farmers receiving price supports, would owe the same "debt."[20]

That is my first criticism of the gratitude version of the argument from status: either it does not apply to scientists like "me" or, if it does, it does not apply to them because they are scientists.

My second criticism begins with the observation that any ordinary debt of gratitude can be paid off. There is supposed to be some proportion between the good you do me and the gratitude I owe you (although this notion of proportion is vague). For example, I should, it seems, be able to escape any gratitude-imposed responsibility to reveal what I know simply by doing society a certain number of good turns. (Perhaps, in my long career, I have already done enough for society to owe me rather than the other way around!) Anyway, the responsibility would not be mine because I am a scientist (knowing such and such) but because I am someone who has not yet paid off my debt (however contracted).

Third, and most important, debts of gratitude do not seem to impose responsibilities (that is, requirements) in any straightforward way. Gratitude seems a creature of *principle*, the principle that you should benefit those who benefit you. Principles do not state responsibilities. I do not, for example, fail in any responsibility if, owing you a debt of gratitude, I favor someone else today. I show my gratitude simply by giving enough weight in deliberations to what you did for me. Debts of gratitude lack the pre-emptive quality of responsibilities.

Indeed, the language of gratitude does not fit well with "debt." Debt, unlike gratitude, creates (well-defined) obligations. Debts do that because, unlike "debts of gratitude," real debts are the product of agreements (or other legal or quasi-legal transactions).

Perhaps (it might then be thought), the argument from status might better be understood as (something like) an argument from *social contract*. Scientists undertake certain responsibilities by becoming scientists. Among these responsibilities is reporting information one develops when so reporting would be in the public interest.

This is an appealing argument if, but only if, we know how to determine what the contract says. We can, of course, *imagine* circumstances in which determining what such a contract says is easy. If, for example, before becoming a scientist, one had to take an oath (as lawyers do), we could examine the oath to determine whether a certain responsibility was there (express or implied). Or if, instead, the law simply required scientists to do certain things (for example, to report certain information, as the law now requires physicians to do), we would know that the requirement was part of the "social contract," society having clearly attached the duty to the status.

Despite these appealing possibilities, there are at least two decisive disadvantages to understanding the argument from status in this way. First, there is no contract. Scientists do not take an oath the way lawyers do; and, as we noted earlier, the law does not require me to report my findings to the Senate committee (though it does, of course, forbid me to testify in a way I know to be false or misleading). Second, if there were such a "contract," it would be a mere convention. We would not have derived the special responsibilities of scientists from their nature (or that of science) but from what this or that locale happened to wring from scientists as a condition of practicing science there.

What about a "natural social contract," the terms of which were determined by the nature of science, or by the necessary relation of scientists to society, not simply by what happened to get into an oath or statute? That, of course, is precisely what we are looking for. But calling it a "contract" is misleading. Contracts are made; such a natural "contract" would, in effect, be a permanent relation among things, not a contract at all.

This may seem too quick a dismissal of social contract. After all (it might be said), John Rawls made a career of using the (potentially) misleading language of contract to illuminate central features of our concept of justice. We might, then, be tempted to appeal either (a) to what a Rawlsian social contract would say about the obligations of scientists or (b) to a secondary hypothetical contract between scientists and society. Like most temptations, both these lose their appeal upon closer examination.

The social contract Rawls defends does not mention "scientist" – and, for reasons he makes clear, could not. For him, such details belong in a constitution (or ordinary legislation), not in the social contract.[21] A Rawlsian contract would, then, force us to look for actual conventions, the enactments of a constitutional convention or legislature (constrained by certain general principles of justice), the very opposite of what we are supposed to be looking for now.

A secondary hypothetical contract would, on the other hand, have nothing to do with Rawls' theory. Since Rawls recognizes no such contract, whatever appeal a theory resting on secondary hypothetical contracts had would have to come from some non-Rawlsian source. Where? I don't know. Imagining what might be agreed to under fair conditions is often useful for construing an actual contract ("What would rational contractors have meant by 'chicken' here?"). Given no evidence to the contrary, we justifiably assume actual contractors meant what rational contractors would have meant. But where, as here, we admittedly do not have an actual contract in need of construing, but a hypothetical – ideal – contract, what could working out its terms tell us about the responsibilities of actual scientists? Any contract hypothetical in every jot and tittle could yield only hypothetical responsibilities.[22] That is not our concern. The argument from status has brought us to a dead end.

Arguments from complicity

While American law imposes no general responsibility to come to the aid of another, it does impose such a responsibility sometimes. The time of interest to us is when the person called upon to give aid has had a part in creating the need. Someone who invites another onto his property has a duty to warn of hidden dangers; a motorist who has run down a pedestrian must call for help; and so on. The rationale for such special responsibilities seems to be the same as for tort law generally. While we may owe mere strangers no help, we have a general duty not to make their condition worse. When we fail in that duty, we must put things right. These twin duties, not to make the condition of other worse or, if we do, to put things right, is not burdensome because we always have the option of avoiding them by taking suitable precautions, for example, by not inviting someone onto our property or driving carefully enough to avoid running down pedestrians.

We might restate this insight as a *rule of individual responsibility*:

> Go out of your way to help someone when, however inadvertently, your conduct has unjustifiably put him in need of such help.[23]

This rule offers a basis for (what we might call) an argument from individual complicity. The rule would require me to reveal what I know if, for example, BIN used data I developed to support its proposal. There would, however, be no corresponding responsibility if, as we are assuming, BIN simply ignored my data.

That is one objection to the rule of individual complicity. There is another. The rule makes only the most tenuous connection between my status as a scientist and my responsibility to reveal what I learned. My responsibility derives not from the fact that the information in question is scientific (though it is), or from the fact that a scientist is involved (though at least one is), but from the fact that the information in question, scientific or not, is mine and I have (unjustifiably) put someone in need of it.

There is, however, a version of the argument from individual complicity that may seem to get around this objection. Each of us, it might be said, has a moral obligation to avoid being the source of *mis*information when we can. When someone speaks "as a scientist" and all other scientists remain silent, the public may justifiably conclude that they speak for all scientists (that is, expresses the scientific community's consensus). If there is in fact disagreement among scientists, the silence of each scientist would contribute to public misinformation. Each scientist, by her silence, would have become a source of misinformation when, by speaking up, she could avoid doing so. Hence, each scientist as such would have a moral obligation to break the silence (though the act of one or a few would free the rest from any need to act).[24]

The appeal of this argument, though admittedly great, depends on two doubtful assumptions.

One doubtful assumption is that not speaking up makes one a *source* of misinformation – in other words, that not informing is, under the circumstances, misinforming. The assumption seems to turn a relatively uncontroversial moral rule ("Don't deceive") into a much more controversial rule of epistemic Good Samaritanism ("Prevent deception"). It would then be open to many of the objections already made against Good Samaritan arguments.

The other doubtful assumption upon which this version of the argument from complicity rests is that, in a case like mine, the problem is that one side will have scientists to speak for it while the other side will not. That is generally not the problem. Generally, *both* sides will have scientists to speak for them. The problem is, rather, that unless I speak, the public (probably) will not learn *all* that science has to teach about the effectiveness of computer-assisted radar in a "star wars" defense. What will mislead the public is not misinformation but missing information.[25]

Arguments from *individual* complicity, whatever their merit, thus seem ill-suited to our purpose, defining the special moral responsibility of scientists. That responsibility is collective, not individual (though special responsibilities eventually do fall on individuals). We might, then, want to consider a *rule of collective complicity*:

> Go out of your way to help change public policy when: (a) you have a special competence with respect to the policy in question; (b) that competence gives you special authority or credibility (a special ability to guide deliberations on the policy); (c) that competence also reveals to you a significant threat to the public health, safety, or welfare (relevant to the policy); and (d) you are a voluntary member of the very community of competence that helped to create the threat.

This rule is, of course, a close relative of the Good Samaritan rule offered as the basis for one version of the argument from status. The chief difference is the final clause. No one is subject to this rule unless, *first*, she voluntarily becomes a member of a certain community of competence (by learning the appropriate skills) and, *second*, that community of competence helps to create a threat (for example, by teaching skills to people who then misuse them). Those who do not want to remain in the community can let their competence atrophy. (Their membership is, in this respect, voluntary.) Those who want to remain must either accept responsibility for helping to clean up when their colleagues mess up or take precautions to assure that their colleagues do not mess up.

The rule of collective complicity imposes collective responsibility on even unorganized groups. In this respect, it departs from the common-law theory of tort on which I modeled it. The common law imposes collective responsibility only where there is a "corporation," "partnership," or "company," that is, an organized body claiming to maintain, or at least capable of maintaining, good order among its members. The rationale for limiting collective responsibility in this way is straightforward. We do not want to be held responsible for the conduct of those we neither control nor purport to control. Whatever advantages might come from being able to hold others responsible for conduct over which they have no control does not seem enough to repay us for the burdens we would have to bear if others could hold us responsible in that way.[26]

If, however, we confine the rule of collective complicity to "corporations" (that is, organized groups), it cannot yield the argument we are looking for. Scientists as such are not organized in the way required. There are, of course, scientific organizations of various sorts, everything from umbrella groups like AAAS to various interest groups (the Society for Imaging Science and Technology, for example). There are also political organizations of scientists – Scientists Against Star Wars – a form of organization I shall ignore hereafter. But, I need not, as a scientist, belong to any of them. And, even if I did, I would not belong to one organized to maintain good order in my field or even claiming to do so.

Scientific societies are, as such, not organized to maintain good order in science. Generally, they are technical rather than professional organizations.[27] A technical society is (primarily) concerned with "technique," that is, with competence in the field. In scientific (technical) societies, competence is generally understood as knowledge of the field (whether about "nature" itself or about research methods for learning about "nature"). So, for example, the American Physical Society (APS) has as its objective "the advancement and diffusion of the knowledge of physics." For the professions, competence generally includes more than "science" in this sense (for engineers, for example, it includes knowledge of relevant government regulations). But even a profession may have a technical organization, that is, one concerned to augment the competence of the organization's members (or of the profession as a whole) rather than set standards for the conduct of the profession.

That is not to say that scientific societies, *as such*, cannot have codes of ethics. They certainly can. My point is, rather, about the structure of such societies, what they are organized to do or, failing that, what they claim to do. They are – by definition – *not* organized to maintain order in a field, nor do they claim to do it. They do not, for example, adopt codes of ethics for everyone in their field. Instead, they maintain order, when they do, and claim to maintain order, when they do, merely among the members of the organization. Technical societies differ from professional societies precisely in this, their willingness to claim to regulate a field of activity (for example, the work of all those calling themselves "physicists"). So, for example, one of the major engineering societies, the Institute of Electrical and Electronics Engineers (IEEE), is – on this analysis – a technical society (rather than a professional society) because its present code of ethics (1990), like its predecessor, applies only to IEEE members.[28]

The structure necessary to regulate a field, or at least the structure necessary to make a plausible claim to do so, is what we need in order to apply any plausible version of the rule of collective complicity. A code of ethics is only part of such a structure. Also necessary are procedures for realizing the code in practice, for example, an education committee to inform members of what the code requires or a disciplinary committee to identify, rebuke, and perhaps even expel those who do not conduct themselves as they should.

But, even if a code of ethics were the only structure necessary to regulate a field, the existence of such a code could not support the argument we are looking for. A code is a convention. To make application of the rule of collective complicity depend on the group having a certain kind of convention, much less on what the convention says, would be to give up the approach I have been arguing we should give up and to adopt the alternative I shall now briefly explain.

The profession of science?

I have tried to identify and refute all interesting arguments for the claim that scientist as such *must* have a special moral responsibility. Suppose that I have succeeded: what are we entitled to conclude? We are not entitled to conclude that scientists, as a matter of fact, have no special moral responsibilities because they are scientists. We are, instead, entitled to conclude only that any special responsibilities they have must depend on conventions. For some sciences, such conventions exist. These sciences have, in effect, organized as professions. While the American Physical Society did recently adopt a code of ethics, its doing so will not help here.[29] Its code of ethics does not cover cases like mine.

Could a science have a code of ethics covering cases like mine? Of course. Consider what my responsibilities would have been had I been an engineer: One provision of the engineers' code declares: "[if] their judgment is overruled under circumstances where the safety, health, property, or welfare of the public are endangered, they shall notify their employer or client and such other authority as may be appropriate."[30] Since the Senate committee seems to be an appropriate authority to notify, I would, as an engineer, have had a responsibility to notify them (at least after I had exhausted all reasonable means within my laboratory).

By itself, this first provision does not, however, decide what I, as an engineer, would be required to do. There may be an exception for confidential information. After all, another provision of the code says: "[engineers] shall not disclose confidential information concerning the business affairs or technical processes of any present or former employer without his consent."[31] The information I would disclose is at least arguably confidential because it concerns BIN's business affairs (and is "classified") and BIN has not consented to its release.

Since these two provisions seem to conflict, neither explicitly giving the other precedence, my responsibility is still not clear. The code requires interpretation. Sometimes a code gives little or no guidance concerning how to resolve a conflict like this. The resolution is left to individual judgment. In this case, however, the code is quite explicit. Engineers are supposed "[to] hold paramount the safety, health, and welfare of the public in performance of their professional duties."[32] When the public health, safety, or welfare conflicts with the interests of an employer or client, the public interest takes precedence.

So, if (as we may assume) giving the Senate committee the information I developed will assure a better informed decision concerning public expense, such decisions are part of the public welfare, and the information can be given to the committee without unduly compromising national security, then my responsibility, as an engineer, is clear. If I cannot convince BIN to reveal what I discovered, I have a obligation to reveal it myself. For an engineer, the public welfare pre-empts an employer's (or client's) right to confidentiality. I-the-engineer have "no choice."

For me-the-physicist, however, any special responsibility to report my data to the Senate committee must have another source. And, as I have argued, there seems to be no other. Unless BIN is going to use my data, claiming my authority for it, I am not implicated in BIN's testimony. Nor am I an ordinary rescuer (or Good Samaritan); I can come to the public's aid only by breaching my employer's trust (and risking substantial harm to my own interests). Nor can I justify my conduct merely by pointing to my status as a scientist. I am going beyond what is required of scientists. Indeed, I am going beyond what is required of employees and citizens too. I will, then, have to act as an individual, justifying my act in the way people do when they violate a moral rule for reasons they believe to be good. In this, "I" am no worse off than I would be if I missed class because I stopped to rescue a drowning child at great risk to myself.[33]

Would "I" in particular, or scientists in general, be better off if scientists, like engineers, had a code of ethics speaking to issues like this? That depends on what scientists (at their rational best) want. Do they want to trade individual freedom for corporate responsibility? They may not, preferring (quite rationally) to leave decisions to individual scientists without collective guidance; or only to give guidance in the form of statements of principle or ideal.[34]

Which they prefer cannot be known until standards of conduct have been laid before the appropriate bodies, debated, and voted up or down. I would hope philosophers could contribute to that process not, as I have done here, by considering what can be squeezed from the nature of scientists, but by formulating standards scientists might find attractive and arguments to make clear the attraction.

5

UNIVERSITY RESEARCH
AND THE WAGES OF
COMMERCE

On 12 October 1990, Ralph Nader gave a talk on "The Relationship Between the University and Business and Industry" as part of Wayne State University's conference, *Ethics and the University*. The talk was vintage Nader, a loose argument supported by hundreds of particular details, presented without notes. The conclusion was a call to arms: declining federal support of scientific research has tempted institutions of higher education (hereafter "universities") to turn increasingly to business for help. Particular universities, even particular departments, have forged links with particular businesses. Business interests are taking over the university. The university will lose its soul unless it again becomes a place apart, a source of independent research and impartial judgment. The link between university and business must be broken once and for all.

I was one of two academics asked to respond. My response was not exactly a refutation. Nor will this descendant of that response be. Nader spotlighted an important problem, but he also, I believe, misunderstood it. He did not pay enough attention to its context. In context, the problem is more ambiguous than he made it out to be, and better contained through innumerable small decisions than resolved once and for all, a problem for university administrators rather than for an Old Testament prophet.

What should university administrators do? They should, I shall argue, approve many of the contracts by which university and business create the links Nader fears. However, they should also help formulate general policies governing such links, distinguishing clearly those links with business universities ought to allow or even encourage from those they should discourage or forbid. This chapter may provide a starting point for making such distinctions.

Admission of possible bias

I must begin with three admissions. The first is that the university with which I am affiliated, the Illinois Institute of Technology (IIT), though it now has Ph.D. programs, a law school, a business school, and so on, began as an engineering school and retains something of that spirit. Engineering schools exist to serve industry. They train chemical engineers for the chemical industry, automotive engineers for the auto industry, and so on. They also try to do research useful to industry and devote considerable time to helping industry make use of that research.

While IIT was conceived in what Nader must regard as sin and grew up committed to what Nader fears, I have not seen the effects that would justify his fears. True, IIT's research tends to the applied. (Even our humanists pay much more attention to technology than their counterparts at a liberal arts college do.) But, otherwise, IIT seems much like other universities with which I have been affiliated.

Engineering schools are not alone in having grown up committed to close links with business. Land-grant universities have a similar history. They were established to serve the major industry of their day, agriculture, and to provide "mechanics" (mechanical engineers) for the new steam-driven industries only then becoming economically important. Their job was not simply to educate farmers and mechanics. From the beginning, they tried to do research useful to them. Links with farmers, and those who supplied farmers, were and remain extensive. Industrial research, though less systematically organized, was also considered part of the land-grant universities' function. The land-grant universities have never maintained the distance from the world's work that Princeton or the University of Chicago have. American universities differ from one another in ways English, French, or German universities do not (or, at least, did not until quite recently). We have our ivory towers, but we also have our Silo U's, Techs, teachers colleges, and so on. My response to Nader reflects my experience of that diversity.

That is my first admission. The second is that the Center for the Study of Ethics in the Professions (hereafter "the Ethics Center") at which I work was designed to link philosophers, social scientists, and other academics with the professions. Even if IIT were an ivory tower, the Ethics Center could not be.

Professions, being practical activities, are as inevitably linked to business in this society as human life is linked to the earth, air, and water of this blue planet. Some professions, like law or dentistry, are in fact carried on as businesses. Most members of those professions market their services. They differ from other business people only in formally committing themselves to serve the public in ways beyond what law, market, and morality require. Other professions, especially engineering, serve the public primarily through employment in large businesses. Still other professions – teaching or public administration, for example – though not directly engaged in business or employed by it, must regularly deal with business. Even government must get most of what it uses from "the private sector."

I am, then, institutionally committed to links between university and business. I have also personally benefited from those links. While I am not in the pay of any business, my links with business have served me in other ways, for example, by making it possible for me to interview engineers within large companies as party of a study of ethical problems engineers face on the job.[1] That too must affect my response to Nader.

So much for my second admission. My third explains how I came to be one of Nader's respondents. It too is relevant to gauging how much weight my response deserves.

More than a decade ago, I was asked to serve as commentator for a panel at a meeting of the American Association for the Advancement of Science (AAAS). The panel's subject was the threat business-supported research in biotechnology posed to the integrity of the biological sciences within the university. Apart from being a philosopher, I had only two obvious qualifications for the assignment. One was that the panel's chair was the Ethics Center's director. The other qualification was that I had never before thought about the subject. My five co-panelists had already taken positions in articles or books. I was to offer a fresh perspective.

I undertook to do what philosophers generally do on such occasions, that is, to analyze the arguments, point out weaknesses, and attempt an overall assessment of the various positions. I undertook to do that before I read the papers. When I did read them, I did so with increasing concern. Everything seemed to depend on one's understanding of what was in fact going on in university departments and business laboratories. The footnotes revealed how little was then known about that. I therefore decided to talk to some university researchers and business people directly involved (including my fellow panelists).[2]

I did not do a scientific survey. I did not even formulate my questions in advance, keep notes of what was said, or choose informants in an orderly way. I simply collected points of view until I thought I understood the reality behind them. That reality turned out to be much more familiar than I had surmised from my initial immersion in the debate over university–business research links. While the AAAS panel did not allow me to report much of what I had learned, Wayne State's conference did. I was therefore grateful when, having heard what I might say, the conference organizers invited me to be one of Nader's respondents.

I shall now report what I learned from my inquiries, beginning with what I learned from people in business and then going on to what I learned from university researchers. While leaving to social scientists the job of determining how accurately I have represented university–business links, I shall conclude by pointing out some lessons to be drawn from what I report (assuming my report catches an important part of the reality of relations between university and business).

What business can get from the university

The business people I talked to generally identified three reasons for wanting to link up with university biology departments (including departments of biochemistry, biophysics, bioengineering, and so on): knowledge, students, and stimulation. I shall discuss these in order.

Knowledge Depending on field and journal, the time between scientific discovery and publication can be between six months and two years. In many fields, even six months is now a long time. Those who depend only on journals for information about their field will forever be behind those who depend on word of mouth, fax, electronic mail, or other informal means of communication with those working at their field's developing edge. This is at least as true of "applied science," including biotechnology, as of "pure science." Indeed, in many fields, the distinction between pure (or basic) research and research in applications is all but gone. Even abstract theory may have immediate applications, and many applications generate new theory.

So, a biotechnology company with close links to the appropriate biology department can gain a lead of anywhere from six months to two years over competitors who lack such links. That advantage need not be gained by excluding competitors but simply by establishing links competitors could also establish but, for one reason or another, do not. The advantage differs little from that a company might gain by subscribing to journals another company does not. Because the advantage is primarily a function of convenience of communication, proximity is important. For that reason, biotechnology companies tend to cluster around universities doing the appropriate research.

What in principle is there to object to in close links between business and the appropriate biology department undertaking to achieve such competitive advantage? The competition involved seems to be in the public interest. The time a company saves by receiving information sooner through informal channels ultimately means that useful products should reach the market that much sooner, making our lives that much better. That public benefit should increase as competition forces companies one by one to copy the links competitors have with a particular department, either by developing similar links with that department or with a similar department elsewhere. In the long run, even as the competitive advantage of links with the university tends to disappear, both the necessity of those links and the public benefit deriving from them should continue to increase.

Students The second reason biotechnology people gave for wanting to link up with a particular biology department was access to graduate students. Biotechnology is not only a "science-driven" field; it is a field in which biologists (biochemists, and so on) are deeply involved at every stage. In some biotech companies, even some large ones, nearly half the employees are PhDs. Such companies need PhDs in biology in the way the auto industry needs mechanical engineers. They want the best people they can get. Their experience is that they are more likely to recruit a PhD who worked with them as a graduate student than one who did not. They therefore want their links with the university to include research involving its graduate students. They view these links as analogous to those often established with universities as part of an undergraduate "co-op" program.

The business people I talked to believed students benefited from contact with them. Graduate students often arrive at an industrial laboratory sure that they are dealing with people who care nothing for science, people whose academic insufficiency forced them out of the university into the world of dreary money-grubbing applications. What they find are scientists not so different from themselves, working under conditions not so different from those in the university. For the first time, taking a job in industry comes to seem an attractive possibility. The students now have an option they did not before.

Stimulation The third reason people in biotechnology companies gave for wanting close links with a university biology department was intellectual stimulation. Though researchers in the biotechnology business think of themselves as scientists much like those in biology departments, they are none the less aware of certain differences.

Some of these differences are like those that exist within a university between, say, a chemistry department and a department of chemical engineering. University researchers, being less concerned with application, tend to see particular problems against a broader horizon. Contact with university researchers helps to break down the tunnel vision that comes from working too long in a single direction or too close to a particular technology, something more likely to happen in an industrial laboratory than in university laboratory.

Though some differences between university and business researchers have this benign origin, others do not. For business, knowledge is primarily a source of wealth rather than reputation or public service. To produce wealth, knowledge must be controlled in ways it need not be to gain reputation or to serve some community of users. Businesses therefore tend to be more secretive than universities, their research something to be discussed freely only "in the company" (or even only within a unit of the company). University researchers generally move in a wider world, talking as freely with researchers at other institutions as with those down the hall.

The problem of secrecy is, however, not unknown even within the university. Some university researchers do classified research. Such researchers, especially those working within separate laboratories under contract with the Department of Defense, may work under conditions more secretive than those under which the ordinary scientist in business works. Such university researchers tend to be cut off from other university researchers. While they may benefit from hearing what ordinary researchers are doing, they can freely discuss their own work only with those having the appropriate government clearance. They cannot engage in the give-and-take of ordinary science.

Most university researchers tend to view those among them whose research is largely, or entirely, classified as outside their community even when they work in the next lab. For that reason (among others), universities have generally discouraged classified research on campus. When they have allowed it, they have usually tried to make the research as open as possible, for example, by settling in advance what will be publishable and how long publication can be delayed. Universities have done what they could to prevent the intellectual isolation secrecy within the university tends to generate.

Researchers within biotechnology companies have tried to do something similar because, even within a business, secrecy tends to impede the free communication on which science – and engineering – thrive. One benefit these researchers derive from profitable links with a university department is an argument for keeping controls on information within the company to a minimum. Since university researchers tend to resist secrecy on principle, the same secrecy that impedes scientific communication within the company tends to make it hard to maintain close links with university researchers.

Something missing? Notably missing from this list of reasons for wanting closer links with university researchers is access to equipment. Biotechnology companies may be unusual in this respect. But that was not a consideration they mentioned. Why not? The explanation does not seem to be that business research is better funded than university research. No one with experience of both made such a suggestion. What they did say suggests the following explanation. A company developing a particular technology is likely to have many more researchers working in a small field than is even a large biology department. So, even if the amount spent on equipment per researcher were the same, the biotechnology company's aggregate fund for equipment suitable for a particular *field* would be greater. The biotechnology company would be more likely to have the full range of equipment needed for work in that small field (while having far less in the way of equipment needed for other fields, even those closely related but not part of its research plan). As in other respects, so with equipment, the university tends to be the generalist, the business, the specialist.

What the university can get from business

The few university administrators I talked to either were willing to do whatever the "research community" wanted or talked primarily as researchers rather than as administrators. While pleased whenever income from research increased, they did not view the administration as initiating profitable links between university and business. The initiators were individual researchers (or research groups). These researchers generally identified three reasons for their links with business: placement, technology, and stimulation.

Placement   American universities have been on short rations for a long time. Since the late 1960s, placing PhDs in university positions has become increasingly difficult, even in relatively hot fields like biotechnology. A department that does not do well placing its graduates will eventually find itself with fewer graduate students. Fewer graduate students would mean less university support, more undergraduate teaching, fewer colleagues, older equipment, and eventually less interesting research. Faculty therefore have reason to want their students to have good jobs upon graduation. Today, many of those jobs are in industry.

A faculty member's close links with a particular biotechnology company gives a student a better chance of being offered a permanent position there after graduation. Instead of a rushed courtship in the few months before graduation, the student can spend two or three years working beside the company's researchers, giving everyone adequate time to make a full assessment. This is especially important for those many students who are more impressive on the job than at an interview.

Technology   Basic research in biotechnology itself depends heavily on developments in applications. A particular line of research may require inserting certain biological materials into a cell. Procedures for producing large amounts of that material and "vectors" for inserting the material into a cell are today at least as likely to be developed in the laboratory of a biotechnology company as in a university laboratory. University scientists closely linked to the right company may be able to get the procedures or vectors they need much more quickly than those without such links. Hearing of them much earlier, they may save several years of work.

That a particular university researcher will benefit from the work of a particular biotechnology company is today relatively easy to predict. If the researcher is working with the same organism as the company, the company is likely to have (or be developing) equipment, procedures, or materials the researcher will find useful and otherwise unavailable. Because their research is related to what the company is doing, the researchers are also likely to have something to bargain with. Collaboration is therefore likely to benefit both. In return for being allowed to monitor a researcher's progress (that is, to see the research well before publication), the company may agree to alert the researcher to what it develops, provide them with new products at cost, and otherwise help the research along.

Stimulation   Those opposed to university–business research links seem to worry as much as anything about the redirection of university research such links tend to produce, what they view as "warping of the research agenda." This worry is not baseless. Even university researchers with close links to business agreed that their research should be determined by the probability of scientifically interesting discoveries, not the profit it might generate. They also agreed that greed does sometimes lead university researchers to seek profit rather than knowledge. They none the less thought their links with business justified.

Why? They did not justify their links with business simply by the access to technology or placement of graduate students that resulted. Those benefits, though substantial, were not, they thought, enough, even taken together, to justify the risk of being drawn into research having no inherent interest for them. They were sure that, if necessary, they could find ways to obtain much the same technology and student placement while putting somewhat more distance between themselves and business. The one benefit they did not think they could obtain if they put more distance between themselves and business was the intellectual stimulation they got from working closely with business researchers on particular projects.

I must admit that, at first, I found this claim suspicious. How convenient! They knew that working with business had changed their research. Why not ascribe the change to intellectual stimulation rather than to the warping effect of too much concern with marketing? As the Greeks used to say: "Whom the gods would destroy, they first make mad." Eventually, however, I decided the claim of intellectual stimulation should be taken seriously. There were two reasons for this.

One reason was empirical. The researchers not only claimed to be more productive scientists as a result of their links with business, they provided anecdotal evidence, stories of how their work with business called attention to particular possibilities they thought they might otherwise have overlooked. Such anecdotes are not the only empirical evidence for their claim. There is statistical evidence as well. For example, one survey reports that "faculty...who were receiving industry support tended to publish more, patent more, earn more, serve in more administrative roles, and teach as much as faculty without industry funds."[3]

The other reason I eventually put aside my suspicions was that I realized that I had had much the same experience myself. I had initially studied applied ethics as an adjunct to teaching courses in that field, courses which, from the outside, looked like "pandering to the student market." Yet, over the years, as I attempted to apply my theoretical views to the practical questions on which such courses focus, I found my theoretical views changing. Much that made sense in the abstract turned out to be nonsense in practice. As my sense of moral practice changed, others, including some died-in-the-wool theorists, found my views on ethics growing more interesting. My publication rate improved substantially. Perhaps all this would have happened had I never had anything to do with applied ethics, but I do not see how.[4]

So, I now think we should take university researchers at their word when they claim they benefit intellectually from working closely with researchers in business (at least until their publications tell us otherwise). Once we accept that claim, we can see why Nader's call to break all links between university and business must be rejected. Some of those links are paying for themselves in scientific knowledge, the one coin even an ideal university must honor.

Money? Notably absent from this list of reasons is money, a reason upon which Nader laid great stress. The researchers I talked to suggested three reasons why money as such is not important. First, for them, money is primarily a means of getting equipment and supporting students. Money is thus implicit in the reasons they did list. Second, they thought that biotechnology companies generally wanted to link up with the best biology departments, that is, those whose researchers were also most likely to win government grants. Links with business did not so much increase their research support as change its source and, with its source, the arguments necessary to justify it. Third, and perhaps most surprising, most biotechnology companies did not seem to have vast pools of money to dump into new research. Getting money out of a company was at least as hard as getting it out of the government. Indeed, the major difference between the two was that getting money out of a company was a much more personal affair, with memos, phone conversations, and meetings often taking the place of a formal application.

Conclusion: what's to worry?

I do not wish to sound too cheerful about links between universities and business. Like Nader, I think those links can endanger a university's soul. I none the less differ from Nader in two ways. First, I have a more pluralistic conception of the university's soul. Second, and in part because of that, I deny that the danger is inherent in most links between university and business.

Universities are not only learned places, places where the learned congregate; they are as well, and indeed primarily, places for learning, whether by discovery or by being taught. The university will not lose its soul so long as its links with business serve learning. The question, then, is which links between university and business are likely to serve learning and which are not. Those links likely to interfere with learning should be forbidden or, where that is impossible, discouraged.

I shall conclude this chapter by pointing out three links between university and business that can endanger learning. While the list could be lengthened, I do not think lengthening is necessary here. These dangers are enough to make my general point.

One danger comes from within the university itself, from university researchers who want to get rich and will stay at the university only if university policies make such enrichment possible. For example, some researchers want to benefit personally from the patents they are credited with. They want to use university facilities, including graduate students, to work on projects from which they will, they hope, eventually make money for themselves. University policy should be designed to encourage such researchers to go elsewhere, for example, by providing that all patents developed in university facilities become the property of the university. The university might then put the income from patents back into research, even into research in the particular researcher's laboratory, but not into the researcher's pocket.

Why discourage the greedy in this way? The university, unlike the market, is a place where riches are (or, at least, should be) suspect. The rewards the university offers are the pleasure of learning something new, the fellowship of those who value knowledge for itself or for the public good it can do, and (ultimately) the honor of doing something for knowledge that the fellowship considers important.

University researchers do sometimes become rich, as do professors who simply write text books. But those who want riches should go into business, not as researchers (for whom, like university researchers, a precondition of employment is generally signing an agreement giving the employer all property rights in what they discover during their employment) but as entrepreneurs, holders of equity, who may go broke in the market instead of growing rich. The university should not go out of its way to make room for those whose purposes are alien. They can be friends outside; but, inside, they are enemies, seeking personal profit where they are supposed to discover and teach.

A second danger comes from those links between university and business which, whether or not entered into to make university researchers more than a reasonable academic income, would raise doubts about the independence of the researcher's scientific judgment. The worst example I know of was a professor who, in partial payment for overseeing FDA-required testing of a new drug, was to receive stock options in the company producing the drug. The options would have been worth nothing unless the test turned out positive.

While lawyers have long been sensitive to conflict of interest, academics are only now beginning to think in such terms. Universities need to provide policies for identifying potential conflicts, for avoiding those that can be avoided, and for disclosing to interested parties those that cannot (or need not) be avoided. Though the government has begun to force universities to have policies on certain conflicts of interest relevant to government-supported research, universities probably should go well beyond what they are now required by law to do.

The third danger, the last I shall identify here, concerns information the university produces for business or receives from business. A university exits to teach what its faculty knows. Secrecy, however justified outside the university, is inconsistent with that commitment to spreading knowledge. Classified or proprietary research may be excused, especially if the secrecy covers only a small part of a research plan, is of brief duration, or is confined to laboratories separate from the university proper. But a university should view even excusable arrangements with untiring distrust. Such arrangements should never become so normal that the income they generate becomes sufficient to justify them.

This list of dangers may sound surprisingly like Nader's. Yet it follows from what I suggested and justifies many of the links Nader condemns. The stimulation that both business and university researchers cite as the one advantage that cannot be achieved except by close links between them, presupposes important differences between them. So, for example, a university researcher would not be nearly as likely to be helpful with a problem that a business researcher has been working on if the university researcher were just as concerned with marketable applications as is the business researcher. Similarly, a business researcher is not nearly as likely to stimulate ideas for new lines of research in a university researcher who has been thinking like a business researcher all along. If (as I believe) what makes the university useful to business depends on such differences, the long run interest of business (as well as of the university) is in preserving those differences. University–business links should not include any that endanger the fundamental difference between university and business.

6

OF BABBAGE AND KINGS: A STUDY OF A PLAGIARISM COMPLAINT

Claiming as one's own what one knows to be the discovery, idea, or writing of another is certainly plagiarism. But what about merely failing to acknowledge the work of another where one does not give the impression that the discovery is one's own? Does it matter how one came upon the knowledge in question, whether in a book, as a referee for a journal, or from private correspondence? Does it matter how easy it was to make the discovery? This is a gray area both in research ethics and in professorial ethics.

While I shall be concerned with this gray area here, I shall not try to provide a definitive answer to the questions just posed. Instead, I shall describe what happened when an independent scholar, believing himself to be the victim of "gray" plagiarism, sought a forum in which to make his complaint. What happened suggests a need to think more deeply about how we assign credit within the university and to scholars outside and about what how we should respond to complaints about misassignment of credit.

The discovery

My story begins with a footnote in the history of mathematics. The July 1983 issue of *Annals of the History of Computing* carried an article entitled "Babbage's Letter to Quetelet, May 1835." The article's heart was a modern translation into English of a much older French translation from English. The French translation, printed in 1835 in the *Bulletin of the Royal Academy of Arts and Sciences of Brussels*, is significant because it contains the first mention in print of Babbage's Analytical Engine, a precursor of today's computer.[1] The "Babbage" of my title is the author of that letter (the same Babbage who wrote *Reflections on the Decline of Science in England*). One of my title's "kings" is the present King of

Belgium; the others are the chief personages of various academic fiefdoms.

The article's introduction noted: "The exact date of the letter is not clear, and the original is not known to exist." The article's author, Alfred W. Van Sinderen, was a long-time collector of Babbage's manuscripts, of his published works, and of works about him. Though Van Sinderen earned his living as chief executive of the Southern New England Telephone Company, his judgments carried weight with Babbage scholars.

Herman Berg, the chief character of our story, shared Van Sinderen's interest in Babbage. Without a college degree, he corresponded with many academics, museums, and libraries concerning common research interests. He also studied mathematics and foreign languages. During the academic year 1971-2, he was studying Japanese at the University of Kansas. There, at a meeting of the Scuba Club, he met an accountant from Kansas City who, hearing he lived in Detroit and was interested in computers, urged him to look up a brother-in-law, "Buzz" (Bernard) Galler, at the University of Michigan's Computing Center in Ann Arbor (an hour from Detroit).

Berg looked Galler up during the winter break. Galler gave Berg "the grand tour" and urged him to come to Ann Arbor as a student. Berg, indicating an interest, pointed out that he had another year's commitment to Japanese at Kansas. They did not meet again for a decade; by then, Galler was editor-in-chief of the *Annals*.

In August 1983, Berg got permission to sit in on a course in software engineering that Galler was to team teach. Galler's teammate actually granted the permission (on condition that Berg explain a software project to be assigned), but it was this class that reintroduced them. While Galler was not often in class, he did see much of Berg's presentation of a topological sorting algorithm. After class a few days later, they had a long conversation. Berg told Galler of his life during the intervening decade, including studies at the University of Wisconsin, and of his interests in the history of mathematics. Berg was then reading the *Proceedings of the 4th International Statistical Congress, London, 1860*. Like the reading of Babbage's letter to the Belgium Royal Academy in 1835, this congress was an important event in the early history of computing. The Scheutz computing machine (a realization of Babbage's idea) was in use at the General Registry. Babbage invited congress attenders, including Florence Nightingale, to see it work. Quetelet was there as well.

Seeing how excited Berg was about the *Proceedings*, Galler told him something of the internal workings of the *Annals*, including the history of Van Sinderen's still unpublished article, and gave it to Berg, suggesting he see what he could do with it.

Why did Galler do that? Berg offers this explanation (based on what Galler told him at the time): both reviewers had wanted to delay recommending publication until sure the original letter could not be found because, if it could be found, the translation would be unnecessary (and therefore not worth publishing). Neither reviewer was quick to give up the search. Meanwhile, Van Sinderen gave Galler a good deal of grief for the long time it was taking the journal to make a decision. Eventually Galler forced a decision from the reviewers, leaving both them and him not quite satisfied. Apparently, Galler saw Berg as an opportunity to put to rest remaining doubts about publishing Van Sinderen's paper.

Early in January 1984, Berg "tackled" the paper. He soon realized that Van Sinderen had missed some holdings of Babbage correspondence. Using indexes at the University of Michigan, Berg was led from Babbage to a file of Quetelet's correspondence in Belgium (in the Archives of the Royal Academy). Berg wrote for a copy of the file on 22 February. By 26 March 1984, he had before him a photocopy of the missing English version of the letter, in Babbage's own hand and dated 27 April 1835.

Complications

Pleased with what he had found, Berg called Galler the next day (while in Ann Arbor on other business). Berg expected warm congratulations. He got something else. As Berg remembers their talk, Galler almost immediately changed the subject to a letter Berg had written to Van Sinderen in February. It was, Berg recalls, a long letter in which he praised Van Sinderen's translation, explained how he came to examine Van Sinderen's paper, and told Van Sinderen about some sources he had discovered. Berg also mentioned the delay in publication, sketched what he knew, and concluded that Van Sinderen was owed an apology (which, apparently, Van Sinderen took as an apology).

Galler said Van Sinderen had "laid it in to him" for telling tales out of class. Why had Berg, of all people, been offering an apology for something the *Annals* had done? Galler seemed to view the letter both as a breach of his confidence and as hurting Berg's relationship with Van Sinderen. His tone was severe: Berg had no business offering an apology to Van Sinderen, and no business repeating what Galler told him about the workings of the *Annals*.

Badly shaken by this exchange, Berg tried to repair the damage. As soon as he had hung up the phone, he sent Galler a copy of the Babbage letter (through campus mail), hoping that seeing the document might help Galler regain perspective. Berg then went to the office of the University's Vice President for Academic Affairs, looking for an explanation of what he had done wrong and advice about what to do next. A secretary made an appointment for him with Robert Holbrook, an economist then serving as Associate Vice President for Academic Affairs (and a member of the University's Joint Task Force on Integrity in Scholarship). The appointment was for a few days later.

When they met at the appointed time, Holbrook treated Berg cordially, heard him out, and then declared that Berg's ignorance should excuse the breach of editorial confidentiality. And, he added, Berg's discovery was in any case significant enough to outweigh such a small sin. Berg left with the impression that Holbrook might "straighten Galler out."

Berg also wrote letters of apology to Van Sinderen and to the two outside reviewers (whom he had referred to by name). Berg's letter to Van Sinderen seems to have worked. In a letter dated 25 June 1984 ("cc – Galler"), Van Sinderen thanked Berg for "your 'peace offering'," adding that it was "not really necessary, as I always have positive thoughts about people who are interested in Charles Babbage."

Soon after mailing these letters, Berg dropped by Galler's office. This visit went no better than the phone conversation. Galler tried to convince Berg that the discovery was not important enough to warrant publication in the *Annals*, certainly not worth a note, and not even a letter to the editor to correct the historical record. After all, Galler argued, the letter differed in only small ways from the translation Van Sinderen had made from the French. The differences were not important to the later history of computing.

Berg could not understand Galler's response. Had Berg not found the lost "ur-letter" of computing? Had he not shown that it still existed, dated it, and provided the full text? Until his discovery, who could say how long the original letter was or how well Quetelet had translated it? Scholars would hereafter know that Quetelet had omitted three paragraphs at the beginning and two at the end (and what those paragraphs said). They would have Babbage's exact words. If Van Sinderen's now unnecessary translation had been worth publishing, why not Berg's original?

These questions led to another. Programs in the history of science are rare; programs in the history of mathematics are rarer still. The University of Michigan had neither. Galler's own background was in mathematics (with a PhD from the University of Chicago), not history of any sort. His work was far from the literary or industrial "archaeology" to which Berg's discovery belongs. Could it be that Galler's editorial judgment in this area was unreliable? To answer that question, Berg wrote to others in the field describing his difficulties with Galler and asking their opinion of his discovery.

Galler soon heard of these letters. On 25 April 1984, he wrote Berg asking him to come in to "discuss some of the letters you have written." They met in May. The tone of this meeting was different from the one before. While urging Berg to stop writing "those letters," Galler no longer dismissed Berg's discovery altogether. Instead, he urged Berg to do "more" with the Babbage letter. Berg mentioned a number of archives he could check. The meeting ended.

Berg left dissatisfied. The "more" Galler was asking seemed more or less what Van Sinderen had already done. Berg might turn up something new (as he had just done). But, without a clear idea of what he was looking for, he was unlikely to beat Van Sinderen a second time at what he did best. What was more likely was that Berg would simply waste time. Then one of two possibilities might be realized: either Van Sinderen's false claim would remain in print unchallenged, or another scholar would do what Berg had done. If that other scholar made the same discovery independently and published it, Berg would get no credit for what he had done. (In history, as in science, priority goes to the one to publish first.) Berg felt he could not just do as Galler asked (though he did try to do that, keeping Galler informed of mostly unsuccessful efforts to get access to various archives).

About this time, the University of Michigan issued its first-ever *Guidelines for Maintaining Academic Integrity*. (This was the work of the Joint Task Force of which Holbrook was a member.) The *Guidelines* included advice on maintaining priority for a discovery when publication has been blocked. Berg used the *Guidelines* as a checklist. So, for example, he donated a copy of the Babbage letter (and related documents) to the University of Michigan Library (which the Library duly acknowledged on 14 May 1984). He also wrote anyone active in the field whom he had not already told, sending each an "unprint" (that is, a copy of the original Babbage letter, a brief summary of what Berg had done, and a copy of Van Sinderen's article).

Much of this must have made Galler unhappy. As Berg recalls their next meeting (early July), Galler told Berg he had been receiving phone calls advising him to publish Berg's discovery as a letter. As Galler recalled the meeting (letter of 10 August), he told Berg he would continue to help with Berg's history activities *provided* Berg "dropped the extraneous correspondence dealing with personalities and past events which were really none of your business." If Berg did not drop the correspondence, Galler "would have nothing further to do with you."

Berg did not do as Galler asked. For example, on 24 July he wrote to the History of Science Society, sending them a copy of the Babbage letter, and – by way of explanation – stating:

> Dr. Bernard Galler is in no hurry to publish it even as a letter to the editor announcement to correct the historical record. I find it difficult to separate the mind games he has been playing with me from his editorial judgment. Dr. Galler has backed off from a position giving me no credit to allowing me to publish at some later date when I have an unspecified "more". Feeling initially blocked by him I sent copies to all of those I was aware of [being] actively involved in Charles Babbage studies. Thus, even if I was never published, I would have in some form fulfilled a scholarly obligation to communicate my results to others. Currently, it seems like Dr. Galler is still dissembling with me as he scrambles to cover himself with his reviewers and editorial board members.[2]

These letters did not always have the effect Berg intended. For example, Van Sinderen responded to Berg's letter of 30 July with a two-and-a-half page synopsis of their correspondence ("cc – B. Galler"). While he ended by urging Berg to forget the past, he was clearly upset that Berg should "write me again, page after page of concerns and speculations about who did what to whom containing, among other things, unfounded suspicions that it was [one of the two reviewers], a close friend of mine, who delayed publication of my article in the *Annals*."

On 10 August, after receiving a copy of Van Sinderen's letter to

Berg (dated 31 July), Galler wrote Berg again: "[You] did not take my advice [but] continued to participate in the kind of activity which can only be destructive to your relationships with other historians." Therefore (with "great reluctance"), he had to "terminate" his relationship with Berg. Galler did, however, add that Berg could continue to submit work to the *Annals*. Any submissions would be sent out to reviewers in the usual way: "There will be no bias against you."

This letter did indeed end their relationship. Doubting Galler would treat him better than he already had, Berg submitted nothing to him again. Until Galler retired as editor-in-chief in 1987, Berg's contact with the *Annals* only concerned other matters and these contacts were always with other editors. Berg's two-page note on the missing letter did not appear in the *Annals* until January 1992.[3]

Plagiarism?

In 1989, New York University Press published *The Works of Charles Babbage* in eleven volumes. Volume 3 contains, among other things, Babbage's papers on the Analytical Engine. Pages 12–14 reprint (in English translation) minutes of the general meeting of the Belgian Royal Academy of Science in which Quetelet read the letter he had received from Babbage (and in which Babbage then stepped forward to speak briefly on another topic, namely Sir John Herschel's plans for a meteorological study). An asterisk beside the title signaled a footnote. The footnote began, "This article is an English version (not strictly a translation) of [the famous 1835 letter] which immediately precedes it [in its French version] in this volume." After giving credit to Lovelace's partial translation (1843) and to Van Sinderen's complete translation, the editor indicates that

> [in] preparing this English version…use has been made of a letter from Babbage to Quetelet, preserved in the Quetelet Collection in the Bibliotheque Royal de Belgique, Brussels. This letter, which is written in English and dated 27 April 1835, is believed to be the same that Quetelet read to the general meeting of the Academie, 7–8 May 1835. The text of this letter has been used, lightly edited for readability, in the version below. Van Sinderen's translation has been used for the French text which did not form part of Babbage's letter.

The note gives no credit to anyone for finding the missing original. It just says that the letter is in the Royal Library. Van Sinderen receives two mentions for his translation; Berg receives nothing for finding the original.

Berg first read this note early in December 1989. The more he looked at it, the more disturbing he found it. There was, first, a shortening of the title of Van Sinderen's article. The date, and only the date ("of May, 1835") had been omitted from the reference (replaced by the usual mark of elision). Had the date not been omitted, Berg thought, it would have been obvious that Van Sinderen did not know of the letter's actual date (now indicated in print for the first time). Second, there was that reference to the "Bibliotheque Royal." The Royal Library had, Berg believed, transferred its Quetelet collection to the Royal Academy several decades before. The scholar who found the letter would not have made that mistake.[4]

Last, as far as Berg could see, the letter was (except for light editing and the omission of the first three and last two paragraphs) the one he had discovered.[5] If there was any reason to credit either the French translation or Van Sinderen's retranslation, was there not more reason to credit Berg for finding the original? The original pre-empted all translations. There was also a good reason to get the Academy's permission to publish the letter: scholarly custom. Berg had sought, and received, that permission, which was granted on condition that the Academy receive proper credit in print. *The Works of Babbage* neither credited the Academy for the letter (though apparently relying on it) nor indicated receiving anyone's permission to publish it.

Berg held in his hand what purported to be the definitive edition of Babbage's work, opened to the page supposedly containing the text of the most famous letter in the history of computing. Yet, what that footnote told readers is that they had before them neither the original letter Berg had found nor Van Sinderen's translation of the French version of Quetelet, but something new, a mix of the two "edited for readability." The rest of the original, though available for inclusion, was omitted. What could explain this?

The explanation could not be that the editors had confined themselves to previously published work. They did not claim to have such a policy, and in fact, they had not followed such a policy. (They had, for example, included what seemed to be a previously unpublished "Statement to the Duke of Wellington.") Berg supposed the worst. Someone was trying to slip by without recognizing Berg's contribution to Babbage scholarship.

Martin Campbell-Kelly, from the University of Warwick in England, was the editor-in-chief of the *Works*. He was also a member of the editorial board of the *Annals*. However, he was not personally responsible for the footnote. An editorial undertaking on the scale of the *Works* requires considerable delegation. There were four "consulting editors." One of these, Allan Bromley, University of Sydney, Australia, seemed to take responsibility for the part of Volume 3 relevant here.[6] He was also one of those to whom Berg had announced his discovery. Indeed, Bromley had written a friendly ("Dear Herman") note of acknowledgment on 19 June 1984:

> Thank you for your letter of 22 May and the information enclosed. I was particularly interested to read Babbage's letter to Quetelet, especially the comment "but it will take many months to work out all the details." How true that proved to be![7]

There could, it seemed, be no doubt that, since Bromley was responsible for that section, he had used Berg's research without giving credit.[8] Berg had done a scholar's work; he had not received a scholar's pay. What could he do?

Search for a forum

Berg could see no point in writing to Bromley. What could he write someone he believed guilty of plagiarism? What could such a letter accomplish? So, on 4 January 1990, he wrote to the Australian Academy of Science (AAS), providing relevant documents and asking for an investigation. The AAS responded within two weeks: "The matter to which you refer is exceedingly complex, but this Academy has neither the facilities nor indeed the ability to investigate the possible misdeeds of scientists working in this country..." It was a response that would become familiar.

Berg then wrote the chancellor of the University of Sydney, Bromley's home institution. He received no response, not even a courtesy acknowledgment of receipt. After what he considered a decent interval, Berg wrote to Australia's Prime Minister. The Attorney-General's Department responded on 12 October. Treating Berg's letter as an inquiry concerning copyright infringement, an

Assistant Secretary for International Trade and Law said the government could do nothing. Berg could claim no copyright infringement.

Well before this, Berg had realized that "blowing the whistle" was not going to be as easy as he had thought. He had therefore begun to make complaints wherever it seemed appropriate. He tried Campbell-Kelly's home institution, the University of Warwick. When he received no response there, he wrote to the British Prime Minister, who (on 6 September 1990) referred Berg's complaint to her Attorney-General. A year later, one Detective Inspector Smith wrote to Berg that Scotland Yard had examined the materials Berg sent and could find no evidence of criminal wrongdoing. A month after that the British Patent Office wrote that "there is nothing we can add to Inspector Smith's letter."

Berg also wrote to the *Works*' publisher, New York University Press. When he received no response, he wrote to New York University itself. Again there was no response. Since Pickering and Chatto published the British edition of the *Works*, Berg wrote them as well. On 30 March 1990, one of their directors wrote back, thanking Berg for his letter and adding "I am truly sorry you feel aggrieved over the Babbage letter, but I am afraid that there is nothing I can do about it. If you wish to pursue the matter, I suggest you correspond with Dr. Campbell-Kelly." Though Berg did not then know it, one of his letters, a complaint addressed to Warwick's Office of the Chancellor (29 December 1989) had already reached Campbell-Kelly and another, the one addressed to the British publishers of the *Works*, would do so in May 1990. Not only did Campbell-Kelley not respond to either of these, but he also failed to respond when Berg wrote to him directly (on 9 May 1992) warning that I was soon to publish a paper concerning the complaint.[9]

Berg also sought the help of the Government of the United States, writing to the Office of Science and Technology Policy on 7 January 1990. They advised him on 8 February that because they lacked the "capacity to investigate individual scientific cases," he should take his complaint to "relevant research institutions and sponsoring federal agencies." Berg thereupon began writing every federal agency that might be "relevant": the National Science Foundation (17 February 1990), Department of Health and Human Services (21 February 1990), Department of Labor (15 March 1990), Office of Government Ethics (16 July 1990), United States Information Service [no date], Department of Education (5 October

1990), the Postal Service [no date], Department of Justice (26 September 1991), and Commission of Customs (10 January 1992). The dates indicate the first date of writing; he wrote to some of these agencies several times. All responded each time he wrote. But, by 1992, Berg was receiving responses like this one from NSF:

> We have received your letter of June 19, 1992. This and any future letters, on matters we have already addressed, will not be answered because to do so will waste valuable resources.

This is where the present King of Belgium comes in. He failed Berg as well, handing Berg's letter to his Cabinet Chief who wrote to Berg (3 September 1991) to confirm the can't-do-anything letter that the Prime Minister's Diplomatic Advisor had sent a few weeks before. No one in Belgium seemed to care that a document in the Royal Academy had been published without permission (and without proper credit).

This list of addressees, though interesting in its way, is worth our time primarily because of what it tells about Berg's search for a forum. Whatever we think of the complaint itself, we must agree that Berg's search for an avenue of redress was reasonably thorough. So, to dissolve any suspicion that he might have gotten a hearing had he done a little more, I must tell something more of what he did. Berg sought the help not only of the appropriate universities, the *Works'* publisher, and several national governments, but of some lesser governments, politicians, professional societies, and even the news media.

Because the *Works'* publisher was located in New York City, Berg wrote New York City's Police Department, the District Attorney of the County of New York, and the Citizen's Action Center (an arm of the City's Office of the Comptroller). Each of these thought his complaint lay in someone else's jurisdiction. The State's Department of Law referred him to the State's Department of Education (on 20 August 1991). By then, Berg had exchanged several letters with an Assistant Commissioner for Higher Education Services who eventually suggested (20 May 1991) that Berg write to the editors of the *Works* and, if they did not respond satisfactorily, "consult a lawyer to see whether your claim has any legal standing." Michigan's attorney general gave much the same advice (25 November 1991).

The Center for Law in the Public Interest referred Berg to the law firm of Hall and Phillips (Los Angeles). The opinion of Hall and Phillips was that "while you have a legitimate grievance, this is not the type of grievance we handle" (24 April 1992). They did not say who did.

Politicians showed no interest whatever. The White House referred him to the Office of Government Ethics (30 October 1990). That Office had already referred him to the Designated Agency Ethics Official in the Department of Education (2 August 1990). The Office of the Vice President simply thanked him for writing (10 December 1990). Congressman Dingell, known for his hearings on fraud in science and protection of whistleblowers, declined to help Congressman Conyers' constituent, sending Berg's letter on to him (8 November 1991). On 15 April 1992, Congressman Conyers wrote, "This is an issue that needs to be worked out at universities and other educational institutions." Bill Clinton wrote that he had "turned your letter over to my staff for review and study" (27 November 1991). That was the last Berg heard from Clinton (except for a letter of 5 August encouraging Berg "to work for the changes you want in America"). Berg heard nothing at all from any of the other candidates then competing in the presidential primaries. The President's Office of Management and Budget sent Berg's complaint to the Inspector General at the Department of Education (2 December 1991).

Back in England, Neil Kinnock, Leader of the Opposition, suggested Berg apply to the Patent Office or New Scotland Yard (9 January 1992). Berg already had.

The professional societies might seem a more likely venue than politicians. In fact, they proved no more helpful. Some came out sounding much like the politicians. For example, both the American Association for the Advancement of Science (28 December 1989) and the National Academy of Sciences (29 December 1989) pleaded lack of resources to investigate such a charge in what sound like form letters. (But each also pointed out work it had done to raise ethical standards in science.) The Phi Beta Kappa Society's rejection (18 January 1990) at least sounded like the work of an individual. Noting the society had "nothing to do with your difficulty," the letter concluded it would be inappropriate to get involved now. The letter closed by suggesting that Berg write to the American Historical Society's newsletter *Perspectives* (18 January 1990). The American Historical Association "[did] not feel that it can intervene in this situation and is unable to advise you regarding other courses of action" (7 May 1990).[10] Among the professional societies responding in this way were the New York Academy of Sciences (30 May 1990), the Mathematical Association of America (13 November 1991), the (British) Institution of Electrical Engineers (26 November 1991), and the Computer Society of the Institute of Electrical and Electronic Engineers (January 1992).

While most professional societies gave noncommittal responses, a few offered comfort (without offering help). The Secretary of the Industrial Mathematics Society responded (18 January 1990): "Your bull dog tenacity is to be admired and, like one person wrote, 'You'll have difficulties because you don't have the important three letters after your name: Ph.D'." The (British) Royal Society for the encouragement of Arts, Manufactures and Commerce (or, rather, the editor of its journal) wrote (9 March 1990):

> I was most interested to receive your letter and documentation about your discovery of the Babbage letter. It is extremely sad as well as wrong for discoveries not to be correctly attributed. In case it is any help I am forwarding copies of your material to our reviewer because of his special interest in Babbage. I am sorry I cannot do more.

The Chairman of the International Commission on the History of Mathematics wrote in a similar vein (23 May 1990):

> I wish I could say that the kinds of difficulties you mention in regard to your research on Quetelet and Babbage were relatively uncommon in academic circles, but as you've discovered, they are not so uncommon as most people suspect.

More telling, perhaps, was the response of the Executive Director of the Commission on Professionals in Science and Technology (13 May 1992). Having informed Berg that, though already "familiar with your story," she could not help, she added:

> It is surprising that academic institutions, which usually jump all over people for plagiarism, have not hastened to give you credit for discovering the Babbage-Quetelet correspondence.... Your situation is not uncommon for women, who often are not credited with their work, while one or more men claim it as their own.

Yet, to the (British) Council for Science and Society must go any award for the best reason for doing nothing. Having thanked Berg for the documents sent, the Council's chair observed (6 December 1990), "Unfortunately, the Council is now being forced to shut down, as we are caught in a financial crisis."

Berg even tried to go public. Mary McGory (*Washington Post*) declined, pleading "[it] is over my head and out of my line" (4 October 1991). William Buckley (*National Review*) thought Berg's case "too far removed from too many of our readers' understanding and interests" (15 October 1991). John Maddox (*Nature*'s editor) was "sorry to have to echo what your other correspondents have had to say, that I am afraid there is nothing we can do to help" (18 May 1992). Dear Abby was sorry too, "but since legal matters are out of my area of expertise, I cannot help you" [no date]. Dennis Selby, Assistant to the *Nation*'s editor, judged that "it is a question of attribution rather than plagiarism [but, in] any event, *The Nation* is not the most appropriate venue for this matter" (30 June 1992). *Time* simply thanked Berg for writing (2 July 1992).[11]

"Blowing the whistle" is not as easy as generally thought.

Ironies and insights

The ironies of this story are many. I will note only four here.

First, following the (good) advice of the University of Michigan's *Guidelines for Maintaining Academic Integrity*, Berg informally published what he could not publish in a journal. Informal publication was supposed to assure him appropriate recognition. Perhaps it still will. But, initially, it may have had the opposite effect, allowing others to use Berg's discovery without crediting him. The *Guidelines*' advice presupposes a willingness of scholars to credit unpublished work.

Second, those institutions best situated to investigate the charges seem to be the very institutions least likely to respond to a complaint; or, at least, a complaint made by a non-academic outside the institution. Those responding to Berg's complaint, everyone from the Australian Academy of Science to Scotland Yard, from the National Science Foundation to Bill Clinton, were generally those least well situated to investigate, whether for lack of resources, jurisdiction, or knowledge. How odd that Dear Abby should have more to say about Berg's complaint than did the Universities of Sydney or Warwick, or New York University Press!

Third, the silence of the institutions that should have responded has not been good for anyone. The complaint did not die but faded into a shadow, darkening the reputation of everyone connected with *The Works of Charles Babbage* (until I published my first article on the subject). That cannot be good for them or for scholars generally (or for anyone else in research). What explains the silence? A clear conscience? Guilt? A dislike of controversy?[12]

The fourth, and last, irony is one common in cases of whistle-blowing. We, the public, have only half the story, a complaint resting on clear and substantial evidence, but still only a complaint.[13] Until the other side has been heard, any judgment we make must be provisional. But, though the other side does not defend itself, we must make a judgment (however provisional). And what can we conclude except that Berg was wronged? Silence is a poor defense.[14]

But ironies do not justify retelling that story in a work on ethics and the university; only insight into ethics in the university can. I think we may state those insights as five lessons.

The first lesson of Berg's story is that there is a *geographic* misfit between the field in which we would hope to maintain research ethics and the institutions we have for maintaining it. The sun never sets on those whom Berg seemed justified in accusing. Like the field they work in, the history of computing, they gird the globe. Yet, the institutions that we would most like to have original jurisdiction over a case like Berg's are geographically small units, universities. None has control over more than one important party in the case.

The second lesson is that many universities do not know what to do with a complaint like Berg's. Only in the last few years, primarily in the United States, have universities begun to establish formal procedures for dealing with cases of faculty research misconduct. Though largely designed to deal with wrongdoing in the laboratory rather than in the library, a university having such procedures should also have a routine for responding to a complaint like Berg's. Such a university might give Berg no more satisfaction than did the King of Belgium, but it would not have fallen into the embarrassing silence of the Universities of Sydney or Warwick.

A third lesson to draw from Berg's story is that there is a problem of what lawyers call "diversity of citizenship" for procedures designed to maintain research ethics. The scholarly world is not, as we often suppose, coextensive with the academy. In some fields, the history of computing being only one, there are significant numbers of non-academics. We need to imagine cases involving, for example, the CEO of a power company, a journal editor with academic standing, and a mathematician working in industry. Some of the non-academics will not have a PhD. Yet, as several of Berg's correspondents noted, academics seem to discount the work of non-academics, especially if they do not have a doctorate, and to feel no obligation to credit a non-academic's work when they would credit the work of an academic.[15]

This prejudice, if it exists, would make problematic the grant of original jurisdiction to universities in cases where one of the parties is not an academic. The U.S. Constitution addresses a similar problem arising when the citizen of one state sues the citizen of another. Rather than force citizens of one state to appear in a court where they would have the disadvantage of being outsiders, the Constitution allows either party to the case to remove the suit to federal court. Every citizen is entitled to a forum not likely to be biased by state citizenship. Perhaps the academy needs to develop something similar to hear cases like that of Berg.

A fourth lesson to be learned from Berg's story is that the boundaries of plagiarism are far from settled. No one responding to Berg doubted that failing to attribute the discovery of Babbage's letter was wrong (assuming the editors derived knowledge of the original from Berg). There were, however, several who thought that the wrong in question was not plagiarism but (as Dennis Selby put it) a failure to attribute.[16] In fact, while everyone seemed to think they knew what the standards of attribution were, there was no general agreement. Stating standards is part of determining what they are (or shall be).

A fifth lesson is that scholars do not yet agree on *how* serious the wrong Berg complains of is (whether or not they think it is plagiarism). Even among Berg's academic correspondents, a common view seems to be that the wrong done Berg is (like Berg's breach of Galler's confidentiality) quite petty. So, for example, one professor of history at Cornell commented: "If it were a straightforward case of plagiarism, we could raise some hell, but it is only neglect of the courtesy to acknowledge that you found the letter...[which is only] inexcusably rude."[17] A senior administrator at Boston University drew much the same conclusion (26 November 1991):

[You] were rather shabbily treated by Professor Bromley, who should have had the courtesy to acknowledge you in print as the individual who located the original English version of Babbage's letter...however, this does not appear to be a case of plagiarism.

My own view on this is quite different (as is Berg's). There are, it seems to me, degrees of failing to credit (as there are degrees of plagiarism). For example, failing to credit when giving credit would only be saying what everyone already knows is not wrong at all; but, using the work of another, where people might well assign you credit for it if you do not tell whose work it is, is, I think, as bad as much plagiarism (and, indeed, is hardly distinguishable from it). Silence can be a default claim of credit.

But that is a topic for another book. What is clear, I hope, is that we need more discussion of both what plagiarism is and of how bad failing to credit is (whether or not called "plagiarism"). Discussion of these questions should go on in every academic department. However, as Berg's story warns, we cannot be satisfied with settling such questions department by department, or even nation by nation. Scholarly communities – even small ones like the history of computing – cross departmental, national, and even continental boundaries. What is needed is international discussion of standards detailed enough to give insight into cases like Berg's.

That probably means examining more cases like Berg's, as well as the few headline cases usually called up when plagiarism is discussed. Though the poet William Blake said otherwise, we cannot, I think, expect "[to] see the universe in a grain of sand." We shall need to examine many grains of sand.[18] Part of understanding research ethics will be the collection of dozens of cases like this for each category of problem, cases to be used both to develop explicit standards and to teach those standards.

Part III

TEACHING ETHICS

7

ETHICS ACROSS THE CURRICULUM

In 1990, IIT's Center for the Study of Ethics in the Professions received a grant of more than $210,000 from the National Science Foundation to try a campus-wide approach to integrating professional ethics into the technical curriculum. In 1996, the Center received another $100,000 to continue the project, with the emphasis on passing on to other institutions what was learned at IIT.[1] I was the principal investigator under both grants. In this chapter, I describe what we at IIT did, what we learned, and what others, especially philosophers, can learn from us about teaching professional ethics in the university. We set out to develop an approach that others could profitably adopt. I believe that we succeeded.

Background: the problem

Professional ethics are – as I have said – special (morally permissible) standards of conduct governing members of a particular profession because they are members of that profession. Engineering ethics applies to engineers, legal ethics to lawyers, and so on. Institutional ethics, though similar, are still distinct. Institutional ethics are special standards of conduct governing all those connected in a certain way with a particular institution because they are so connected. Business ethics applies to all those in business (whatever their profession), research ethics to all those doing research, and so on. Though important for some purposes, this distinction is not important here. I shall therefore ignore it in what follows. I shall use "professional ethics" to refer to both professional and institutional ethics.[2]

Because they are special standards, professional ethics are more than mere ordinary morality or common sense. Like other special standards (for example, law), they cannot be learned in most families, religious institutions, or primary or secondary schools. Generally, they must be taught as part of a formal professional education or learned in some less formal way (for example, by copying what others do in a workplace).[3] Over the last few years, a consensus seems to have developed that professional schools are not doing enough to teach professional ethics.[4]

Beginning with the founding of the Center for the Study of Ethics in the Professions in 1976, IIT has recognized the importance of teaching professional ethics, experimented with various ways of connecting ethics with professional education, and learned from the experiments. We may distinguish six ways IIT has tried to make ethics a part of professional education.

One way is "independent study." Independent study merely provides materials, leaving students to make of them what they can. Since professional programs in the sciences are only now beginning to confront the need for ethics training, they are the ones most likely to use this approach. So, for example, in 1990, IIT's Pritzker Institute of Medical Engineering distributed copies of Sigma Xi's *Honor in Science* to all its graduate students and research staff.

Another way to connect ethics with professional education is by extracurricular events. Student professional associations, the administration, or others on campus might invite an outside speaker, set up a faculty panel, or show a movie (for example, *China Syndrome*) dealing with an issue of professional ethics, following it with an open discussion of the issues raised, either as part of the event or later in smaller groups in the residence halls.

These two approaches share three important disadvantages. The first is that they treat ethics as extracurricular, something distinct from the professional program (narrowly defined). That ethics is extracurricular suggests that problems of professional ethics are rare, not built into the day-to-day work of a profession. The second disadvantage is that both extracurricular approaches treat professional ethics as voluntary, something good to know, *not* something necessary for minimal competence in the profession. The third disadvantage is related to the second. Few students will read handouts they are not to be tested on or attend many "heavy" extracurricular events. The curriculum itself, as well as part-time jobs and ordinary social life, leaves most students little time or inclination for independent study or extracurricular activity. It is not surprising, then, that almost everyone now seems to agree that, whatever is done outside of class, professional ethics has to be brought into class.

One extracurricular approach that may seem free of these disadvantages is the honors code. This is an illusion. An honors code is not *extra*curricular but *super*curricular, operating within the classroom as well as outside. It belongs to a category I shall not discuss here. I have three reasons for ignoring it. First, while some IIT faculty lovingly recall their own experience with an honors code, my impression is that honors codes are a wave of the past. Students do not seem interested (though they do seem interested in the idea of creating a more ethical environment). Second, I have no direct experience of an honors code. IIT does not have one (except in ROTC). Third, an honors code (for example, "I will not lie, cheat, or steal, or tolerate those who do") is a kind of institutional ethics (usually limited to students). The connection that teaching students an honors code has to teaching another code (whether that of a profession or another institution) is mysterious. The idea seems to be that practicing an honors code helps build good character and good character is part of understanding professional ethics. While plausible (though by no means empirically verified), that claim still leaves unexplained how practicing one code teaches the *content* of another. And as far as I am concerned, our primary concern here is how to teach content. I think we must assume that our students, though far from perfect, are of generally good character. But that is an issue beyond the scope of this chapter.[5]

The simplest way to bring professional ethics into the class is the "guest lecture." The instructor in an ordinary professional course invites an "ethicist" to speak on ethics at the appropriate point in the semester ("ethics day"). The ethicist may be a member of the profession, either another faculty member or a practitioner involved in some way with ethics (for example, a member of the local grievance committee). In my experience, however, the ethicist is more often than not someone from the philosophy department with an amateur's knowledge of the profession in question.

The guest lecture is certainly better than nothing. It does get ethics into the curriculum. But the connection it makes between ethics and professional education has a forced look. If ethics were really important to this course, students may reason, wouldn't our instructor be able to teach it along with everything else? In addition, the connection the guest lecture makes between ethics and professional education is generally weak and necessarily limited. It is weak because students are generally not tested on their understanding of the guest lecture. (The same faculty who do not feel comfortable teaching ethics are likely to feel uncomfortable grading an exam question on ethics.) The connection made between ethics and professional education is necessarily limited because there is only so much one can pack into an hour or two of guest lecture. Having been raised, the topic is dropped, never to be raised again that semester.

The "outside course" is not limited in this way. It is generally a full-length course with the requirements and grading usual in other courses in the department. Usually, that department is philosophy (though, occasionally, religion, political science, or sociology). Since the late 1970s, IIT's philosophy section has offered four such optional courses: Business Ethics, Moral Issues in Engineering, Moral Issues in Architecture and City and Regional Planning, and Moral Issues in Computer Science. We recently added Medical Ethics (as part of a joint program in engineering and medicine). Many other universities have similar courses (as well as courses in journalism ethics, agricultural ethics, and so on).

Some professional programs give their students the option of an outside course in the ethics of their profession (or even in "generic" professional ethics) as a "technical elective." Few require such a course. Generally, students take one of these outside courses as a "humanities elective." Because it must compete with other humanities electives, only a minority of professional students learn the ethics of their profession in this way. At IIT, such students represent less than a quarter of any graduating class. And IIT is, I think, well ahead of most institutions of higher learning in this respect.

Cynics will suppose that resistance to requiring the outside course comes primarily from the professional programs, jealous of their turf. That is not my experience. While much of the resistance has come from the professional programs, the concern seems to be not turf but the humane treatment of students. This is especially true in engineering where current requirements are already so demanding that almost half of all students take five years to complete what purports to be a four-year program.

Perhaps more surprising is the resistance of philosophy, the "section" of the Humanities Department that would gain turf if an outside course were required of all students. The philosophy section believed that they could not possibility teach all the undergraduates such a requirement would generate without either (a) enlarging class size from the present maximum of 25–30 to 100–50, or (b) doubling the size of the section, with almost everyone required to teach at least one required ethics course (along with the required humanities introduction and one other course). Neither option (or some combination) seemed attractive.

The first option was unattractive because it would change the way courses in professional ethics are taught. Quadrupling class size would make impossible the three to five writing assignments (or, at least, their careful reading and close grading) customary in philosophy classes. Quadrupling of class size would also reduce substantiality the opportunities for an instructor to question any one student, for a student to defend an opinion, to hear how others evaluate it, and so on. In short, quadrupling class size would make courses in professional ethics relatively poor philosophy courses.

That was philosophy's objection to the first option, radically increasing class size. It had four objections to the second option. First, no one in the philosophy section likes teaching students taking a course because they "have to." There is already one such service course, Humanities 102 (shared with English, History, and Foreign Languages). Requiring a course in professional ethics would mean that every member of the department would every semester have to teach at least one (and perhaps two) more required courses. Second, philosophers not in ethics disliked teaching so much ethics. Third, even with a doubling of the philosophy section, the usual offerings of non-ethics courses would have had to be cut back somewhat. Students who wanted to study philosophy would face an impoverished program (in a enlarged section). And fourth, no one seriously expected the administration to come up with the money necessary to double the section. A required outside course was simply unrealistic.

The outside course must therefore be voluntary. Voluntary and outside the professional program, it suffers one disadvantage of the guest lecture. It looks optional (because the curriculum treats it that way). Voluntary or not, it also suffers from another disadvantage of the guest lecture; it seems to teach something members of the profession (as represented by faculty in the professional program) need not know.

The in-house course can overcome both these disadvantages. The in-house course, even if optional, is part of the professional program, taught along with other technical electives by members of one's profession. Clearly, some professionals (the ones teaching the course) know the profession's ethics well enough to teach it. And, in most institutions, requiring such an in-house course would be easier than requiring an outside course. All staffing and budgeting decisions would be within the program. There would, of course, still be costs, either giving up some other requirement or wiping out an elective, but these are matters individual programs manage all the time.[6]

Nonetheless, the in-house course, even if required, has at least one important disadvantage. It treats ethics as a distinct field, not as integral to all professional practice. Some professional programs have therefore sought to supplement or even replace their in-house course with the "pervasive" teaching of ethics. ROTC has long used the pervasive method (along with most of the other methods already discussed) to teach military ethics. While IIT's law school, like most others, has had a required in-house course since the early 1980s, it has recently begun trying to integrate ethics into core courses such as Civil Procedure.[7]

The pervasive method has, however, proved hard to implement. Few faculty in professional programs were trained to teach professional ethics. Few can even recall a mentor explicitly discussing ethics. Faced with the unknown, even the best of intentions falter. No one likes to teach outside their competence. No wonder, then, that when law schools substituted the pervasive method for the in-house course during the 1950s, ethics faded from the curriculum (until the in-house course was reinstated two decades later).

Administrators have been aware of this problem for some time. For example, in 1987, the Dean of the University of Pittsburgh's Graduate School of Business frankly acknowledged that "[though accredited business schools] pay some attention to ethical issues in the courses they teach, faculty...are ill-equipped to deliver a flow of materials about ethics."[8] The chair of a major civil engineering department was even harder on his colleagues: "most faculty members who are asked to include ethics in their courses think that reviewing the rules of the code of ethics is the sum total of what is available to be taught; they are totally unaware of the rich lode of classical and modern ethical thinking."[9]

The pervasive method, as traditionally applied, also shares a disadvantage with the other five approaches: extracurricular events, independent study, guest lecture, outside course, and in-house course. Each treats the ethics of one's own profession in isolation from the ethics of other professions. This is certainly understandable, both because one course is barely enough time to teach students the basics of their own profession's ethics and because even professors who know about the ethics of their own profession seldom know much about the ethics of any other. Yet, in practice, cooperation across the professions is common; and many ethical problems arise from the failure of members of one profession to understand the professional ethics of another.[10] Training in professional ethics would therefore be better if a way could be found to help entrants in each profession understand the professional ethics of others.

That is the problem we set ourselves. How did we solve it?

Outline of a solution

What we proposed to NSF in 1990 was a four-step four-and-a-half-year program.

Step One was to develop and offer three summer workshops for IIT faculty in how to teach professional ethics in technical courses (one workshop each summer, fifteen faculty each workshop). These three workshops would train about one-fifth of IIT's faculty. Our hope was that one-fifth would be enough both to have an immediate and substantial impact on what students learn and to make teaching ethics seem routine enough in professional programs that those who had not taken the workshop would copy from those who did. (We have, however, sought support to continue the internal workshops for several more years.)

These workshops were expensive, costing about $40,000 a piece, with three-fourths of the cost being stipends for participating faculty ($2,000 for each participant). While paying faculty to improve their teaching strikes many people as odd, especially when what will be taught is professional ethics, we believe such payment to be both necessary and proper; necessary, because many faculty could not otherwise afford the time the workshop demands or, at least, would not choose to put aside important paying projects for one that paid nothing; and proper, because the university always finds money to support what it considers worth doing.[11]

Step Two is providing institutional support for faculty trying to introduce professional ethics into their technical courses. "Support" included consultations with those experienced in teaching professional ethics, collecting problem sets a faculty member might draw on for class, purchases of films, videos, and books for use in class or for background, and a few meetings of workshop graduates each term to continue their education (and to keep them from feeling isolated).

Step Three was redesigning existing "capstone" courses in the professional programs to include a "cross-disciplinary" component.

A cross-disciplinary component is a design problem requiring ethically difficult cooperation among students in two or more professional programs – for example, business and civil engineering. Our budget included enough money for one pilot. We regarded this step as an early experiment in overcoming disciplinary isolation.

Step Four was to capitalize on, and disseminate, what we learned in the three preceding steps through, first, a small day-and-half working conference for staff and volunteers dealing with continuing education in various professional societies; second, a week-long version of the IIT workshop for faculty of other universities; and third, presentations at meetings of professional societies and publication in professional journals of the results of our project.

The goal of the IIT part of our program was to assure that every professional student graduates with a basic understanding of professional responsibility, even if she never takes a course in professional (or business) ethics. We could, we thought, achieve this goal if students meet professional ethics issues in many of their technical courses. Success did not require total penetration of the curriculum.

Our goal was not to replace separate courses in professional ethics, whether in-house or outside. Such courses are too valuable. Entrants to a profession, especially its future teachers and leaders, seem likely to benefit from the systematic and extended analysis only such a course can offer. Such courses also help to support scholarly interest in professional ethics which, in turn, supports the literature on which good teaching of professional ethics ultimately rests.

Insofar as we are successful at integrating ethics into technical courses, students taking a separate course in professional ethics will begin already knowing something about the ethics of their own (and other) professions. They will be ready to discuss the theoretically interesting questions that much sooner. Ethics across the curriculum should complement the separate course.

We have so far held three workshops for IIT faculty (1991, 1992, and 1993), provided support services for half a decade, given a number of talks to professional societies (out of which this chapter has grown)[12], held the workshop for staff and volunteers in continuing education (2–3 April 1992), and held three external summer workshops (1994, 1997 and 1998). This chapter will, however, focus only on Steps One and Two, the internal faculty workshops and support services. What did we do? What happened?

Developing the workshop

The workshop was open to any IIT faculty member teaching in any "program" (that is, degree-granting course of study) with a professional purpose. These programs range from architecture to physics, from business to design, from engineering to psychology. Though most programs give a bachelors degree, a few (like law) give only a post-baccalaureate degree. We ignored this distinction. We chose not to define "profession" narrowly or limit the workshop to faculty teaching undergraduates. We thought that the more varied the professional background of those participating, the richer the program was likely to be. We would be laying the groundwork for understanding professional ethics across disciplines. While most of the workshop participants each year came from engineering, computer science, and business, the participation of those from other programs (including ROTC, biology, mathematics, law, English, psychology, and public administration) clearly improved the discussion of issues cutting across disciplines.

Many workshops carried out under the banner of "Ethics Across the Curriculum" are basically a philosopher's course in ethical theory capped with some applications to professional ethics. We had heard that, while participants generally enjoyed these workshops, relatively few thereafter integrated ethics into their technical courses. Such workshops seem to support research in professional ethics (and perhaps in-house courses), not integration of ethics into technical courses. Our workshop, on the other hand, was supposed to teach professional faculty enough ethics, and enough about teaching ethics, to make them both willing and able to discuss issues of professional ethics in their courses, to give assignments with an ethical dimension, and to hold students responsible for the work assigned. So, our workshop had to be different from its predecessors.

To find out how it could be different, we met over sack lunch almost weekly for more than a year (1989–1990) with eight faculties from computer science, engineering, psychology, and public administration (and a few philosophers, of course). About half had been associated with the ethics center for a long time. At first, the discussion was quite abstract, but soon it began to focus on particular readings, some suggested by us and some by the other faculty. Some faculties also tried writing and presenting a case. In this and similar ways, we used the lunches to "test market" ideas (ours and theirs).

"Test marketing" was extraordinarily useful. I was often

surprised both by what these faculty knew and by what they did not know. While most knew quite a lot about their own profession's ethics, and several knew a good deal of philosophy, all had trouble with activities I do almost without thinking. For example, asked to write a brief ethics case for discussion, most came in unsure whether they had done as asked, when in fact they had.[13]

We concluded that what blocks teaching professional ethics in professional courses is primarily lack of experience with teaching ethics. Professional faculty will teach professional ethics when they have enough background to feel confident that they can teach ethics. That background consists of such nuts-and-bolts matters as how to devise problems for homework or class discussion and how to grade work consisting almost entirely of non-mathematical reasoning.[14] Ethical theory, though occasionally helpful, is relatively unimportant.

We planned a workshop requiring about thirty hours in class (five morning sessions back to back in June and then two all-day sessions, one in July and one in August). There was also to be substantial reading and two required presentations (one at each of the all-day sessions). In the next section, I describe the workshop day by day; in the section after that, the support rendered during the academic year; in the penultimate section, the student evaluations, faculty evaluations, and other evidence of success (or failure); and, in the concluding section, what I take to be the important lessons to be learned from what we did.

The workshop day by day

A week or two before the workshop began, we distributed a loose-leaf notebook with an agenda for each day, including the day's assignments, eight articles (and two other handouts), and three paperback books.[15] Participants were asked to bring the notebook and accompanying materials with them. Each presentation began with the handing out of an outline of what would be said, with holes already punched to fit the notebook. This reduced the need for notetaking while assuring participants a handy reference when they actually sat down to figure out what to do in class.

Day One began at 8:30 in the morning. The workshop co-leader and I introduced ourselves.[16] Participants introduced themselves and briefly described what they hoped to get from the workshop. I then presented the plan of the workshop, explained how the notebook worked, and stressed that this was an attempt at "technology transfer." We would teach them what we knew about teaching professional ethics. We would help them figure out what to do in class. But they would have to figure out how to adapt what they learned from us to the special circumstances of the courses they taught. They knew far more about their courses than we ever would.

The first two readings – a brief history of teaching ethics and a brief summary of methods and problems of teaching professional ethics – provided general background.[17] The third reading was a short case for discussion.

From 8:45–9:45, I presented definitions for terms common in discussions of ethics (right, good, fair, law, rational, prudent, just, and so on). After noting the existence of thirteen senses of "values" (and presenting three), I recommended dropping the term as too ambiguous. I defined "morality" in a way that should now be familiar, that is, as those standards of conduct everyone (every rational person) wants every other to follow even if everyone else's following them would mean he had to follow them too. I then distinguished "ethics" (as we have been doing). Ethics (the ethics of a particular group) consists of those morally permissible standards of conduct each member of a group wants every other to follow even if their following them would mean he had to follow them too. For our purposes, ethics is "special morality." Both "morality" and "ethics" have other senses, of course, but these serve us better. For example, relying on these definitions, I easily explained why a morally decent person should be ethical.[18]

I began the hour by claiming that nothing I said should be controversial, and that anyone who thought I had said something not obviously true should interrupt me immediately. The interruptions were frequent. But, by the end, everyone seemed agreed that I had cleared up a good deal of confusion while telling them only what they already knew. We had a common vocabulary for the rest of the workshop.

Starting at 9:45, we discussed "Catalyst B: Phase 1," the case assigned for the day. In it, a manager seems to be asking a young engineer he supervises to withhold relevant technical data from higher-ups.[19] Though designed for a course in engineering ethics, this page-and-a-half case proved general enough to engage everyone. (One of the business faculty, a former chemist, said that he had himself been in such a situation.) Neither my co-leader nor I did much to guide the discussion. Our contribution consisted almost entirely of reminding participants to use the terms just defined in the way they had been defined. Our purpose was to let workshop participants experience what students would experience in class if left more or less on their own. By 10:15, participants were agreed on what "you" (the young engineer) should do (write the report as requested, taking care to say nothing false, but start looking for another job).

After a fifteen-minute break, we reconvened for a discussion of how to analyze an ethics problem. My co-leader presented a seven-step method (identify problem, check facts, and so on).[20] First someone from business, then an engineer, and eventually everyone recognized the method as basically the "rational decision" procedure of their own discipline. The method was not peculiar to philosophy.

By 11:00, we were ready to look again at Catalyst B. This time we proceeded step by step, following the method. This discipline seemed to change the focus of discussion. While most participants ended with the same position as before, everyone seemed to feel that the discussion went better this time. Clearly, a discussion of ethics need not be a free-for-all. Far from hurting the discussion, disciplining it had actually helped. Many expressed satisfaction at having an outline (the seven-step method) they could use to lead class discussion of an ethics problem.

The morning ended with my co-leader giving a preview of issues in professional ethics. Does it matter in Catalyst B whether any of the chief characters is an engineer or other professional? What is a professional, anyway? Does a professional owe special loyalty to employer, coworkers, public, profession, or what? What might such loyalty require? What part should a code of ethics play in answering such questions?[21]

Day Two was "moral theory day." The "recommended" (that is, assigned) readings were accounts of utilitarian and Kantian moral theories. In addition, we suggested Kant's *Foundations of the Metaphysics of Morals*, Mill's *Utilitarianism*, and a brief discussion of relativism.[22] We were surprised, especially the first year, at how many faculty took our suggestions.

Explaining the day's plan at 8:30, I stressed (to the evident relief of participants) that moral theory was not something they should teach. We would teach them enough about it to make clear that they need not know more to integrate ethics into their technical courses. In particular, they should notice the dialectic of criticism and correction by which seemingly radically different theories ended up (in the hands of an expert) giving much the same answer to practical questions. This is no accident. A moral theory that gets results much different from the others is open to counter-example (and so, refutation) to which the others are not. I did, however, admit that theory has its uses. Many teachers find that some one theory suits them better than the others, that it provides them with a comfortable framework for guiding class discussion or thinking through a problem on their own.

The session on utilitarianism began at 8:45 much like any class in moral theory. I pointed out that the foundation of any utilitarian theory is an analysis of (non-moral) good. While there are many analyses, "happiness" will serve for our purposes. Utilitarians define the morally right ("right all things considered") in terms of the good. This makes their theories "teleological." But utilitarians are not (as we shall see) the only teleologists.

Maximizing the good is the most popular, but not the only, way utilitarians have of defining the right. The good for utilitarians is objective, a certain state of the world. But, because we cannot know how our acts will in fact turn out, we cannot actually know what good our acts will do. Choosing acts must therefore be done based on something more subjective than actual outcome, that is, on what we are justified in expecting our acts to accomplish. We may then summarize the "utilitarian method" in this way:

1 Identify all courses of action open to you.
2 For each course of action, identify all parties affected.
3 For each party, identify the contribution of each course of action to that person's happiness. (Generally, the first three steps must be carried out more or less together.)
4 *Ignoring all other considerations*, compare courses of action, taking account of the *number* of persons affected and *how* each is affected but not of who is affected.
5 Choose that course of action most likely to maximize overall happiness.

This lecture took about half an hour, including some good questions. I then showed a five-minute segment of the Ethics Resource Center's video, *A Matter of Judgment*. The video consists of five independent vignettes, each involving a conflict of interest. In the part I showed, "Jeff," an employee with significant management responsibilities, sees an opportunity to start a business of his own, perhaps with great advantage to himself, his wife, and a software inventor. Should Jeff seize what may be the opportunity of a lifetime if doing so means taking advantage of contacts made through his employer (possibly to the employer's disadvantage)? The vignette provided a test case for each moral theory (as well as giving faculty an example of the videos available for use in class). How might a utilitarian handle such a situation?

Trying to answer that question had three interesting outcomes. First, several faculty noted that using the utilitarian method forced them to think carefully about all the possible outcomes of what one did, who one might hurt and how, who one might help and how. Second, one faculty member noted, with great dissatisfaction, that we had listed clearly immoral options along with others. Our calculation of consequences was all that stood between us and choosing an immoral outcome. And third, as we attempted to carry out the calculations, everyone soon became aware of how complicated the process had become and how prey to estimates of probabilities. The discussion ended at 9:45 without a clear conclusion.

My co-leader then presented Kant's theory as a way to get around many of utilitarianism's weaknesses. For Kant, what is important for doing the morally right act is not what will or probably will happen but what the agent intends. She then explained Kant's three formulations of the categorical imperative as providing three distinct tests of conduct (consistency, human dignity, and autonomy). For example, the test of consistency might be summarized:[23]

1   identify your act (what you are actually proposing to do), for example, tell someone something you believe to be false;
2   identify the end you have in view (what is actually moving you to do the act in question), for example, getting something without paying for it;
3   consider whether (assuming the world otherwise remains as you believe it to be) you could still achieve that end if everyone is permitted to act the same whenever he has the same end in view;
4   reject the act if you find it would not achieve the end you have in view in a world where everyone were permitted to act the same when he had the same end in view.

We then tried to apply Kant's tests to Jeff's choice. This turned out to be harder than expected. We had to consider carefully what Jeff's act and motive were to apply the test of consistency; whether Jeff's employer, presumably a corporation, counted as a person for purposes of the test of human dignity (or whether the relevant persons were superiors, stockholders, and other individuals associated with the corporation); and, for the test of autonomy, what the world would be like overall if employees took advantage of contacts in the way Jeff proposed to do. We had to "get inside Jeff's head" (something Jeff would have found easier). The question soon became whether Jeff could both do what he wanted to do and satisfy the Kantian tests. For example, would he do enough if he notified his superiors of the new software, clearly stating its value and, if they declined to act, act on his own?

Discussion again ended inconclusively (at 10:45) with comments about how different the moral landscape looked when surveyed from Kant's perspective. After a fifteen-minute break, I undertook to present pluralism, social justice theories, virtue theories, and relativism all in one hour. This would, of course, be foolhardy if I intended to do more than give a sense of the wide range of possibilities we could not explore. I began with pluralism, noting its rejection of Mill's insistence on a single (absolute) standard of right conduct. Pluralist theories are inherently less tidy. I offered Bernard Gert as a representative pluralist. Morality, for him, is defined by a *list* of ten moral rules. No rule takes precedence over any of the others. The rules are universal but not absolute. There can be exceptions. Gert gives a list of considerations relevant to determining exceptions. This list is not a decision procedure, but it nevertheless provides a framework for discussion. I passed out a copy of the ten rules and of the list of considerations. Many faculty, especially those from business, thought these two lists might prove useful for guiding discussion.[24]

Social justice theories reject utilitarianism's indifference to who is benefited (or harmed). They accept some reduction in overall happiness in order to assure "better" distribution. John Rawls, though not a moral theorist, can be read as imposing a distributive condition on deriving the right from the good. Nothing can be a moral rule for him unless its adoption would improve the condition of even the least well off. David Gauthier provides another example. His distributive constraint is a bit weaker. Nothing can be a moral rule unless its adoption would benefit some without worsening anyone's condition overall.[25]

Virtue theories reject utilitarianism's connection of the (objectively) right with the actual outcome of an act (or actual outcome of the practice of following a rule). For these theories, the objectively right act is the one a person of a certain type ("the virtuous

person") would choose. Virtue is a complex of virtues (good dispo-
sitions), including justice, courage, temperance, and judgment.
Some virtue theorists (for example, MacIntyre) define the virtues
historically. The virtues are what we have come to believe contribute
to overall happiness (or, as virtue theorists prefer, "human flour-
ishing"). Other virtue theorists (for example, Becker) hold instead
that the virtues are not historically defined; they are those disposi-
tion that *in fact* contribute to overall happiness (or, at least, would if
commonly shared).[26] For a virtue theorist, deciding what "Jeff"
should do would require determining what a virtuous person in
those circumstances would do.

Relativism is the name for two distinct entities. One is a theory of
how we should act, or "moral relativism"; the other, an attitude
toward all moral theories, or "metaethical relativism." Moral relativism is in fact consistent with some other moral theories (for
example, MacIntyre's). In any case, moral relativism is no bar to
teaching ethics (which, as I defined it, differs from morality
precisely in being relative to the group it governs). The students'
favorite form of moral relativism, "Do what society says," is a
problem for teaching professional ethics only because it usually
does not come with any idea how to do determine what society says.
Consider this example: in Chicago not long ago, it was a practice at
the County Clerk's office that any lawyer seeking a document would
have to attach a $10 bill to the back; otherwise his request would be
"lost." This social practice violated both state law and the Illinois
Bar Association's code of ethics, yet the practice was both well-
known and publicly unchallenged. What did society say? Did
society forbid it (because its law forbid it)? Or did society permit it
(because it was a common practice)? Did society change its mind
when the new (reformist) County Clerk publicly threatened to fire
any employee accepting a payment?

Metaethical relativism, on the other hand, is merely a challenge
to moral *theorists*. Metaethical relativism does not rest on any proof
that moral theory cannot be true, only on a skeptical attitude. For
the purposes of teaching professional ethics, or even using ordinary
morality, it is enough that we can agree on certain basics, for
example, at least the first eight of Gert's ten rules (and all of Gert's
reasons for exceptions). Even if part of morality does vary from
place to place, our students share enough of it to make moral
discussion possible and moral agreement on many questions likely.
And, on that welcome note, we adjourned for the day.

Day Three focused on professional ethics (with the first real discussion of how to teach it). The two readings offered two ways to think about professional ethics, code-based and role-based.[27]

From 8:45 to 9:15, my co-leader presented the standard analysis of professions: they are occupational groups delivering important services, making a commitment to serve the public in ways beyond what market, law, and morality demand, requiring judgment and training not easy to acquire, and characterized by evolving standards of conduct expressed in a code of ethics. She also provided an analysis of "responsibility" (as in "professional responsibility"), talked a bit about the history of professions (and their codes), noted differences in the structure of professions (for example, the way clients are much less central to engineering than to lawyering), and identified some problems in the concept of "professional autonomy."

At this point, about 9:15, we distributed a copy of an engineering code of ethics (ABET, 1989, including Guidelines), and returned to Catalyst B. The assigned reading for the day included Phase 2 of that case, reporting events over the month after the first decision. This gave faculty a chance to see the possibilities in a case in stages. Choices have consequences. One consequence of a particular moral choice may be harder choices later. But the primary purpose of looking again at Catalyst B was to see what difference treating it as a case of professional ethics made. "You" (and perhaps those around "you") are not simply employees now but representatives of a profession with special obligations beyond what other employees have.

Many of the engineering faculty had not seen their profession's code of ethics before (and of those who had, none had seen the long version we handed out). The other faculty were in much the same situation. As we used the code to analyze Catalyst B, they expressed surprise at how the code affected their judgment of what "you" should do. The situation had more structure than they had supposed. And that structure suggested they should have taken a tougher initial line than they did. Because they had not, they now faced a more difficult Phase 2. They saw clearly the potential value of a code in shaping class discussion.

At 10:00, after a fifteen-minute break, I offered advice on how to identify ethical issues in technical courses. Ethics, I argued, is part of the normal context of professional practice. Ethical standards are similar to other professional standards in at least three ways: (1) They have the same purpose as other standards, that is, to standardize the profession's work for the public's benefit; (2) ethical standards develop in the same way other standards do, beginning with common sense, getting modified as the profession's experience grows, and never becoming final (since experience continues); (3) most important, like other professional standards, ethical standards need practical context to make sense. They are, after all, guides to professional judgment. Judgment can only be exercised in a context. Teaching professional ethics is, in fact, part of teaching professional practice.

How then do you find ethics issues in a technical course? You must see the course material in its professional context. How do you do that? I then made a number of suggestions to be found in Chapter 8: read the profession's code, draw on your own experience, and so on.

Having identified some issues, how can you make room for them in a technical course? You can:

1   Rewrite problems so that they include relevant context (for example, including the name of a chemical in place of "fluid" and the name of a local river in place of "basin"). After going over the problem in the usual way, you can point out ethical issues the problem (so revised) raises. ("Did you notice that this problem involved dumping a large amount of poison into the city's drinking supply? Do you have an obligation to flag the danger even though no one asked you to?")[28]

2   You could also develop "mini-design" problems by converting similar problems already side by side in the book into alternative solutions of the same practical problem. (Usually, you can do this simply by providing a bit more context, for example, "think of these pulley problems as alternate ways to pull a tractor out of the mud".)

You ask the students to do the usual calculations and then recommend one method, giving a justification in addition to the calculations. The problems should force them to balance several different kinds of consideration (for example, speed, cost, and safety).

3   Assign students to study one or more disasters or scandals involving principles being taught in class with an eye to avoiding a similar occurrence.

4   Assign students to study a technical standard relevant to the course. Why do we now draw the line here?

5   Reorganize lab or field work so that both standards of conduct and standards of evaluation are closer to professional practice.

At about 11:00, my co-leader took over. Her subject was methods for doing ethics in class. The line between her subject and mine was, of course, far from sharp. No one seemed to mind. My co-leader's presentation differed in two respects from mine. First, she systematically went through a list of methods, giving an example or two of each from her own experience. This both augmented my list and reorganized it. Second, she gave the advantages and disadvantages of each method. For example, case studies can be long narratives, short vignettes (or scenarios), mere hypotheticals (what if I did x?), or slight modifications of problems already in the course (for example, mini-design problems). Narratives can have substantial impact, but they take time to lay out; vignettes, such as Catalyst B, take much less time but are therefore less realistic; hypothicals take even less time, but tend to invite students, especially if inexperienced, to doubt that such-and-such could happen; mini-design problems probably will not have much impact unless there are a lot of them during the semester (for more on this, see Chapter 8).

In much the same way, my co-leader discussed projects, films, computer simulations, role playing, discussion (whole class, small group, debates, and so on), and writing assignments (again, see more about these in Chapter 8). Having demonstrated that there are a great many ways to teach professional ethics, we adjourned.

Day Four dealt with cognitive and moral issues of teaching professional ethics. Can ethics be taught? Should it be? Where does what one person does in the classroom on one day fit into institutional goals? All three readings for the day dealt with the empirical literature on teaching ethics. What works? What does not work? How do we know? The third reading, while summarizing this literature, tried to deal with specific fears faculty may have about teaching professional ethics (indoctrination, appearing holier-than-thou, and so on).[29]

At 8:45, my co-leader began summarizing the empirical literature. The good news is that moral development does not end in childhood. We go on developing moral judgment (and picking up relevant moral information) well into adulthood. Ethics certainly can be taught. The bad news is that we know little about how to teach it, especially about how to affect conduct. What do we know? Most important, the lecture method common in technical courses is unlikely to contribute much. Discussion of cases, especially when guided to bring out clashing arguments and force their evaluation, is necessary to improve judgment. These discussions should be integrated into the wider discussion of related technical issues, with some examples of how others have handled similar problems and with information about resources a professional might be able to mobilize to evaluate his own position or that of others.

There are a few other rules we can derive from our experience as teachers: Avoid theories alone (pure philosophy), too many dilemmas (for example, either lose your job or cause a thousand innocent people to die), and too many hypotheticals. Stress the similarity between technical issues and ethical issues. In both, we need to define the problem, gather facts, develop options, inventory resources, consider costs, and so on.

At 9:45, we considered whether, assuming we could teach ethics in the ways open to us, we *should*. As teachers, we are committed to imparting information, skill, judgment, and the like in order to benefit the recipient, our students. Teaching ethics should not be mere training, that is, imparting information, skill, judgment, or the like for the benefit of a third party. How can teaching ethics benefit students? There are, I argued, four benefits teaching ethics can bestow on students: (1) increased ethical sensitivity; (2) increased knowledge of relevant resources and standards of conduct; (3) improved ethical judgment; and (4) improved willpower (ability to act ethically when they want to) (for a fuller explanation of these benefits, see Chapter 8). Whatever students want to do with what they are taught, they will not want to get into ethical trouble because they did not see the ethical element of the situation or were ignorant of the relevant standard, because they showed poor judgment, or because they lacked the resources to say "no" when they wanted to (or to say "yes" when they wanted to).

Teaching ethics is, in part, like teaching more technical material. What we teach gives power, a power that can be used for evil as well as for good. While we cannot know how our students will use what we teach, we have good reason (in general) to believe that they mean well. The problem of what to do with a student who does not mean well is the same whether we are teaching ethics or more technical material.[30]

Can we teach ethics ethically? Indoctrination is unethical. A teacher, or at least a university professor, should not get students to believe a claim or recognize a standard by means that bypass their reason. But the methods that teach ethics successfully, that is, those discussed earlier, do not involve indoctrination. They appeal to reason in much the way more technical teaching does. So, faculty need not try to appear neutral with respect to their profession's ethics any more than they need appear neutral with respect to technical standards. Faculty need only make clear what is simply their opinion (something about which respectable members of the profession can disagree) and what is in fact settled among members of the profession. Even settled questions can, of course, be reopened. But those wishing to reopen them bear a heavy burden of proof (just as, for example, would a student who wanted to reopen discussion concerning the location of oxygen in the periodic table).

What about the bright student who really does have a fundamental disagreement with the profession; for example, an engineering student who does not care about the safety of the public? A faculty member can still grade the student's work, evaluating it for awareness of issues, knowledge of standards, and so on. The faculty member should give the student a good grade if she has mastered the material, but also probably should take the student aside and urge her to consider whether she really wants to work in a field where she does not share the fundamental commitments of those with whom she will be identified. Joining a profession is not the only, or even the surest, way to make money.

After many questions and a fifteen-minute break, the last hour was devoted to strategies for teaching ethics. The emphasis was on *strategies*. Faculty should not try to do everything all at once. Instead, they should try to build on what came before and to lay the groundwork for more later. So, for example, faculty teaching a first-year course might naturally emphasize increasing ethical sensitivity, for example, by raising an ethical issue now and then (by vignette, war story, or forensic case). The theme would be, "Here is something that can come up." Someone teaching a second year course might instead work at increasing ethical knowledge, for example, by handing out a code of ethics at the beginning of the term, raising easy ethical issues early in the term for which students must find answers in the code, and raising harder ethical issues later in the term for which students can provide an answer only by interpreting provisions that are not directly on point. Faculty teaching third-year courses might in addition allow discussion of ethical issues in class, give homework assignments requiring students to make a recommendation taking those ethical issues into account and providing a defense of that recommendation going beyond a mere citation of relevant code provisions (and including perhaps even a justification or critique of the provision). Faculty teaching a fourth-year course might in addition send their students out to various employers in the area to find out how questions like those discussed in class are handled there (including what resources a young professional might call on should she disagree with a supervisor on how to handle the question).[31]

I presented this as only one model. By the second year, I had to warn IIT faculty that most of their sophomores would, as freshmen, have seen a copy of their profession's code, have had some experience working with it, and have participated in significant classroom discussions of professional ethics. Faculty would have to adjust the model accordingly. Nonetheless, the basic idea was still sound. Don't try to do everything at once. Start small. Push on. Know what colleagues are doing. Coordinate with others when possible. Have a long-term plan (subject to change as experience suggests). Check for impact by testing, graded assignments, or the like.

Day Five continued the focus on pedagogy. After describing what we intended to cover and taking questions left over from the day before, we turned to practical matters. Both readings for the day combined discussion of the importance of teaching ethics with ideas for how to do it.[32]

The first year we had several workshop participants who had tried to teach professional ethics in technical courses describe what happened. Participants found the ROTC instructor's description most interesting, since ROTC had tried to integrate ethics systematically and seemed to have been reasonably successful. Although even the ROTC instructor admitted to considerable dissatisfaction with what he had done, these reports had the effect of reducing general anxiety about teaching ethics. Some technical faculty had done it and lived to tell the tale. This took about an hour.

We felt no need to reduce anxiety this way in later workshops. By then we had faculty who, having graduated from our workshop, had much more satisfying experiences. So, we took a different tack. From 8:45 to 9:15, an English instructor who, having taken the workshop, described four techniques she had used to integrate writing into coursework (without much work for her), for example, the "one-minute essay" (asking students at the end of an hour to write two sentences summing up the discussion, as a way both to provide faculty with some quick measure of what students had heard and also as a way to help students to organize and retain the experience before it began to fade). Along the way, she gave examples of how such techniques might help faculty trying to integrate ethics. She also noted that these techniques helped to satisfy the faculty's responsibility for integrating writing into technical courses.

At 9:15, another of the graduates of the 1991 workshop came in.

He told how he introduced ethics into CS 105, the basic computer course taken by almost all IIT undergraduates in their first year. His presentation had two purposes. First, it was a success story (complete with a few failed experiments). Second, it set a baseline for what other faculty could expect of sophomores in the coming fall, of juniors the year after that, and of seniors the year after that. Every student who took CS 105 would have participated in several discussions of computer ethics, have had an assignment requiring use of the code of ethics of the Association of Computing Machines, and have had to go to the Ethics Center's library to find a copy of the code of ethics of his or her profession and answer some simple questions concerning it.

At 10:00, after a fifteen-minute break, we began looking at typical assignments faculty had brought in. Our purpose was to look for places to insert ethics. In the first year, most faculty came in with textbooks, seeking help. In the second and third years more than half came in with ideas as well; and a few had actually worked out tentative assignments, complete with handouts and overheads. We went through as many of these as we could, giving some priority to faculty who thought they were more worried than the others about what they were going to do. My co-leader and I generally spoke only when there was dead silence. In general, workshop participants had good advice for one another. There were several points in discussion where I thought the advice they gave was better than what I would have given. Plainly, they were well on their way to integrating ethics into technical courses.

At 11:30, we reminded participants that we would be meeting twice more this summer, once to hear something they would be doing in class in the fall and once more to look at an assignment they intended to grade.[33] We then went over to the Ethics Center's library where the librarian described the library's resources (including videos, on-line search capacity, and code files).

Day Six had only the structure that individual faculty presentations gave it. What was important was that workshop participants showed up with classroom presentations to try out among friends and left feeling the presentations worked (or could be revised so that they should work). The best way to appreciate what happened is to examine some examples. I will give three drawn from different levels and fields. The first two are from the second year; the third is from the first year.

Example 1. How do you introduce professional ethics into a calculus course? First-year students are taught a routine for deriving coordinates for the tangent to a curve. For unusual curves, the routine will give an incorrect result (a line not in contact with the curve). The only way students have of knowing whether a particular curve is unusual is to sketch it and the supposed tangent. Students seldom bother even though they are regularly told that checking their calculated result against a curve is part of doing such problems.

Since most of his students are would-be engineers, one of our workshop's participants, a math professor, thought to use engineering ethics to explain what is wrong with not checking. As engineers, his students are responsible not only for the accuracy of their calculations but for the usefulness of the answer. Unless they do the sketch, they cannot honestly vouch for the answer's usefulness. But, because they will be engineers, anyone to whom they gave the answer would quite properly expect the answer to be useful. So, to give the answer without checking it against a sketch (or without warning that they have not checked it) is deceptive, a clear breach of engineering ethics. Should students get credit for such dishonesty? (While he planned to say just this and go on, he was ready to pull out an engineering code of ethics and read appropriate sections should students object. He was also prepared to suggest students verify his claims with engineering faculty.)[34]

Example 2. An engineering professor revised a problem from a text in applied thermodynamics (a third-year course). The original problem asked students to determine the evaporator and condenser pressures, the mass flow rate of refrigerant, the compressor power input, and the coefficient of performance for two refrigerants (freon and 134a), given a certain vapor-compression refrigeration system. To this, our workshop participant added information about cost, advertising department hopes for the new non-freon system, and some other typical context, and asked students to recommend a refrigerant and justify the recommendation. Students could get extra credit for research beyond the text (though the text in fact contained more than enough about the refrigerants, ecological information and economic information).

Because the freon system would have a 3 percent cost advantage over the 134a system, students could not just choose refrigerant 134a. Their recommendation would have to take environmental impact into account, the economic costs of developing a system using freon when freon systems may well be prohibited by law in a few years, and perhaps other considerations as well. As part of going over the problem in class, the instructor should go beyond the calculations and generate a discussion of what should go into an engineer's recommendation.

Example 3. A professor of finance, having read Gauthier's *Morals by Agreement* at my suggestion, proposed to have students in his senior course, Financial Markets, study the Japanese stock market scandal (then in the news). Most of the large Japanese brokerage houses had, it seemed, a policy of secretly covering part of the losses of their largest customers. His students were to use market theory to explain what, if anything, was wrong with such a practice (for example, whether it was unfair or biased the market's assessment of risk). They were also to consider how such scandals would affect the willingness of rational investors to enter that market if other markets ruled out such practices.

The business professor hoped in this way to bring out the long-term benefits of strict standards of conduct for brokers in a market. Individual brokers might benefit from shady practices so long as these did not become public (as they would eventually) or just too common. But markets depend on trust; and trust, once lost, is hard to regain. He thought the Japanese stock market a particularly good example. It had remained depressed after the 1990 slump while most other markets had recovered. Because his students do not think of themselves as professionals, he could not bring in ethics through a professional code. But, since his students do take market rationality very seriously, he thought they would respond to an explanation of ethics relating it to market rationality. He hoped to lead a discussion of these issues after students turned in the paper. He could lay the groundwork for such a discussion with very little change in the way he teaches the course.

Day Seven was supposed to differ little from Day Six, except that the emphasis was to be on grading. In fact, Day Seven differed a good deal from Day Six. The same faculty who had so confidently presented their classroom plans were visibly nervous about grading the assignments. Over and over I had to ask (something like), "What did you teach your students about professional ethics?" When they had no trouble answering that question, I would ask, "Can't you grade them on whether they learned that?" After I received an uncertain nod, I would say (something like): "You were trying to make your students sensitive to issues of safety; so, where in this problem could a student show such sensitivity?" When they listed several places, I would suggest giving a little credit should a student say something about safety at any of those places and a little more if she said something about more than one or if what she said was particularly good. There would then be a smile of under-standing.

I do not want to give the impression that workshop participants were dull. They were overall by far the best students I have ever had. The only time I had any doubt about their ability was on this ques-tion of grading. I now think that the problem is that, despite everything we had been through, many faculty still *felt* that "grading ethics" must mean either grading character or grading philosophy. They had not yet fully assimilated how much like other grading the grading professional ethics was. They were to look for sensitivity, knowledge, or judgment. This could be shown in words (for example, a note on the side pointing out the toxicity of an effluent in a routine problem), but it could also be shown in, say, the presence of a sketch in a calculus problem of the sort I described earlier.

I said that they still *felt* that grading ethics meant grading char-acter or philosophy, not that they *believed* that. The problem went deeper than belief. Going through a problem or exam question with one workshop participant, making clear how easy grading ethics was in the context of his own course, did not seem to help the rest much. I generally had to start over with the next. And, for all this one-on-one effort, my success was, I now know, only partial. I gave most workshop participants enough confidence to try grading an ethics assignment, no more. Most faculty left the workshop not quite convinced that they could do it, and they remained uncon-vinced until they actually gave an assignment, graded it, and found that neither they nor their students found any cause for complaint. There is no substitute for that experience.

Supporting ethics across the curriculum

We planned three sorts of support for participants after the work-shop: a) *material* (books, videos, and case files); b) *social* (continuing seminars); and c) *technical* (consultations with Ethics Center staff). Technical support was almost an afterthought. While we had always been willing to consult with faculty, few faculty had ever taken advantage of it. We did not expect workshop partici-pants to be much different. We thought the most important support we could provide was material. We were wrong.

We bought a good number of books (and a few videos) at the suggestion of workshop graduates and a smaller number with their advice. This substantially improved the Center's library in a way visitors appreciated. But *our* faculty only occasionally used the new acquisitions (and that use seemed only slightly greater than in past years). We gained more from their involvement in the library than they did. Material support was not crucial to getting ethics into their courses.

Neither was the continuing seminar. It worked well in one respect. Those attending the two sessions we held during the first term enjoyed them. In another respect, however, the seminar worked badly. We were never able to get even a bare majority of workshop graduates to attend. The usual excuse, "too busy," though honestly made, none the less seemed less than the whole story. My impression, and it is only that, is that faculty whose courses were going well had no need of a "support group." Other things squeezed out the continuing seminar because it had a low priority for them.[35]

Those who did attend attended out of general interest, the same reason they would have attended any other event the subject of which was professional ethics. Indeed, many of these attended a sack-lunch series on research ethics we organized the second term (independently of ethics across the curriculum). Attending the workshop increased their interest in professional ethics, making them more likely to attend other ethics-related activities (whether or not specially designed for them). They found their own social support. We therefore scheduled no sessions of the continuing seminar after the second term.

Our experience with "technical support" was quite different. The first year, most workshop participants were at one time or another glad to call on me as an experienced teacher of ethics willing to answer a few questions, look at a proposed assignment, suggest a source of cases, or the like. The questions were never hard; the time required to answer them never more than a few minutes; the total time devoted to such consultations probably did not exceed six hours. The consultations were in fact a natural continuation of Day Seven. Yet, I often had the feeling that, had I not been there to consult, the faculty member would have given up. After the first year, I had only a few such consultations.

Learning to teach professional ethics is, I now think, a lot like learning to use a new computer (or new software). "Technical backup" is crucial. For those with the appropriate experience, much of what is necessary to use a new machine (or program) is intuitive; the manuals seem to devote page after page to the obvious. But for those lacking that experience, the same manuals (and prompts) often seem cryptic. I have sat in front of my computer, manual before me, at a loss how to proceed, given up and called an expert, either the "help number" the manufacturer provides or the helpful hack in the next office, and after a brief exchange suddenly understood what the manual had been telling me in what now seemed relatively plain English. I believe many workshop participants have had a similar experience with teaching ethics.

By now, most departments at IIT have a helpful "ethics hack" just as they all now have at least one computer hack. But, for a few years, the Ethics Center provided a crucial service, "an ethics help number." Participation in the workshop seemed to give faculty permission to use resources always available to them. No ethics-across-the-curriculum program should be without provision for this sort of consultation.

Evidence of success

Evidence of success may be divided into three categories: (a) faculty reports, (b) student evaluations and (c) institutional response. I shall here limit myself to evidence from the first workshop, in part because evidence from later workshops is much the same, but in part because presenting evidence from all the workshops would make exposition substantially more complex without compensating insight.

We had sixteen participants who completed the program in 1991. Fourteen of these were official participants (that is, they received a $2000 stipend).[36] The other two were unofficial. One, an ROTC instructor, could not accept the stipend; the other, a business professor, intended to take sabbatical leave (and so could not sign the agreement promising a report for the fall term). Neither unofficial participant submitted a report.

Of the fourteen official participants, two did not submit a report on time. One spent the academic year 1991–2 elsewhere, for reasons beyond his control, but reported (with some prompting) after the Spring 1993 term. The other non-reporting participant simply put off reporting until the end of the grant provided an absolute deadline for receipt of the last quarter of his stipend; this even though we asked for the report several times and had independent knowledge that he was doing professional ethics each term.

So, eventually, we had reports from fourteen out of sixteen faculty. All those reporting reported success. Most, especially those in engineering, did more ethics in class than they had prepared by summer's end. All indicated in their final report that they intended to do at least as much the following semester. Many, especially in engineering, intended to do more next time (whether more in that course or something similar in another course). The following comment (for IS 326, an advanced course in information systems in the business school) was typical of those of most faculty:

> With one exception, everything I did seemed to work well. The one problem I had was that my spreadsheet case was not as clear as it should have been. My explanation of the cost justification problem confused many students. I don't believe this had any effect on how the students approached the ethics question in the case however. I liked how the mini case worked (The First Bay state bank case). In the future, I plan using written mini cases. A written mini case would provide a maximum of one page description of a situation that can be discussed in the same class period in which it was handed out.

In 1995, we resurveyed these faculty. Most responded. Of those responding, none was doing less professional ethics than in the first year after the workshop. About half reported doing more. All still regarded the workshop as well worth the time.

Every workshop participant was supposed to conduct a student evaluation of the ethics component of the class and transmit the results as part of the final report. I provided a suggested form. While all reporting participants did an appropriate student evaluation, only half used the suggested form. So, to avoid unnecessary complexity, I will focus on those that are strictly comparable (though I do not think results on the others differ materially).

The suggested form had seven questions. Three required a yes or no.[37] After each yes-or-no question was an open-ended question. The first six questions were as follows:

1 Did this course increase your awareness of ethics issues likely to arise in your professions or job?
2 If "no," what might have helped increase your awareness of such issues? If "yes," please explain how it increased your awareness.
3 Did this course do anything to change your understanding of the importance of professional or business ethics?

4   If "no," what might have helped the course change your understanding? If "yes," please explain how the course changed your understanding.
5   Did this course increase your ability to deal with the ethical issues it raised?
6   If "no," what might have helped the course increase that ability? If "yes," please explain how the course changed your understanding.

There was also a catch-all question, and finally, a question asking about previous experience with ethics:

7   In your opinion, did this course spend too much time on professional or business ethics, too little, or just the right amount? Is there anything that should have been done differently? Explain.
8   Did you have any professional or business ethics in a class before this one?

What can we learn from these student evaluations? For most classes, the student responses were quite favorable. Variations seem to have little to do with discipline, class size, or level. Consider, for example, CS 105 (a large first-year class), MAE 205 (a mid-size second-year class), and CBK 504 (an MBA class). For question 1, the number answering "yes" out of those answering was (in order) 101 out of 110; 15 out of 19; and 15 out of 24.[38]

In general, the responses tended to be more negative for questions 3 and 5 – but "negative" must be used carefully here. The comments accompanying "negative" responses were generally positive. For example, a substantial number of students, having answered "no" to questions 1, 3, and 5, might answer question 7 in some such ways as this: "We spent a short chapter on ethics – just right." In fact, very few students can accurately be described as "turned off" by the ethics component.

That brings me to the last category of evidence of success, the most subjective but also the most interesting. Starting about the October after the first workshop, various university publications began coming to us to do stories on Ethics Across the Curriculum. We would tell them what we knew and then refer them to workshop participants. Eventually, favorable stories appeared in IIT publications. I was invited to sit on two university committees, one to propose ways to integrate creativity into the curriculum and the other to do the same for quality. But, the high point of expressions of administrative regard occurred at a faculty meeting when IIT's president observed, with obvious pleasure and awe, that one of our workshop participants had integrated ethics into Thermodynamics. In short, it seemed that, even in the first few months after our first workshop, the administration had received enough feedback from our graduates to conclude that we knew what we were doing.

But something more subtle was also happening. Faculty who had thought that the engineering curriculum left no room for the innovations they wanted, began to talk about integrating this or that into standard courses. They regularly referred to Ethics Across the Curriculum as a model for what can be done. They had a new way to look at curricular change.

Concluding lessons

What lessons can we draw from all this? The most important is that the barriers to integrating ethics into the professional curriculum are not what they have commonly been supposed to be. That most faculty know little moral theory is, for example, not a barrier to teaching professional ethics (except insofar as an unjustified fear of not knowing moral theory intimidates scholars who like to know a field before they teach it). The barriers are much more mundane, deriving in large part simply from lack of classroom experience (for example, knowing how to respond when a student challenges a code provision). Because teaching, like other professions, is largely a matter of judgment, and "judgment" is a shorthand for "what we learned from exercising poor judgment," the focus of any effort to integrate ethics into technical courses must be on getting faculty to start doing it as quickly as possible. There is no substitute for experience.

This is not to say that faculty in business, engineering, biology, or any other academic discipline cannot benefit from moral theory. They certainly can. Indeed, some participants of our workshop have suggested an advanced workshop on moral theory. Having a better sense of what philosophers do, they can see how knowing more philosophy might be relevant to what they do in the classroom or just worth study for its own sake. What our experience shows, however, is that those reasons for studying philosophy are largely independent of integrating ethics into technical courses. If you want to integrate ethics into technical courses quickly (and effectively), a workshop in moral theory is not what you want. You want a workshop focused on how to teach ethics such as that described here.

Our success also suggests another lesson. Insofar as we succeeded more than others before us, we did so because our workshop was different from theirs. It was different because we worked out its contents in close cooperation with faculty like those who would eventually take it. (Indeed, most of the faculty who helped to design the workshop eventually took it.) Not only careful planning, but careful "market research" is necessary to provide what faculty actually need to include ethics in technical courses. Those planning a workshop should take care not to assume they have more than good hunches about what the workshop should include until they have consulted with their potential students. Designing ethics workshops is still a field where nobody knows much, and those who claim to know a lot usually turn out to know nothing. We need all the help we can get.

8

CASE METHOD

While much has been written about "the case method," most of it is about the teaching of law or business.[1] Little has been written about teaching practical (professional or applied) ethics. Of that little, most has been rather theoretical – concerned, for example, with comparing case-based with theory-based teaching.[2] The instructor who looks for guidance on how to develop an ethics case, how to use one in class, or how to write or grade a homework assignment or exam question involving such a case will find only a few scattered remarks.[3] The instructor who would like to use a few ethics cases in a course to which "the case method" is foreign will find even less.[4] The purpose of this chapter is to begin to fill that gap in the literature.

A brief history of "the case"

For lawyers, a "case" is something quite specific, a legally significant event with a client. Where the event has not actually occurred (or the client has not yet sought a lawyer), the case is only "hypothetical." Sometimes lawyers will even contrast cases ("real cases") with hypothetical cases, for example: "That's not a case, that's only a hypothetical."

While the ordinary lawyer has always organized his life around (real) cases, the first law school to adopt something called "the case method" (Harvard) did not do so until the 1870s. The cases of that method were only a small part of what lawyers call "cases." The law school's cases were published decisions of an appellate court, the Olympus few legal cases reach (and most clients are happy to avoid). Published legal decisions contain a digest of the facts of the case, the court's ruling with supporting argument ("the opinion of the court"), and any minority opinions ("dissents" or "concurring opinions").

There was a practical reason for limiting the cases that Harvard's new method used to this small subclass of the cases lawyers deal with. Confidentiality generally keeps lawyers from publishing *their* cases. Since trial courts generally do not publish their decisions, the appellate courts provide the only large pool of cases available for study.

Much can be said in criticism of using only appellate decisions. Lawyers have said it all.[5] Law schools have responded in many ways, for example, by opening "legal clinics" to provide "living cases" to study along with the "frozen" ones in books. For our purposes, however, what is important is not these details of the law's case method. What is important is first, that the law's case method was contrasted with the method it replaced, the study of jurisprudence (legal theory) and summaries of the law (treatises or hornbooks); and second, that the new method proved successful, that is, it appealed to students (after some initial resistance), seemed to train them at least as well as the old method, and had a "scientific" quality that helped the law faculty fit into a Harvard that was already changing from a nineteenth-century religious college into a twentieth-century research university. The case method, insofar as it worked with primary sources, resembled laboratory work, much as the old method, insofar as it relied on secondary sources, resembled the appeal to authority characteristic of religion.

By 1908, the law school's method was so obviously successful that Harvard's new business school adopted it in its commercial law courses and even expressed the hope that cases might also be used in its other courses. That hope was only slowly realized. Use of cases in non-law courses proved difficult for at least three reasons. First, published legal cases tend to focus (not surprisingly) on legal issues. Legal issues are only a small part of what business schools teach. However inadequate the pool of published cases may be for teaching law, it is many times less adequate for teaching business. Second, business people do not think in cases (as lawyers do). The categories of business are "customers," "personnel problems," "deals," and so on, not "cases." Hence, business faculty began without a clear idea of what a non-law case would be. They had to invent the "business case." Third, having invented the business case, the business school still needed to find the equivalent of the law's publication: eventually Harvard itself became a publisher of "cases."

At first, a "business case" might be no more than a faculty member's war story, a company's annual report, a guest lecturer's recounting of some significant business transaction in which he was involved, or even a wad of newspaper clippings. By the 1940s, however, the writing of business cases was becoming a specialty. Today, business school cases are generally the result of extensive research, often including on-sight interviews and detailed examination of public records. While (almost) always about actual events, the names used in a case may be fictitious to preserve confidentiality or to fend off libel suits.

The business school's case method took several decades to perfect. In time, however, many other business schools adopted it (more or less). Starting in the 1950s, other Harvard programs began to adopt it as well.[6] The adoption was often signaled by the writing and publication of a new line of "Harvard cases." Once Harvard had published enough cases for a certain program, programs of that sort at other universities could follow Harvard's lead.

Except perhaps for providing a hospitable background, this history has, I think, little to do with the cases used to teach practical ethics. The people who began the boom in practical ethics were not trained in law or business. They were philosophers (or theologians) with little or no contact with law or business school. They seem to have developed their own "case method" independently, as part of the fruitful exchange between philosophy and medicine that also produced the specialty we now call "medical ethics." Teaching ethics by use of cases came to business schools relatively late.[7]

Philosophers have a long history of using "examples," that is, facts or stories, both in teaching and in writing. Philosophical examples generally have one of two purposes. One is to illustrate an abstract point ("Consider any violation of a moral rule, for example, Jones saying that his wife is not at home when she is"). The other purpose of a philosophical example is to prove a point ("Of course it is sometimes all right to lie, for may I not properly lie to a would-be murderer if that is the only way to keep him from finding his victim?"). Philosophical examples (and "counter-examples") tend to be short, sharply focused, and sparing in detail.[8] A philosophical example may be an actual event, though most are not. Some – like Putnam's world in which everyone is only a "brain in a vat" – seem barely possible. Though a philosopher's example may provoke discussion, its purpose is to kill it. Where an example succeeds, it either clarifies the point in question or proves (or disproves) it, allowing discussion to leave that point for the next. In short, whatever the analogies between the philosopher's example and the law school's or business school's case, a philosopher's example is not a case.

Like lawyers, physicians have cases. In the early 1960s, when physicians began asking philosophers for help with problems of medical ethics that the new technology of medicine had already begun generating, they presented the philosophers with "cases," just as lawyers might have done.[9] For physicians, however, a case is a medical problem, a particular patient with a certain set of symptoms, not a legal problem.[10] The physicians' cases were never "hypothetical." Often the patient still lay in bed across the street. These living cases were seldom short, spare, or sharply focused. Often they were not even fixed. The patient might reveal some important detail of her life between one discussion of the case and the next, or take a turn for the worse, or make a new demand. A philosopher could even go and look if he wanted to, adding to the facts of the case himself.

Those philosophers who made peace with the responsibility that goes with helping physicians decide what to do in actual cases, found the narrative, the unexpected details, the ambiguity, and the practicality of these cases exhilarating. They were also impressed by how much both they and the physicians seemed to learn from the discussion, even when there was no agreement on what to do.

Not surprisingly, some of these philosophers tried to introduce (something like) these discussions into their own teaching, especially into the new undergraduate courses in medical ethics and social issues then taking shape. Because the physician's case contained too much technical information and assumed a good deal of institutional knowledge, the philosophers could not just bring the physician's case into an undergraduate, or even a graduate, class in philosophy. They had to rewrite the case. The rewrite was usually shorter than the typical law school or business school case, much less technical than the physician's. The philosopher's "case" was, however, not just a new version of the philosopher's example. The case was designed to provoke discussion rather than to kill it. If a case had a right answer, it would not be immediately obvious or easy to demonstrate. Often there was (or at least seemed to be) no unique right answer, only several pretty good ones (and several pretty bad ones too).

It is, I think, easy to gloss over this history, to see the ways in which everyone's cases are the same and miss the ways they differ.

So, let me offer two experiences of my own to illustrate the importance of the differences.

First, there is the difference between the lawyer's case and that of the philosopher. During the fall of 1974, when I was preparing to teach legal ethics for the first time, some of my colleagues in law warned me that the course had proved hard to teach because there were so few ethics "cases." What they meant, of course, was too few "published appellate decisions concerned with legal ethics." Whenever I heard that, I asked, "Well, haven't you ever had a case raising an ethical issue?" Seldom was the answer no. Those who answered yes usually went on to describe a case. I put those descriptions in writing, just as had my colleagues in philosophy who taught medical ethics. Many of the cases, suitably disguised, eventually made it into class and a few, into a collection of readings and (what I called) "problems."[11] The course went well, but a fair number of students asked why we read so few "cases" and so many "stories." They had no trouble seeing the difference between the usual law school case and mine.

I had a less happy experience with business school cases. A few years ago, an association to which I belong asked a member of the faculty of Harvard's business school, Prof. X (as I shall call him), to give a demonstration, at the annual meeting, of teaching ethics by "the case method." The plan was for half a dozen of us, all experienced teachers of practical ethics, to lead warm-up discussions in small groups, after which Prof. X would lead a plenary discussion. Everyone attending the meeting was to receive a copy of the case in advance. Prof. X was to meet with the discussion leaders the evening before the small groups met to offer advice, answer questions and otherwise coordinate what would happen in the small groups.

Prof. X's meeting with the leaders was interesting. Many of us voiced doubts about his case, in particular about its length, about thirty typewritten pages; its format, an unstructured mix of narrative and documents; and its lack of focus, the absence of any question to answer – indeed, of any indication who might be given this material or why. Here, it seemed, was a case in something like the literal sense, a container with lots of related stuff tossed in, some useful, some not. Prof. X, smiling kindly, assured us the case was perfectly normal and advised letting the discussion group provide the focus: "You might, for example, begin by asking what issues this case raises." We followed his advice, since we would have done what he advised even if he had not advised it. None of us had trouble leading a good discussion. But nothing Prof. X said, or anything that happened during our group's discussion, did much to change our negative judgment of the case.

When his turn came, Prof. X did not do so well. His audience, mostly philosophers or other academics without business school training, found his unstructured style of discussion so irritating that several of them said so in asides while trying to participate. Prof. X shrugged off these asides with some equivalent of, "Well, that's how we do it at Harvard." Halfway through his time, however, he switched from trying to lead a discussion that was not going well to explaining how it should have gone. The audience then felt free to evaluate the case. To the complaint that the case seemed too long for what it did, Prof. X answered that it did not seem so to him. To the complaint that the case should have a point of view, he responded that he found the you-are-there approach "hokey." To the complaint that the case did not present a problem, he observed that reality seldom does present anything so well defined; we must sort through the facts to develop the problem, if there is to be one.

In short, he had an answer for every objection, most pretty good answers. Yet, the fact remained that the discussion did not go well, by our standards or his. What he had done wrong, I think, was to assume that the business school's method, including the kind of case it uses, is *the* case method of teaching practical ethics. In fact, the business school's method is only one method among many, at home only in a business school where everyone uses cases much like Prof. X's and uses them much as he does. Those of us who use different cases, and use them in different ways, were – PhD's and teaching experience notwithstanding – quite unprepared to do what even first-year MBA students do with relative ease.[12]

The beginning of wisdom in the use of cases is, I think, appreciating how different cases can be. This, then, is a good place for an orderly consideration of the chief differences.

What is a case?

The purpose of this section is to demonstrate the useful variety among cases. I shall make fifteen distinctions. Since most of the distinctions are independent of the others, the number of combinations possible is quite large. While I doubt that the fifteen exhaust the list of potentially useful distinctions, I do believe the list to be long enough to discourage defining "case" too narrowly. I also believe the list to be long enough to remind anyone writing a case of some useful possibilities that might otherwise not come to mind.

Long (and very long) v. short (and very short). Business school cases can be quite long, many times longer than Prof. X's thirty-pager. Such very long cases are worked through over several days or weeks, the instructor focusing first on one aspect of the case (some problem of finance, say) and then on another (a problem of personnel or legality). Very long cases generally contain a good deal of background material, not only records of the company involved and other case-specific information, but also material typical of a text in economics, history, psychology, or sociology. Very long cases may, in fact, be no more than a way for business schools to have their cases and textbooks too.

I have never seen a hundred-page ethics case. Indeed, until Prof. X's case, I had considered a ten-page ethics case quite long. In this respect, ethics cases seem to resemble legal cases. While published decisions can be several hundred pages, the cases in a legal case-book are generally only a few (carefully edited) pages; few cases are even twenty pages. But even most of the cases in legal texts are long compared to most of the ethics cases I use. Mine are generally only a paragraph; few fill a single typewritten page. And, though certainly short, they are not as short as ethics cases can be. A case can be a single sentence, for example, "What would you do if you were in a two-person life boat on an empty, ice-cold sea with a lawyer and doctor and the boat could not long stay afloat with all three of you on board?"

What length a case should be seems to be entirely a matter of what an instructor wants to accomplish, how much time is available, what the students already know, and how much they can be expected to read. So, for example, I generally use short cases because I generally assign a substantial amount of reading along with the cases.[13] Cases provide an opportunity to use ideas in the accompanying readings. They are the equivalent of problem sets in a math course.

Perhaps I need not add that making a case long does not mean that it will be any more real (or realistic). The decision to add a fact is as much a pedagogical judgment as the decision to leave one out. No matter how long (or short) we make a case, we have to make decisions of relevance, suitability, and readability. Except where relevant information is skimpy, we will always leave out far more than we put in, no matter how much we put in. Length *guarantees* nothing but additional cost to print the case, additional demands on student time, and so on. Length, as such, is a disadvantage. All else equal, the shorter the case, the better.

Documents (or pseudo-documents) v. summary. By "document," I mean any writing (graph, photo, or the like) that existed before the author of the case in question set to work on the case. A legal opinion is a document (in this sense), whether complete or abridged. A "pseudo-document" is a writing that, though resembling a document, is the creation of the case's author. Lon Fuller's "The Case of the Speluncean Explorers" is a "pseudo-document" (in this sense).[14] Though not meant to deceive, it has the look of an actual reported decision (as well as a literary power most actual decisions lack). By "summary," I mean an author's description of a situation offered without any pretense that it is the work of anyone else. The following is a typical summary-style case (for medical ethics):

> Dr. Derva Marcus quit her job at a health maintenance group (and went into private practice) because she did not like the idea that the cost of any specialist to whom she referred a patient would come out of a special fund the residue of which would be, at year's end, her annual bonus. "I didn't want to think about whether I would be losing money if I ordered an ophthalmologic examination," she explained. Is the practice Dr. Marcus describes unethical?

Generally, summaries present a set of facts (or "pseudo-facts"). Discussion starts with the assumption that the facts are as presented.

Documents are useful for helping students to appreciate that "facts" must come from somewhere, that they are not necessarily as presented, that it is always worth asking, "Why am I being told this rather than that?" and so on. Where time allows, the reconstruction of reality that documents invite can be quite useful (allowing, for example, an instructor to provide information about the institution that generates documents of that sort). Document cases are especially useful in business school where much of what is being taught is how to turn into business decisions the motley array of documents that cross a manager's desk. Where, however, a course has another purpose (as most courses outside a business school do), and time does not allow a long detour, a summary can bring students directly to the question, or questions, the instructor wants to consider.

Single perspective v. several perspectives. A document or summary can embody one or more perspectives. A published legal case, with majority and minority opinions, is a good example of a single document with several perspectives. A summary can embody several perspectives by reporting the different views of different participants (and omitting to add a "God's eye" alternative).

Single-perspective cases allow an instructor to go directly to the specific ethical issue he wants to discuss. A case with more than one perspective forces a preliminary discussion of what the problem might actually be, which interpretation of the situation, if any, might be the right one. Like documents, multiple-perspective cases teach students to see ethical issues as coming with an interpretation which need not be accepted. Though multiple-perspective cases tend, all else equal, to be longer than single-perspective cases, they too can be short. Here, for example, is a good, short two-perspective case (from legal ethics).

You are the "ethics officer" in a medium-size law firm. Today you have before you one of the firm's most successful negotiators, Allen Dirblock, and the very angry credit manager of the largest department store downtown. The credit manager has accused Dirblock of "lying, swindling, taking advantage of my good nature, conduct unbelievable even in a lawyer." Dirblock described what he did in this way:

"This was a *pro bono* client. She owed $3000 on a couch destroyed by fire. She had only $1000. I knew the store's policy: at least half, or the debt goes to a collection agency. So, before going to the credit manager, I asked the client to give me $500. I removed all my money from my wallet and put that $500 in. Then we went to the credit manager. After the usual dancing around, I offered to settle for $500, all the money she had. He refused. 'I can't go below $2000,' he says. We go around a couple more times and then I say, 'Look, this women lost everything in the fire. What say we settle?' I then take out my wallet, remove all the money in it, and gently place the bills in a rough pile in front of him, saying, 'I feel really strongly about this case. She could be my mother. How about $1000, the $500 she has and all the money I have in my wallet?' He agreed. I didn't lie the way he did when he said he couldn't go below $2000. I *did* mislead him, as he tried to mislead me. But that's negotiation." The credit manager agrees that's what happened, but adds that when he heard "through the grape vine" how

Dirblock had tricked him, he couldn't believe even a lawyer would stoop that low. What, if anything, did Dirblock do wrong? What should you say to him? To the credit manager? Now? Later? Why?

Narrative v. dialogue. A narrative is a sequence of events told in one voice (or several voices that do not respond to one another). A narrative can consist either of documents (say, one or more newspaper articles) or a single summary (as in the Marcus or Dirblock case). While a narrative can quote conversation, if the conversation dominates (as in the Dirblock case), "the narrative" will differ little from dialogue.

Dialogue consists (largely or entirely) of two or more voices in one or a sequence of conversations (with perhaps a few stage directions). A play is a good example of dialogue, but so is a legal opinion in which one or more judges concur or dissent. Dialogue is the easiest way to present a multiple-perspective case, each voice presenting its side. Dialogue does, however, have uses other than providing several perspectives. It can simply give a fly-on-the-wall view of what happened, infuse more life into events than a narrative would, or provide the opening lines for a role-playing situation. Though narrative is a much more common case format than dialogue, many narratives might just as well have been dialogues.

Pure fact v. descriptive commentary. A case is "pure fact" if its author does not explicitly include his own analysis. Most cases are pure fact (in this sense), whether they are document or summary, single perspective or several perspective, narrative or dialogue. Both the Marcus and Dirblock cases are pure fact (in this sense). A descriptive commentary provides a framework for discussion that the instructor might otherwise have had to provide. It gives students help in thinking about a case, whether by winning belief or by offering a target to shoot at.[15] While descriptive commentaries are seldom short, they need not be (what I have called) long. Sometimes a few pages is sufficient.

Realistic (hypothetical) v. real (actual). Philosopher's *examples* need not be real or realistic; perhaps they need only be logically possible. They are adjuncts to theory, interesting only because of what they illustrate or prove. Cases, in contrast, must be real or at least realistic. They must, that is, be enough like actual events to be treated as practical possibilities. The easiest way to assure that a case will be treated as a practical possibility is explicitly to use actual events (whether or not the names are changed). Whatever actually happened must be possible in practice. The other way to achieve realism is by imagining a case but imagining it within the bounds students consider plausible. The case will then be realistic but not real, "a hypothetical." A case that fails even the rest of realism is a "*mere* hypothetical."

Generally, hypothetical cases are much easier to write in a way that focuses on a specific question. But they do not expand the student's sense of what is possible; and they are always subject to being dismissed as "unrealistic." While I do sometimes risk a hypothetical, especially on an exam, I generally prefer actual cases, often with the names changed (as in the Dirblock case) and the facts modified in small ways to fit the class. I like responding to a student who claims, "That couldn't happen," that it did. I think it important for students to learn that the plausible does not define the real.

Stories v. problems. A story has a beginning, a middle, and an end. The Marcus case (above) is a story. It ends with Dr. Marcus leaving her job at the health maintenance group. Stories can come in documents (for example, as a law case or series of letters) or in a simple summary; stories can be narratives or dialogues, single perspective or several perspective, hypothetical or actual.

Problems may be thought of as stories that stop without ending. A problem "ends" by asking what should be done next. The Dirblock case (above) is a problem. The difference between stories and problems is not fundamental. Any story can be turned into a problem.[16] For example, the Marcus case (above) would become a problem if, instead of completing the story with her resignation from the health maintenance organization, I had written the case with her hearing of the new bonus plan and asked what, if anything, she should do in response. Stories can also be "stopped" before their end. For example, an instructor can ask a class (about the story version of the Marcus case), "What would have done if you had been in Dr. Marcus' place when her employer announced the bonus plan?"

You (agent) v. they (judge). Cases (whether stories or problems) can be written with the reader as a participant (the "you" of the Dirblock case) or as an outside judge (as in the Marcus case). Caroline Whitbeck has recently criticized cases with the "judge perspective" because they allow students to treat ethics as, in effect, a spectator sport. The student need only decide whether the conduct was right or wrong (and provide arguments in support of that decision). Second-guessing the actual decision maker is far easier than working out the details of a decision when it is your own and you do not know how it will turn out.[17] That, of course, is true. But it is also true that being able to think about how a decision will look to those not directly involved (especially if it turns out badly) can sober a decision maker who might otherwise succumb to too narrow (or too hopeful) a view of what she is doing. Students probably need help not only in learning to make their own decisions, but also in learning how to evaluate those of others and how to see their own as others might. So, the best strategy may well be a judicious mix of the two kinds of case, along with an occasional switch in the middle: "You say that is what she should have done, but what would you have done if you had been in her place? What should *you* have done?"

Would v. should. "They" cases seem always to ask what *should* be done or have been done (when they do not ask what is the "right," "moral," or "ethical" thing to do). "You" cases, however, are sometimes written with "should" and sometimes with "would." I do not like "would" for two reasons. First, "would" seems to ask for a prediction. Since I do not teach students how to predict their own conduct, but how to choose it, I do not think it fair to ask them to make such predictions. Second, "would" seems to ask students to reveal something about themselves beyond what they know about ethics. Asking them to do that seems to me to invade their privacy.

Those are my reasons for preferring "should" to "would." When I have offered these reasons to instructors who use "would," they usually tell me that I have a point *but* a) asking students what they would do often helps clarify their thinking about what really matters (what should go into a "should" judgment), and b) that students seem to regard the "would" as asking for neither prediction nor self-revelation but for a kind of "personal should." I see their point, but – .

Top v. bottom. Most cases in the news, most of the Harvard cases too, involve decisions near the top of an organization. Our students will, however, graduate into jobs much closer to the bottom. Only after many years, and only with a good deal of luck, will they rise to be in a position like Thiokol's expert on booster rocket seals, the Du Pont vice-president asked to decide whether to bar women from certain hazardous jobs, or the like. Should not our cases reflect that reality? Should not our cases be drawn solely from first-job experiences?[18] I think not.

Many top-level decisions are simply more dramatic versions of low-level decisions; they are first-job reality written large. Why give up the dramatic large print? Some top-level decisions may, of course, have no (exact) counterpart lower down. Still, studying them may help students to see high-level decisions as ethical decisions, to see their own first job as part of an ethical career at the end of which may wait those top-level decisions, and to think about how first decisions may help to shape later decisions. My students do not find the top-level cases boring, though they often need a good deal of background information to understand what is at stake. The top-level decisions seem to be the equivalent in practical ethics of Homer's heroes or Shakespeare's kings. First-job cases may, all else equal, be better for enhancing judgment than top-level decisions, though even that remains to be shown.[19] Since top-level cases may be better for other purposes, for example, for enhancing sensitivity or knowledge, I see no reason not to use both kinds of cases. Indeed, given student interest in the big cases, I think it unwise to restrict one's cases to those originating at the "bottom."

Success (the positive) v. failure (the negative). Ethics *stories* may be divided into two categories, those that turn out well (successes) and those that turn out badly (failures). Because ethics *problems* have yet to turn out, they cannot be categorized in this way. They can, however, be categorized in an analogous way. What makes some problems is that the agent has the opportunity to do something good (for example, save lives that would otherwise be lost). No one has done anything wrong; indeed, wrongdoing is not among the live options. The problem is produced by a conflict of considerations all of which are (more or less) good. These are the analogues of success stories. In other problems, the source of the problem is someone's (at least apparent) wrongdoing (usually that of the agent's superior, colleague, or client). The problem may seem to pose a "dilemma" (in the strict sense), two choices, both bad. These are the analogues of failure stories.

In many fields, the primary source of ethics cases is the newspaper. Newspapers seldom report ethical success (presumably, because, short of heroism, such success is too common to be news). Most newspaper accounts concerned with ethics are reports of ethical failure: scandals, crimes, disasters. An instructor who relies only on newspapers for ethics cases may end with a collection of cases consisting entirely of failures. Students fed entirely on such cases may become cynical about the very possibility of ethical conduct: "What do we learn in our professional ethics course? How bad we are!"

While failures, both stories and problems, are important for teaching what can go wrong (a part of expanding a student's

155

"moral imagination"), success stories have at least three additional uses. First, success stories show that ethical conduct is possible, thus reducing cynicism. Second, they may provide examples of *how* to conduct oneself ethically – and live to tell about it. That is, they may contain insight into the "art of ethics," for example, that you will do better if you develop a reputation for accuracy, if you have an alternative to the proposal you think objectionable, or if you build a coalition before confronting a superior. Third, just as failures provide a vocabulary for what can go wrong ("a *Challenger* situation"), so success stories provide a vocabulary for what can be done right ("Horatio at the bridge"). Success problems, in contrast, have only one use, to give students an opportunity to practice judgment in situations where no one has done anything wrong.

Single issue (poor) v. multi-issue (rich). Cases can be narrowly focused. The Marcus case, for example, is about conflict of interest; once you have discussed what to do about the conflict of interest the bonus plan creates, there is not much left to say about the case. Other cases are about several ethical issues. They are "rich" in possible uses. Prof. X's case was rich (in this sense). Generally, the shorter a case, the poorer it will be. But even a relatively short case can have several issues, as, for example, the Dirblock case does. Rich cases are better for examinations, where you want to see how many issues a student can spot. Poor cases are better for a class where you want to focus on identifying, analyzing, and responding to a particular issue, not several.

Single stage v. multi-stage. In real life, problems often grow. We make a small decision, without much thought, thinking that will be the end of it. Our decision has consequences and, a few days or weeks later, we have the same problem on our desk, somewhat more complicated now. Again we decide. We may hear nothing more of the decision, or it may have new consequences producing yet another decision. And so on. Generally, cases – both problems and stories – have a single stage: we decide the case and go on to another. We are not later asked to clean up the mess we did not foresee. A diet of single-stage cases may leave the impression that (in Macbeth's words) "it were done when 'tis done," whereas often:

> . . .we but teach
> Bloody instructions, which, being taught, return,
> To plague the inventor.

Multi-stage cases try to teach that, because no decision is necessarily "final," it pays to think about what new decisions this one might generate, especially those it might generate if things do not go as we hope or expect. Multi-stage cases invite computer simulation, but can be done well on paper. The first stage is a conventional problem (for example, a situation where "you" are faced with the question whether you should obey what you believe is an unethical order). You resolve it, say, by obeying under protest. You go to the next stage: A few weeks later your boss' superior asks why you did what you did. Do you tell her the whole truth, including the protest, or just some part? Why? You decide. There may then be a third stage, a fourth, and even a fifth. Indeed, in principle, nothing prevents a multi-stage problem from being as long and complex as a novel.[20]

Ordinary v. technical language. The philosopher's case is typically put in language allowing someone not trained in philosophy or any other particular discipline to reach the ethical issues. Such cases are in "ordinary language." Cases can also be given the characteristic format of a particular discipline. Some disciplines, especially engineering, accounting, and many of the sciences, organize their teaching around numerical problems. Other disciplines have a less formal equivalent, for example, the rendition of symptoms in medicine or the details of site measurement, tagging, and logging in archeology. Those who hope to make a discussion of practical ethics seem continuous with a specific technical education probably should use some ethics problems where the ethical issue must be reached through the typical techniques. Here, for example, is a typical ethics case in technical language (for a first course in environmental engineering):

> Ellerbe Creek receives wastewater from the 10 mgd Northside Wastewater Treatment Plant in Durham, North Carolina. The creek has a mean summertime flow of 0.28 m^3 m/s. The wastewater characteristics are: temperature = 28°C; ultimate BOD (L) = 40 mg/L; k_1 = 0.23 d^{-1}; dissolved oxygen = 2 mg/L. The total stream length is 14 miles, at which point it empties into the Neuse River. Should the State of North Carolina be concerned about the effect of this discharge on Ellerbe Creek? Explain and justify.[21]

In general, technical language cases are better for technical courses; ordinary language cases are better for courses, especially those in philosophy, where students do not all have the same technical training or where the instructor does not share the technical background of the students.

Personal v. policy. For some cases, all the likely responses are what one or a few people should do (or should have done). For others, all the likely responses are what an organization or other large group should do (or should have done), especially, what rules they should have (or should have had). Cases of the first sort concern what is often called "personal ethics"; the second, what is often called "social ethics" or "policy." Many cases have both a personal and a policy aspect, that is, "you" should do such-and-such now, but your organization should make such-and-such changes so that you don't have to make such a decision again. Where "your" organization is a government, policy issues are also political issues. The line between practical ethics and politics is not sharp. The best rule of thumb for distinguishing them is that a case belongs to politics rather than practical ethics if all the likely responses require new laws.

The line between ethics and politics is not sharp because the line is primarily a convenience for teachers. A particular problem may have a personal resolution, a policy resolution (a new corporate rule), and a political resolution (a new law). The line between ethics and politics is none the less important because courses in practical ethics (as distinct from courses in political philosophy) tend to focus on what individual agents, or some private organization to which they belong, can do, rather than on what government can do.

Living v. frozen. A "living case" is one that is still in progress. Most cases, especially published cases, are "frozen"; they will always be as they are now. Generally, the ordinary classroom must make do with frozen cases; the clinic's living cases belong to another realm. But, there are exceptions. For example, someone teaching engineering, business, or journalism ethics during the semester when the *Challenger* exploded would have had a chance to treat that disaster as a multi-stage case, returning to it every few weeks to review the events, make a new evaluation, say what should be done, and then see what happens. Instructors can also create living cases, for example, by having students write and adopt a code of ethics for the class (or laboratory) at the beginning of the term and then, from time to time, describing cases arising under the code and asking for guidance, including suggestions for revising the code. An instructor can even create a fair imitation of a living case, for example, by presenting a multi-stage case over several days, stage by stage.

That, I think, is enough variety to free up thinking about cases. We are now ready to consider what can be done with cases of one variety or another.

What is "the case method"?

Many discussions of "the case method" treat "the Socratic method" as a necessary part. In law schools, the two methods are quite distinct. The case method defines *what* can be studied – cases rather than statute books, legal treatises, and the like. The "Socratic method" defines *how* the study should be carried out. The "Socratic method" is instruction by a certain sort of questioning rather than by lecture. The "Socratic method" can be applied to statute books, legal treatises, or any other non-case material just as easily as to cases.[22]

I have kept the law school's term "Socratic method" in scare quotes because I want to suggest that any connection with the method of Socrates is problematic. Socrates asked others questions in order to teach himself, not in order to teach them. He professed ignorance, not – as a professor of law necessarily does – expertise.[23] Beyond this fundamental difference, there is as well a difference in style. Those who have seen the movie *Paper Chase* will remember Prof. Kingsfield's bullying questions, the way he humiliated students, and the way some students learned to fight back. While an extreme, Kingsfield has his counterparts, however drab in comparison, in most law schools. That is because one function of the law's "Socratic method" is to teach law students to respond quickly (and correctly) under pressure (as they might have to do in a courtroom). The "sarcastic method" (as I have heard law students call it) is, at its best, a kind of legal calisthenics, a hardening independent of its content. At its worst, it is what engineers call "testing to destruction." *The Paper Chase* had a reminder of that, a student so broken by failing that he took his own life.

The law school's "Socratic method" has another peculiarity. Though the questioning begins with an actual case, it often moves on to hypotheticals, sometimes reaching hypotheticals almost as strange as the strangest philosopher's example.[24] Principles or theories of a case (instead of, or as well as, students) are tested to destruction. Viewers of *Ethics in America* will have some idea of what that process is like. Arthur Miller, a law professor who served as the discussion leader, responded to any consensus about what should be done in an ethics case he put with a new variation on the case, one in which the situation was less probable and the decision harder, until the situation became unlikely indeed and the panelists just scratched their heads. While useful for teaching students how to probe legal theories, this testing to destruction is probably a poor way to teach ethics. Students are likely to develop an exaggerated sense of how much disagreement about ethics actually exists on questions they are likely to face.

The business school's version of the "Socratic method" is more closely linked to cases than the law school's. The business case is supposed to be an ordinary business decision. The business school's "Socratic method" is supposed to be a method a manager could use in dealing with that decision. A good manager asks questions of subordinates, colleagues, or even superiors because she wants to know the answer. She leads discussion to a resolution none may have foreseen. Learning to ask the right questions, to probe a position until understood, is a skill managers should have. Business students who learn to do what their business professors do will probably be better managers than those who do not.[25]

Lawyers can, of course, turn the "Socratic method" they learned into (something like) the manager's questioning. They will, however, have to give up the sarcasm (which tends to alienate others rather than to help with problem solving); they may also have to learn how to overcome the tendency of legal colleagues to respond to questions in the defensive way they learned in law school. And, like managers, they will have to omit the truly strange hypotheticals with which law professors test theories to destruction.

Because the business school's "Socratic method" corresponds to the way managers approach a problem, business professors can, and frequently do, claim not to know what the "right answer" to a case is. That is a modest claim, one worthy of Socrates. Sometimes they claim there is "no single right answer" (meaning that there may be several), a claim that tends to keep discussion going after students have found one good answer. Sometimes, however, business professors claim that there is "no right answer" (meaning not even one). This last claim seems dubious: it must rest either on a theory of knowledge or on evidence.

The theory, whatever it is, would presumably have to be right about what there is to know. The professor who used such a theory to defend his claim that there are no right answers would, then, have to explain why theories can be right but decisions cannot be. He would find himself in a forest of mirrors from which few return.

The alternative, defending the claim that there is no right answer by appeal to evidence, is only slightly more attractive. Since we do believe that some of our decisions were right, even some business decisions, the business professor who claims to know that there is no right answer to the problem under discussion makes an extraordinary claim, one we should reject until shown strong evidence to the contrary. That he, his colleagues, and his classes have not yet found the right decision would be evidence for that claim, but only weak evidence. We often have trouble finding the right answer and yet go on to find it. Any claim to *know* that there is no right answer must rest on an examination of all the possibilities leading to a determination that none is right. Examining all possibilities, not just all that have been thought up so far, is plausible in mathematics and other fields where the set of possible answers is relatively well defined. But business is not such a field. Imagination can always add to the number of possible answers. So, to know that there is no right answer to this business case would seem to require knowing that no new courses of action can be invented. The claim to such knowledge is both implausible and un-Socratic.

Why then do business professors so often claim that there is no right answer to a case? The explanation, I think, is in the purpose for which they use cases. Business professors use cases to approximate actual business decision making. In practice, managers will seldom know more than that they made the best decision given the information and alternatives available; and often they will know less: for example, that they made the decision they thought best when others, whose judgment they respect, thought some other decision was better but (so far) things seem to have gone the manager's way. There is generally no way to *demonstrate* that a decision was right; there are merely more or less plausible arguments one way or the other. Much of business school is preparing future managers to enter this epistemic vacuum. The claim that there are no right answers turns a (reasonable) epistemic point into a metaphysical nullity.

The business school's method of teaching cases, though closer to that of practical ethics than the law school's, is still (as the story of Prof. X illustrates) not typical of practical ethics. So, what method is typical? Actually, I do not think any single method is typical. There are several methods, each more like most of the others than any is like the method used in law or business school. In part, instructors use one method or another depending on their own style of teaching. In part, though, the method they use depends on the kind of ethics they wish to teach, the cases available, and their purpose in using cases. This, then, is a good place to consider what kinds of ethics there are, what teaching can accomplish, and what role cases might have in that teaching.

What can you accomplish with cases?

The term "ethics" can, as we have seen, be used in at least one of three senses relevant here: (a) as a synonym for ordinary morality, (b) to name a field of philosophy, and (c) to refer to those morally permissible standards that apply to members of a group because of that membership. Those concerned to teach ordinary morality tend to focus on moral judgment; those concerned to teach philosophical ethics focus on moral theory, and those concerned to teach the special standards of a group focus on those standards, their interpretation and application. Their use of cases should differ accordingly.

I shall say no more about using cases to teach ordinary morality for three reasons. First, teaching ordinary morality is primarily a pre-college enterprise; my concern here is teaching ethics in college, graduate departments, and professional schools. Second, the literature on using cases to teach ordinary morality is substantial, including a good deal of empirical evidence that it works. I have little to add here.[26] Third, much I shall say about teaching special standards applies to teaching ordinary morality as well. So, little, if anything, is lost by not dealing further with the teaching of morality as such.

I do, however, want to say a little about the use of cases in teaching philosophical ethics. What is important for us is that such teaching uses cases in two ways different from the use of traditional examples.

First, there is a pedagogical use. So, for example, one might begin a course in ethical theory with an ethics case rather than a theory to help students see the point of theories: theories should help us solve problems like this.

Second, there is a theoretical use. One can, during the semester, bring various theories to bear on this or that case, asking which theory gives us the most insight. This use of cases, though close to the use of traditional examples (and counter-examples) differs in one important way. Examples are chosen because they are "clear," that is, because we agree on what the right answer is; the theory is tested against the example. Cases, in contrast, are chosen because they are "hard," that is, because we disagree about what the right answer is. Cases help us to probe the theory, to compare one theory with another, to gauge their power. Theories do not pass or fail depending on whether they give the right answer to a case. The case has a right answer, of course, perhaps even more than one. But, insofar as we have chosen the case because it is hard – that is, because we do not agree on what the right answer is – we cannot test the theory against the case in the way we can test a theory against an example.[27]

This theoretical use of ethics cases resembles the business school use of business cases in at least two ways. First, a philosophy instructor can use a case while claiming not to know what the right answer is (how a problem should be resolved or whether a character in a story did what she should). Second, a philosophy instructor cannot use cases to test moral theories to destruction. Examples, not cases, test theories to destruction.

This theoretical use of ethics cases does, however, resemble the use law schools make of legal cases rather than the use business schools make of business cases in at least one way. In a course in moral theory, the instructor uses cases to build an argument against one theory or in favor of another. The cases are not offered simply to train judgment.

That is enough about courses in moral theory. Courses in moral theory, however they use cases, are not courses in practical ethics.[28] What then is a course in practical ethics? We may distinguish at least three kinds: social issues courses, professional ethics courses, and institutional ethics courses. A course in social issues takes up controversial questions of social policy: abortion, euthanasia, war, terrorism, and so on.[29] It seeks to clarify the issues, to evaluate arguments, and (if all goes well) to justify adoption of certain social standards.[30] A course in professional ethics focuses on the special standards of a profession rather than on general social standards (special standards that do or should exist): nursing ethics, police ethics, accounting ethics, engineering ethics, or the like. A course in institutional ethics focuses instead on special standards of an institution (those that do or should exist): academic ethics, business ethics, criminal justice ethics, research ethics, or the like.

The distinction between professional and institutional ethics, though not important here, is worth recalling for clarity's sake. Physicians, for example, both belong to a profession (medicine) and work in an institution (the health care system). It is therefore at least theoretically possible for "medical ethics" (in the sense of the special standards physicians as a group apply to themselves as individuals) to conflict with "medical ethics" (in the sense of the special standards that the health care system applies to anyone providing health care). Indeed, such conflicts explain why many courses in "medical ethics" include both professional and institutional ethics.

A course in practical ethics (of whatever kind) is concerned not with moral theory as such but with special standards of conduct that apply, or might apply, to members of a certain group. The same is true of a course on some other subject (Thermodynamics, say) in which a segment is devoted to practical ethics. A practical ethics course, or practical ethics segment of some other course, can have at least four purposes (all quite different from the purposes of a course in philosophical ethics):

First, the course might seek to raise the ethical *sensitivity* of students. That is, the course might try to teach students to recognize that some professional, institutional, or other special standard may be relevant to a decision. The study of cases is an obvious way to raise sensitivity. Students may, for example, read a case, see no ethical issue, and come to class wondering what the point of the case was. If, during class, the instructor (whether by lecture, by "Socratic" questioning, or by some other method) helps students see that the case raises several issues they missed, the students should be more likely to see those issues next time they read a similar case – and probably the next time they are in a situation resembling the case. This use of cases is analogous both to the law school's use of legal cases to teach students to identify legal issues and to the business school's use of business cases to teach students to identify business issues.

A second purpose a course in practical ethics might have is increasing the ethical *knowledge* of students. The course might try to add to what students know about the special standards in question, not only their content, interpretation, and application, but also the resources available to help realize them in practice. A case can contribute to this purpose either by itself containing the information (as some business and law school cases do), by providing an occasion for the instructor to provide the information, or by providing an occasion for the students to seek the information, in their texts, in the library, or in the world.

A third purpose a course in practical ethics might have is improving the ethical *judgment* of students. The course might, that is, try to increase the likelihood that students who apply what they know about ethics to a decision they recognize as ethical will get the right answer. All university courses teach judgment of one sort or another. Most find that discussing how to apply general principles helps students to apply those principles better; many also find that giving students practice in applying them helps too. Cases are an opportunity to exercise judgment. The student who has had to decide how to resolve an ethics case is better equipped to decide a case of that kind than one who has never thought about the subject. If she has also had to present her decision, hear it criticized, and respond to that criticism, she will be even better prepared to think through an actual problem of that kind – and so, more likely to make the right choice in practice.

A fourth purpose a course in practical ethics may have is enhancing ethical *willpower*. By "enhancing willpower" I mean no more than making more likely than would otherwise be that a student will do what he thinks right. A case discussion can contribute to ethical willpower by helping students appreciate that a view they thought was their own idiosyncracy is in fact common among members of their society, profession, or institution, and that they will probably have support if they try to act accordingly. Even writing a paper on a case can enhance willpower. A student who believes he has thought through a particular problem is more likely to make his arguments to others, more likely to win allies, and less likely to be cowed by appeal to arguments of the form, "well, that's just how we do it here."

These four purposes share a common assumption, that there are right answers in practical ethics and that (often at least) we can know what they are. This assumption does not imply that there are no hard cases in practical ethics. Certainly there are. The assumption implies only that not all situations of practical ethics are hard cases, that there may be a half continent of settled cases as well as a frontier in flames. A course in *philosophical* ethics might well never discuss an easy case. But a course in *practical* ethics probably should discuss a good many to avoid leaving the impression that there are no right answers. The course should also make clear why some answers are settled, so that students understand that they are settled for reasons that can be challenged, that the standards in question are not arbitrary commands or inexplicable artifacts, but the work of practical people trying to use their experience to achieve certain aims.

Cases rather than theories?

The previous section drew a sharp line between philosophical ethics and practical ethics, and between the way cases would be used in one or the other of those courses. Yet many texts in practical ethics begin with a long section discussing moral theories, and many teachers of practical ethics feel obliged to introduce a good deal of moral theory into their practical courses. While the line between philosophical ethics courses and practical ethics courses need not be as sharp as I have drawn it, I think there are at least four good reasons to avoid the use of moral theory in courses that really are in practical ethics, reasons which become decisive when the question is not a course but a segment of a course or when the instructor does not in fact know much about moral theory.

One reason not to teach moral theories in a course in practical ethics is that moral theories are complicated. Teaching one theory in a reasonably sophisticated form can take several weeks, pass over the heads of most students, and consume time better used for the substance of a course. Teaching a theory in simplified form, while avoiding most of these disadvantages, has another: it tends to reduce the theory to caricature, leaving students to wonder why anyone would want to hold such a view.

A second reason not to teach moral theories in a course in practical ethics is that (explicit) theories are generally unnecessary for good decision-making. What a teacher of practical ethics needs is some framework for orderly discussion of ethics cases, one including the substance of common sense. While a moral theory can provide such a framework, there are many other frameworks. Here is one I use.

Seven-step guide to ethical decision making

1   *State problem*. For example, "there's something about this decision that makes me uncomfortable" or "do I have a conflict of interest?".
2   *Check facts*. Many problems disappear upon closer examination of situation, while others change radically.
3   *Identify relevant factors*. For example, persons involved, laws, professional code, other practical constraints (e.g. under $200).
4   *Develop list of options*. Be imaginative, try to avoid "dilemma"; not "yes" or "no" but whom to go to, what to say.
5   *Test options*. Use such tests as the following:

- *harm test*: does this option do less harm than alternatives?
- *publicity test*: would I want my choice of this option published in the newspaper?
- *defensibility test*: could I defend choice of option before Congressional committee or committee of peers?
- *reversibility test*: would I still think choice of this option good if I were adversely affected by it?
- *colleague test*: what do my colleagues say when I describe my problem and suggest this option as my solution?
- *professional test*: what might my profession's governing body or ethics committee say about this option?
- *organization test*: what does the company's ethics officer or legal counsel say about this?

6 *Make a choice* based on steps 1–5.
7 *Review steps 1–6.* What could you do to make it less likely that you would have to make such a decision again?

- Are there any precautions can you take as individual (announce your policy on question, change job, etc.)?
- Is there any way to have more support next time?
- Is there any way to change the organization (for example, suggest policy change at next departmental meeting)?

Step 4, "Test options," uses ideas from various moral theories (harm, reversibility, and so on) to evaluate options. The tests are not necessarily decisive; they are supposed to call attention to relevant considerations. In this way, the core of most moral theories can be brought into decision making in an uncontroversial form (that is, without the exclusiveness and technical paraphernalia of explicit moral theory).

A third reason not to use moral theories in a course in practical ethics is that in practice people seldom explicitly appeal to moral theories. They may do so "implicitly," that is, by saying something that can be understood as appealing to one moral theory rather than another. But telling them that they are so relying is seldom an effective way to get them to think sensibly about the practical problem before them. Indeed, thinking explicitly with theory is a special skill, one few have and perhaps not many more can develop. Even many philosophers are not competent to do justice to a moral theory. Given how short a single course in practical ethics is, its time seems better used dealing with practical ethics directly. Insofar as students need a framework for dealing with practical problems (as they certainly do), the best framework would seem to be one – like the seven steps – that both has a theoretical foundation (however implicit) and guides reasoning in ways likely to convince those to whom the reasoning is addressed.

A fourth reason not to use moral theories in a course in practical ethics is that different people tend to prefer different theories as soon as they understand them well enough to see the differences. Getting agreement on a particular course of action, even in a relatively hard case, is usually much easier than getting agreement on which moral theory to apply. In this respect, moral theories resemble religions; their explicit use in practical decisions tends to be divisive.

These four reasons are all practical. They do not establish that moral theories are useless in principle or that they should never be used in a course in practical ethics. Together, the four establish no more than a general presumption against moral theories in courses in practical ethics, a presumption that can be overcome where time, the preparation of students, the skill of the instructor, and the specific question under consideration together create circumstances making the introduction of theory clearly helpful. However that may be, neither these reasons nor my own experience suggests that instructors may not benefit from reading theoretically informed work in practical ethics, from applying theory in their own thinking about hard cases, or from using theory to organize what they do in class.

Some ways to use cases

When time allows, the best use of cases in a practical ethics class (or class segment) is certainly guided discussion (guided, that is, by something like the seven steps). Not only does discussion engage students in a way lecture generally does not, it also improves judgment in ways lecture cannot.[31] Guided discussion also allows an instructor to break in now and then with informative mini-lectures providing information, ideas, or approaches at just the moment when students feel the need. Guided discussion is less formalized than the "Socratic method" of law or business school; but insofar as it has a distinct form, what most distinguishes it from the case method of business and law school is the inclusion of mini-lectures.

The following ways of using cases may both supplement guided discussion, where such discussion is possible, or accomplish some of what guided discussion would accomplish were it possible. Some of these ways of using cases are especially useful in classes the subject of which is *not* practical ethics.

Hit and run. In "hit-and-run," an instructor simply points out a problem or source of problems and goes on. Generally, the case used is quite short or integrated into a larger technical problem. For example, during a discussion of crowd psychology, an instructor in criminal justice might describe a situation where an attempt to arrest in fact set off a riot (without telling students the outcome) and ask how to make the arrest using various theories of crowd behavior. After the students have made their suggestions, the instructor might describe what the officer in question did and what happened (connecting the outcome with one or another theory of crowd psychology), concluding with the question, "Why didn't anyone here suggest not making the arrest? After all, police have discretion to make arrests precisely because there are times when making a justified arrest would be disastrous." The instructor should do this hoping that at least one student will point out that the class was only asked *how* to arrest, the means, not *whether* to arrest. If a student does point that out, the instructor can reply: "A police officer need not be bound by the form in which a question is put. If there is a problem with the end, an officer should so indicate. Police are not mere instruments of policy; they are also moral agents." Even a few such comments in the course of a semester can help students get used to looking for the morally significant decision concealed by a discussion ostensibly about means.

Homework problem. Students can be asked to read a problem or story outside of class. In a course where students routinely prepare for class by doing problems at home (whether or not for a grade), students may also be asked to write a response to a case (turning that in if they turn in other homework). Such ethics homework assignments should offer some general guidance about how to respond to the problems posed (for example, the seven step guide) or a series of more specific questions. The process of thinking through a case, perhaps in consultation with other students, forces a student to use judgment, to look for sources of ethical information (for example, for help from a code of ethics), and to marshall reasons. Responses need not be long. In a science course, for example, students might be told that no response should be more than a hundred words.

Exam question. An exam question is an in-class version of the homework problem. The student is given a story and asked to identify the ethical issues, to evaluate the responses of participants, and to defend that evaluation. Or the student might be given a problem and asked to identify the ethical issues, develop a response, and defend that response. Ethics questions can stand alone or be built into larger·technical questions. Answering exam questions on ethics, and receiving a grade for them, helps students appreciate that ethics is something you learn, something that the instructor takes seriously, and something for which there are (objectively) better and worse answers.

Essay. The essay, though a kind of homework problem, is different enough to deserve separate mention. Essays generally take longer to write than a response to an (ordinary) homework problem (a week, say, rather than part of an evening), to be much longer (a few thousand words rather than a few hundred), and to pose a more complex problem (or to leave the student to identify a problem on his own). The advantage that the homework problem has over the essay is breadth: an instructor can easily assign a dozen or two in a semester. The advantage of the essay is depth: while a single essay may take as much time to write as ten homework problems, the student is likely to understand most of the issues in the one essay much better than any one of the issues in the ten homework problems.

Interview. In an (ethics) interview, a student asks questions of someone with more experience. The purpose of an interview is to learn something about how individuals deal with ethical problems of a certain sort, how the organization in which that individual works deals with such problems, or what connection there is between what has been going on in class and what actually happens "in the world." The core of the interview may be a series of questions, a problem for the interviewee to resolve (saying what she "would do" or what her organization "would do"), or some combination of these. After the interview, the interviewers write (or give) a report in which they describe what they asked, what happened, and what they learned. Interviews can contribute substantially to both the student's and the instructor's ethical knowledge.[32]

Role playing (you). In formal role playing, students are assigned roles in a situation (often a day or two before); they come to the front of the class and try to act as they think one should in that role. Role playing can, however, be less formal. So, for example, in the middle of a class discussion, a student can be asked what she would say (or do) if she were so-and-so or were in such-and-such a position or office; another student might then be asked what he would say (or do) in response if he were some other person

170

involved. Role playing has the power of all drama to engage. It also gives students an opportunity to get some idea how various arguments look from a position different from their own, helping them break out of stereotyped thinking.

Ethics committee (they). An ethics committee is a body with authority to advise on the interpretation of a code of ethics. An ethics committee responds to someone else's practical question with a reasoned judgment. Many professional societies, a smaller percentage of governments, and some businesses have such committees (or some equivalent such as an ethics officer or ombudsman). The classroom version of such a committee is a kind of role playing, but one distinct enough to deserve a paragraph of its own. Students are given one or several ethics questions (problems or stories) and asked to decide whether certain lines of conduct are ethical or unethical (and to justify their decision). A committee should have three or more students. Generally, they would have several days or weeks to reach a decision, work out the rationale for it, and commit that rationale to paper. Minority reports are welcome. If time allows, the committee might have to present its recommendation to the class (with the class acting as the parent committee or some other appropriate body), answer questions, respond to objections, and so on. I like to take a vote at the end of such a classroom presentation: should we (the class) adopt this recommendation? The vote provides closure.[33]

What distinguishes the ethics committee from most role playing is that the committee is asked to advise *others*. By itself, this may seem a disadvantage. What compensates for that disadvantage, if disadvantage it is, is that the students are forced to think of ethics as a public undertaking for which reasons are appropriate. They get to see the impact of ethical reasoning on themselves and other members of the committee or class. They are also forced to think about the institutional impact of specific ethics decisions. They must consider everyone whom the decision might affect.

Debate (and ethics bowl). Debate, as distinct from discussion, is another form of role playing. Students are assigned "sides" which they are to defend much as lawyers might. The great disadvantage of debate is that it tends to leave the impression that there are only two sides to any question. Debate also has a tendency to harden opinion when a student is asked to defend a position with which he agrees and to produce caricatured arguments when a student is asked to defend a position with which he disagrees. Debate certainly does not teach students how to resolve ethical disagreement. What sometimes compensates for these disadvantages is that, like other forms of role playing, debate can be dramatic and can help students see a position from another side.

There is, however, a variation on debate that avoids most, or all, of these disadvantages, "ethics bowl." Students form teams of four each to compete, much as on Public Television's College Bowl. The chief differences between College Bowl and an ethics bowl are: (a) the teams must answer questions asking for an ethical decision in a specific situation; (b) the responses are evaluated by a panel of practitioners (as in a diving contest) with the emphasis on the identification of ethical issues, the ingenuity of the proposed solution, and the reasoning offered in its defense, rather than on giving "the right answer"; and (c) the teams have the right to criticize the "official answer" if they believe their own is better (with the panel counting the effectiveness of this criticism in making their final evaluation). After two years of experiment with this format at IIT, the ethics bowl went intercollegiate in Spring 1995, with DePaul, Loyola, and Western Michigan joining IIT to hold a joint ethics bowl (after each held an internal ethics bowl to choose a team to represent the school). A second, and larger, ethics bowl was held in the spring of 1996, and a third and even larger one in the spring of 1997. Several instructors have used a variation of the ethics bowl in class. Students enjoy the competition while appreciating the opportunity the ethics bowl gives them to practice making decisions.[34]

How to develop cases

Developing a case differs little from developing an exam question or homework assignment. You begin by identifying the purpose of the case: what do you want the case to teach? What issues do you want it to raise at that point in the semester? You should then consider what your students will know at that point and what they need to know. If you have trouble thinking of any ethical issues relevant to your class, or any ethical knowledge your students should have, I recommend looking for inspiration in the following ways:

1 Look in the appropriate code of ethics. What is there relevant to what you are doing in class? If it is in the code, it probably comes up.
2 Draw on your own practical experience, especially when you were "learning the ropes": what bothered you about choices related to the matters relevant to this part of the course?

3   Look at ethics cases in textbooks in the field (if there are any).
4   Ask practitioners what comes up when they do work of this sort. Many good ideas can be picked up at what would otherwise be dull parties.
5   Think about writing a report on research, design work, or evaluation of the material you are teaching: what problems arise in reporting technical results? What should be put first? What put last? What buried in a footnote? What left out? Why?
6   Ask your students to identify ethical issues related to work of this sort.
7   If all else fails, ask how someone using what you are teaching could harm someone or embarrass members of your profession (or theirs).

Once you have identified an issue, you are ready to go looking for a case. Often, identifying an issue will also give you one or more cases. So, for example, practitioners will seldom give you an ethical issue without describing one or more times when they themselves faced that issue. If, however, identifying an issue has not given you a suitable case, you should begin looking for one in a file you should have been keeping. This file would contain newspaper stories raising ethical issues relevant to your course, parts of novels or short stories raising such issues, cases out of text books, cases your colleagues have given you, cases students have given you (and given you permission to use), cases you developed for other purposes, and so on. If all else fails, start asking colleagues, students, and practitioners if they know of a case raising the issue. If this fails to identify a suitable case, perhaps the issue you have identified is not live; and so, not worth discussing.

Once you have identified a "case," you must still put it in a form suitable for use in class. Case writing becomes easy pretty quickly, but it is no more a science than writing a paper is. The first step is to draft the case so that it seems to do what you want it to do. When your draft is done, you should be able to answer yes to the following four question:

a   Is the story line clear (clear enough)?
b   Does the case contain enough information (but not too much)?
c   Does it raise the right issues (and not too many others)?
d   Will students care?

If you cannot answer yes to all four, you should keep revising until you can. Once you do answer yes, you should put the draft aside for a few days. That should be enough time to see room for improvement. Make the improvements and then let a student or colleague read the case. A second reader generally uncovers a number of points in need of clarification by addition, subtraction, or wordsmithing. Rewrite accordingly and then use in class. Classroom use usually reveals a whole new set of imperfections. Rewrite accordingly.

Like a paper, a case is never really finished. But, at some point, we decide that the improvements that may be possible are no longer worth the effort necessary. That is the point at which to stop rewriting and to declare the case finished (for now).

Some commonalities in the use of cases in practical ethics

Throughout this chapter, I have emphasized the variety among practical ethics cases and among methods using such cases. That emphasis may suggest that the various case methods have nothing in common. While I am willing to admit there may be nothing all the case methods have in common (except "case" in some sense or other), I do think there are at least three important similarities among most of them. First, the various case methods of teaching practical ethics generally encourage the expression of ethical opinions (in class or at least outside). What a student "thinks" about the case is not out of place. Second, the various case methods generally encourage students to identify ethical issues, to make decisions taking into account practical complexities, and to justify those decisions in ways others are likely to find convincing. Third, the various case methods generally try to develop in students a sense of the practical context of ethics. In practice, a good ethical decision takes into account not only "how things should be" but whether "we can get there from here." Cases provide a way to help students see connections between the clean abstractions of the classroom and the disorderly bustle of life outside.

9

A MORAL PROBLEM IN THE TEACHING OF PRACTICAL ETHICS

> Virtue shuns ease as a companion. It demands a rough and
> thorny path.
>
> Montaigne, *Essays* II.xi

Teaching practical (or applied) ethics invites reflection both on teaching methods and the ethics of teaching. The preceding two chapters grew out of reflection of the first sort. This chapter grew out of reflection of the second sort. While its focus is quite concrete, answering a criticism of something I do in a particular philosophy course, the answer requires sketching a general theory of the ethics of teaching. That theory, though (I hope) familiar once stated, seems to have remained largely unstated until now. I believe its statement will prove useful to those university teachers interested in understanding the ethical fundamentals of the practice to which they are devoted.

I proceed in the following way. First, I describe what I do in class in enough detail to suggest why someone might be justified in registering a moral objection. Next, I try to make the objection plausible. Doing that is complicated. There are many side issues. Sorting through these, I reach a version of the objection resting on two assumptions: (a) that teachers are responsible for what their students do with what they teach; and (b) that teachers have some responsibility for distributive justice between their students and others. Clarifying these assumptions reveals much of the moral substructure of teaching. Clarified, these assumptions also help explain why a questionable teaching practice is in fact morally permissible. The objection misunderstands the context of teaching, especially the division of labor making teaching a distinct activity.

The problem

Whistleblowing is properly an important topic in business ethics. When teaching that course, I used to emphasize questions of definition and justification, but now I emphasize ways to make whistleblowing unnecessary. I shifted emphasis in part because my students do not much care about the difficulty of defining whistleblowing and, given any plausible definition, whistleblowing seems morally permissible (if not morally required). Whistleblowing is not philosophically that interesting.

In part, however, I now emphasize avoiding whistleblowing for two reasons having to do with the effect my teaching may have on my students. Whistleblowers so often end up martyred that, on the one hand, I worry that, if I leave students with the impression that their only choice is between being unethical and becoming whistleblowers, many will become unethical – on Solomon's principle, "Better a live dog than a dead lion." On the other hand, I worry that, leaving the alternatives to whistleblowing unexplored, I would fail as a teacher. I would contribute to my students unnecessarily becoming whistleblowers.

So, I have revised my course to include information on how to make whistleblowing unnecessary. In particular, I tell my students how to identify organizations likely to make whistleblowers of them. I do not name names – I do not know enough to do that – but I do suggest questions that should allow students to assess, for example, how open an organization is to hearing bad news. I present the questions as part of a theory of complex organizations.[1] While an executive might use the theory to reform her organization, the primary use to which my students are likely to put it is to avoid such organizations. And – let me be honest – that is just fine with me. I hope my students will avoid organizations likely to make martyrs of them.

Until recently, I thought my revised course morally unproblematic. I was helping students avoid pressure to do wrong when the cost of resisting would be high. I was smoothing their path to virtue. Perhaps anyone who thinks that what he does is morally unproblematic should think again. Certainly, I should have. Teaching students how to avoid having to blow the whistle at least seems to involve helping them shift moral burdens to others. Even if that is all right (as I think it is), it is morally problematic. It needs a justification.[2]

What kind of justification will depend on what we take to be objectionable in shifting moral burdens in this way. What objection could there be? One likely source of help with that question is utilitarianism; another is Kant. Other moral theories (such as virtue theory or pluralism) seem barren of such suggestions. So, let us begin with the utilitarian objection.

A utilitarian objection

My students will have had a course in business ethics. Most other applicants for a job probably will not. My students will therefore be more likely to be morally sensitive than other applicants. All else equal, the more morally sensitive employees are more likely to identify moral problems that the rest would not and more likely to resolve well the problems they identify.[3] Probably no organization is all bad; even the worst will sometimes, perhaps often, respond to moral objections by changing policy. Whistleblowing may be relatively rare in part because one common response to internal dissent in most organizations is to try to find an alternative that satisfies dissenters. If morally sensitive employees can make a difference even in organizations that are morally relatively insensitive, my students can do something to improve the moral performance of such organizations and thereby make society better than it would otherwise be.

The reverse, however, is not true. The morally better an organization, the more likely it is to provide its own ethics training, to encourage its employees to discuss moral problems as they arise, and otherwise to raise the moral sensitivity of employees. The better an organization, the less need it has of the moral sensitivity that my students would bring to their work. The better the organization, the more likely it is to generate that sensitivity itself. So, insofar as what I teach leads my students to take jobs in morally better organizations, the effect of my teaching is to assure that the organizations most in need of morally sensitive employees will not get them. I am contributing to the moral insensitivity of those organizations. The overall effect of that cannot be good.

Like most utilitarian arguments, this one rests on a good number of shaky empirical assumptions (for example, that morally sensitive people put in a morally insensitive environment will maintain their sensitivity long enough to make a difference).[4] Still, even putting doubts about those assumptions aside, the argument seems morally unattractive. It recognizes no special responsibility to *my* students. They are treated as only so many opportunities that I have to benefit society. They have (according to this argument) no claim on me beyond what every other member of society has. They have disappeared from sight, swallowed by a vast social calculation.

This, of course, is an instance of a general weakness of utilitarianism, a "universalism" recognizing no special relation, not even that between parent and child or promisor and promisee. There is, then, probably no point in pursuing this objection further. The universalism it relies on itself provides a refutation. A more plausible utilitarianism would presumably provide for special responsibilities between parent and child, promisor and promisee, and so on. Such a theory might also provide for the special responsibility of teacher to student. But, since no such theory is now available, we cannot give a plausible formulation of the objection in utilitarian terms. We must look elsewhere. Utilitarians may learn from what we find.

Some Kantian objections

While Kantian ethics is also universalistic, its universalism differs from the utilitarian in at least one important way: it is not aggregative. Kantianism requires me to treat each of my students as a person, that is to say, not as a mere means to overall well-being but as a being with ends to some degree incommensurable with those of others, an "end in itself." Kantianism (whatever the details) thus seems to provide an argument *for* teaching my students how to avoid whistleblowing. Do I not treat my students as ends in themselves when I provide them with information to help them achieve the life they want? If instead I withheld that information in order to keep them from making choices I do not want them to make, would I not fail to respect their status as persons? Would I not be trying to manipulate their choices much as I would if I deliberately lied to them to get them to act as I wanted? Would I not be making them my means, whatever their ends might be?

This Kantian argument relies on the second version of the categorical imperative ("Treat each person as an end, never as a means only"). The same conclusion can be drawn from a quite different argument relying on the first version ("Act only on those maxims you could will to be universal laws"): If every teacher of business ethics did as I do, that is, instructed students how to avoid organizations likely to martyr them (and every student were to act in consequence as I hope mine will), organizations likely to generate whistleblowers could not recruit enough competent employees.

They would either have to improve the way they do business or cease to exist. Can I will that consequence? Certainly. Indeed, I would welcome it. On the other hand, I could not universalize a maxim allowing me to withhold information from students for the purpose of raising social utility at their expense. I would not want teachers to treat me (or those I care about) that way.

These typical Kantian arguments are, however, not quite on point. They ignore too much of what we know, the smoke and sludge of an imperfect world. My problem arises precisely because few others are teaching what I teach (or, at least, because I believe that). My students can shift the moral burden of working in bad organizations to others in part at least because the others do not know what my students know. I would not have a problem if my students could not shift the moral burden in this way. I therefore need to consider what my duties are in world where "bad organizations" (or, at least, the relatively bad) will probably always be able to find enough employees among the morally insensitive (but otherwise competent). The maxim I must be willing to universalize is therefore (something like) this: *Serve your own students even if, by doing so, you both help them to shift moral burdens to strangers and help to make society as a whole somewhat worse.*

Here we have a Kantian version of the utilitarian objection discussed earlier. The maxim forces a choice between the good of my students and that of others (both the good of particular strangers and of society as a whole). If I cannot will that maxim, then (assuming it is the maxim of my act) I cannot go on teaching as I have. Can I will that maxim? I shall need the rest of this chapter to answer.

This Kantian objection plainly has a power the corresponding utilitarian objection lacked. Why? In part, what explains the objection's power is a certain conception of the relationship between teachers and students. Teaching is conceived as somehow different from, for example, selling gasoline to motorists. Teaching is not the mere transmission of information, skills, understanding, or the like from one intelligence to another. The teacher bears some responsibility for what students do with what is taught to them (in a way a gas station attendant need bear no responsibility for what a customer does with the gasoline pumped by the former into a gas tank).[5] Without such a conception of a teacher's responsibility, it makes no sense to include in my maxim anything about what I "help" my students do. I should instead think of my teaching as merely transmitting information, knowing that it might be used for any number of purposes, one of which would be shifting moral burdens to others. I should take no interest in what my students do with what I teach. What they do, we might say, is just not my business.[6]

A certain conception of a teacher's responsibility is, then, clearly one source of the objection's power. There is another: the uncertain place of teaching in achieving distributive justice. We could think of teaching as a relation between just two people, teacher and student. Questions of distributive justice would then be out of place. The objection instead treats teaching as a mechanism for distributing benefits and burdens in society. My decision to teach how to avoid whistleblowing is understood as helping my students bear less of the burden of whistleblowing than they would otherwise while strangers end up bearing more as a result. I am expected to take that fact into account in determining what to teach.

There is, then, what we might call a "political" objection to what I am teaching. My decision to teach my students how to avoid whistleblowing, rather than, for example, what defines whistleblowing, changes the future from what it would have been had I gone on as I had. It shifts moral burdens. Surely, it might be said, I could not possibly be the right person to decide who will be forced to choose between whistleblowing and martyrdom. Since society as a whole (including students I do not have) will bear the burden resulting from what I do in class, should not the decision to teach (or not to teach) something like that belong to some public authority; a government, perhaps, or a least a professional accrediting body?

We can quickly dispose of this political objection. Society has in fact left the decision to me, not simply by accident but as a matter of policy. No public authority – not even an accrediting body – has tried to limit what I teach in business ethics (so long as I remain, as I certainly have, within the outer bounds of the subject). More important, no accrediting body is likely to try to impose limits strict enough to decide whether I teach how to avoid whistleblowing. Considerations of academic freedom stand in the way. So, I cannot determine whether I should be teaching what I am teaching by considering what a public authority, actual or possible, would legislate on this subject. Even the best legislation probably ought to leave me free to make the decision myself. I am, apparently, the proper authority to make the decision; although, of course, I am not morally free to make any decision whatever.

The political objection would have allowed me to escape responsibility for distributive justice by passing it to someone else, to a legislature or accrediting body. There is another escape we need to consider, one calling into question the very existence of a benefit to distribute. If I were doing my students no good by what I taught, or actually harming them, our problem would disappear or at least be quite different. For example, since my students are free to take my class or not as they choose, any burden imposed in taking the class may be voluntary enough to foreclose questions of distributive injustice. My students would bring the burden on themselves. Neither they nor anyone else would have any cause to complain. Since this resolution does not so much escape the problem as ignore it, we should be able to reject it by clarifying how I benefit my students.

I am (we may suppose) helping my students to carry out their life plans. That sounds good. But the life plans we are supposing them to carry out may seem morally impoverished. My students will avoid suffering, but at the cost of giving up a chance to show moral courage. I seem to be teaching "cloistered virtue," an appearance of strength existing only because of an absence of opportunity. Isn't moral courage better than that? How then can I benefit my students by teaching cloistered virtue rather than moral courage?

The answer is obvious: I cannot. But have I answered the right question? Do I in fact face a choice between teaching cloistered virtue and teaching moral courage? That question may suggest that I doubt my ability to teach moral courage. I have no such doubts. Or, at least, I have none so long as "teaching moral courage" is given an appropriately modest sense. While I have no reliable procedure for turning a moral coward into a moral hero, I can, I think, contribute to the ability of students to show moral courage, for example, by demonstrating the possibility of such courage through examination of cases in which people in business behaved as they should when under great pressure to do otherwise.[7]

Why then think that I in fact do not face a choice between teaching cloistered virtue and teaching moral courage? I am (we are supposing) teaching cloistered virtue by providing my students information that makes it less likely that they will show moral courage, because they will decline to take certain jobs they would otherwise take. My alternative is to withhold that information so that they will be more likely to take a job they would otherwise have refused. Withholding the information does not, strictly speaking, teach moral courage. It simply makes it more likely that my students will *need* moral courage. They will then develop it if they can. They will not have learned moral courage from me. Teaching moral courage in this way is teaching only in the sense a parent may be said to teach a child swimming by throwing the child into the water and letting the child sink or swim.

So, we cannot condemn what I teach simply because I teach cloistered virtue rather than moral courage. Indeed, the foregoing argument suggests a defense of what I do. By providing my students information about how to avoid the need to blow the whistle, I give the chance to show moral courage in their choice of job. They need not avoid the organizations I hope they will avoid. What I teach frees them to choose knowingly between entering the morally risky environment of a bad organization and the morally safer environment of a good organization. Those who choose the morally risky environment knowingly (and for the right reasons) thereby show moral courage (as those who choose blindly do not). Insofar as the practice of moral courage is part of learning moral courage, they would be farther along in learning moral courage than students who have blindly stumbled into a job where they will need such courage. In the sense in which a parent teaches swimming simply by throwing the child into the water, I am teaching moral courage by teaching the students how to avoid the need to blow the whistle. I am giving them an opportunity to choose courageously, an opportunity that they would not otherwise have had; and I am giving it to them earlier than if I withheld the information in question.

However, as I said, I *hope* my students will avoid the morally risky environment, even if the effect of my teaching is only to let them know what they are getting into. I cannot so easily escape the charge that I am at least *trying* to harm my students. Nor need I. The claim that teaching cloistered virtue rather than moral courage harms students rests on the assumption that having moral courage is morally better than having cloistered virtue. That assumption seems, in turn, to rest on another, that virtue is an individual strength, like good teeth or endurance. If I act honestly thanks only to social arrangements, I am not really honest. I only appear to be because I have not yet been put to the test.

This is a common assumption, but not a necessary one. We are, after all, social beings, not isolated individuals. Without the social world we take for granted, most of us would quickly starve, lonely and terrified. Those who survived might well envy the baboons in their troop. Since we are social beings, why not think of the virtues, especially the moral virtues, primarily as expressions of social arrangements? Why not, for example, say I am honest if, thanks to social arrangements that protect me from most temptations, I in fact act honestly? Why demand instead that I satisfy some individualistic ideal in which one is not "truly" honest unless that honesty would endure even the ring of Gyges? The virtue that shuns ease and demands thorny paths seems a romantic invention more appropriate to the knights of Malory's *Morte Arthure* than to the business people of today. Why make a fetish of that ideal, seeking test after test until we die or are defeated? What is wrong with cloistered virtue so long as we have in fact chosen a cloistered life? There is no virtue in looking for trouble.

Of course, all else equal, it would be better to be able to resist temptation within any social carapace rather than only within some. I do not deny that. What I deny is much more limited, that is, that such an ability is of a different order from the ability to pick a carapace where the need to exercise that other ability becomes unnecessary. Cloistered virtue is not less a virtue than moral courage nor inherently inferior to it. It is, at worst, a virtue more easily developed because its range is correspondingly narrow. How we rate the two virtues will depend on our assessment of the environment in which the possessor is likely to have to operate.

While this defense of cloistered virtue is hardly decisive, it is, I think, strong enough to leave the problem intact. We have reason enough to believe that teaching students how to avoid having to blow the whistle benefits them.[8]

The discussion so far allows us to see that the problem has two parts. The first is the teacher's responsibility for what a student does with what is taught. Without that responsibility, a Kantian objection to what I teach seems unlikely. However, given that I am responsible for what my students do with what I teach them, our problem has a second part, showing that I am entitled to benefit them even at the cost both to strangers (burdened with choices they would rather avoid) and to society (made worse overall by what my students do). We must, then, turn to the question of responsibility. What is my responsibility for what my students do with what I teach?

A teacher's responsibility for what students do

My students are rational persons, independent agents. They are morally responsible for their own actions. They cannot shift responsibility to me by claiming that what they do results from what they learned from me. Or, at least, they cannot shift responsibility in that way so long as I make clear (as I try to do) that they are to weigh my reasons, not bow to my authority.

However, if my students cannot shift moral responsibility to me, what responsibility can I have for what they do? The answer seems to be: quite a bit. I could not, for example, both teach students how to burgle and deny responsibility if they then commit burglaries. Transmitting that technical skill is not a morally neutral act. The reason is not that the skill can only be put to a bad use or even that its primary use is bad. Most teachers would, I think, still feel shame (or at least embarrassment) if a student got into trouble using a socially approved skill they had taught, such as computer programming. Something similar is true of praiseworthy acts. We do not think it odd for a teacher to take pride in the accomplishments of a student, moral as well as technical, so long as the virtue the student thereby revealed has some connection with what the teacher in fact taught. But how can such an attitude be justified?

The attitude makes no sense if we think of teaching as morally neutral, the mere transmitting of information, skill, understanding, or the like. If that were all teaching is, we could take pride in our students' technical achievements but not in their moral achievements. We would also have no reason to feel shame when students misused the information, skill, understanding, or the like that we successfully imparted to them. Indeed, insofar as they used what we taught effectively, we should feel pride, not shame, at the evidence of our (technical) success.

So, teaching must have a moral structure, a context of presuppositions justifying such pride and shame. Among these presuppositions, the most important is probably that the teacher recognizes the student as a person, a being who can reason and whose acts can be guided by reasons, including reasons of the sort the teacher gives. The teacher–student relation requires the teacher to know something the student does not. In this respect, the relationship is necessarily unequal. That technical inequality is, however, consistent with a deeper equality among rational agents. Here, then, is one difference between teaching and mere training or indoctrination. Teaching can of course address far more than a student's reason (it is a poor teacher who ignores a student's interests, prejudices, or emotions). But, strictly speaking, we do not teach unless we address as well the student's reason. A student is not a mere pupil or trainee. A teacher cannot simply transmit knowledge, skill, judgment, or understanding by some mechanical means ("drum it into the student's head," as we might say); the teacher must actually win the student's faith in it by showing the student that it works or by giving other suitable reasons.

A second of teaching's presuppositions is that learning what the teacher has to teach will (probably) be good for the student. The relation between teacher and student is, as such, morally good (hence the possibility of a profession of teaching). The moment we assume instead that what is being taught is bad for the student, we tend to give up teacher–student language for some other. We might, for example, talk instead of the more knowledgeable person *corrupting* the innocent. "Knowledge," "information," "skill," and even "understanding" are morally neutral in a way "teaching" is not. Even if we assume merely that what is being taught is of no value to the student, we tend to replace student–teacher language with, for example, talk of pedantry. A teacher is, as such, a benefactor.

A third of teaching's presuppositions is that the teacher *intends* the benefit. "Teacher" who did not care whether their students benefited from what they taught would seem mere time-servers, functionaries, or (at best) natural resources. So, for example, we seem to speak of "corporate trainers" rather than "corporate teachers" in part at least because those instructors owe their primary loyalty to the corporation rather than to those they instruct. They are not expected to benefit those they instruct, except insofar as they benefit the corporation. They are, however, also not expected to harm their trainees. "Teachers" who actually intended those they taught to be harmed by what they taught could not even be described as trainers. Such a person would be a trickster, a Mephistopheles. They would not so much teach as mislead.

A fourth of teaching's presuppositions is a corollary of the third: the student must expect to benefit from what is being taught. A "student" who did not expect to benefit would hardly be a student (strictly speaking), that is, one eager to learn. The student would instead be a "drudge," held to her studies by some external force, or a fool wasting time. A student need not love studies for their own sake (as a scholar should), but she must see the point of these studies, that they will make her better in some way (even if only better able to do what she wants). The student cannot be held to her studies by a gun pointed at the head, by the threat that she will be paid less if she gets a poor grade on some test, or by any other consideration external to what is taught.

The last of teaching's presuppositions we need identify here follows from the preceding four: the teacher must intend that what the student learns will serve the student's purposes (even while recognizing that a student's purposes – like her teacher's – are often inchoate, partially inconsistent, and otherwise in need of rational revision). The teacher cannot try to benefit the student in ways contrary to the student's own purposes without treating the student as a mere pupil; nor teach what he thinks will not be useful to a student without becoming a mere pedant; nor declare indifference to how a student uses what is taught without ceasing to be a benefactor. The teacher, as such, is always trying to help the student do something the student could not otherwise do. A teacher is always co-conspirator in the student's plans, however little of the details the teacher knows.

Character therefore limits what we *can* teach (as well as what we *will* teach). We cannot (literally) teach what we think it wrong to use. For example, a teacher of burglary would have to think knowing how to burgle is itself good for the student. A criminal might well think that. Knowing how to burgle gives options the student would not otherwise have. The student will now be able to supplement earnings in a way she could not otherwise. For the criminal teacher, then, seeing the skills that were taught put to such a use should be a source of pride. Such use shows the teachers has done the job well.

If, however, the teacher is a morally decent person, he cannot think in this way. A morally decent person cannot view helping someone become a criminal (or helping him commit new crimes) as benefiting him. Helping someone become a criminal is – except under the most unusual circumstances – corrupting him. A morally decent person could, of course, teach skills useful to a burglar – but only as part of teaching something other than burglary, for example, a course for homeowners in how to protect against burglars.

A morally decent person also cannot teach burglary as a "mere means." No one can. Means are always means to something. Part of being a teacher is taking an interest in the ends one's student is pursuing, for the means should be appropriate to those ends. Students who cannot benefit from what is being taught, even if only by way of simple edification or harmless diversion, cannot strictly speaking be taught, although they might still be trained or indoctrinated. So, for morally decent people, teaching burglary as such (or not caring what they teach) can only be teaching with scare quotes, teaching's counterfeit.

We can now understand why a teacher properly feels shame when a student misuses what was taught. Shame is proper when we fall short of what we should be, when we are weak when we should be strong, foolish when we should be wise. While the teacher is not responsible for what the student did, he *can* recognize their own failure in what the latter did. He can see that he did not do his job as well as he should have. He may, for example, have harmed the student by unintentionally helping her to get into trouble. Doing that may, under the circumstances, have been excusable; perhaps only a brilliant teacher would have done better. The failure is none the less a cause for shame. We do not need excuses where we have been as good as we should be.

The shame the teacher feels may be moral, but it need not be. Shame is still appropriate where the failing is one of technical skill or knowledge; where, for example, we have simply not shown as much insight as a good teacher would. We are not necessarily criminals because our students turn to crime. We must none the less view ourselves as failures insofar as they use what we taught them to commit crimes. A better teacher would have withheld the knowledge, skill, judgment, or understanding to prevent its misuse, or found a way to help the student see how it should be used, or refused to be that student's teacher.

If (as I have argued) my responsibilities as a teacher include providing my student with what we can both recognize as benefits, it may seem that we have a solution to our problem: I cannot morally offer myself as a teacher while withholding knowledge, skill, judgment, or understanding (relevant to the course of study) for any reason but the student's good. To "teach" what I do not think will help a student, especially if I teach it in place of what will help, is, strictly speaking, not teaching at all but its perversion. It is a perversion of teaching even if I do it to be just to others or to benefit society overall. By offering myself as a teacher, I invite my students to believe I intend to benefit them. If, lacking that intention, I still offer to teach them, I deliberately mislead them. I merely pretend to be their teacher.

Though this argument may seem decisive, it is not. We all recognize certain limits on what a teacher must reveal in class, however relevant to the course and useful to the student. For example, we expect the teacher to respect the privacy of others. (Indeed we expect the teacher to respect his own privacy also.) Insofar as we believe our teachers to be morally decent persons, we, as morally decent persons ourselves, understand that there are limits on what they can properly do in teaching (beyond the technical limits teaching as such sets.) We expect our teachers to avoid injustice, immorality, and the like, even if we might benefit but they do not. Such limits are part of the context of teaching. That statement should surprise no one. Indeed, we discussed two cases involving such limits in Chapter 2.

This observation suggests another argument: If considerations of distributive justice can require a teacher to withhold information about how to avoid the need to blow the whistle, a morally decent person would normally withhold that information even if the students would benefit from learning it. Such withholding would not be a perversion of teaching because everyone understands (or at least should understand) that such withholding is the price of having a morally decent person as teacher.

Of course, this argument assumes that a teacher should be a morally decent person (as well as that distributive justice requires withholding that information and that a morally decent person respects distributive justice). A cynic might wonder why we should make that assumption. Why should students not want amoral or immoral teachers? What students want from their teachers is benefit. Why then should they want a teacher of good character? Why not study under Fagin rather than Mr Chips, since Fagin will not let justice to strangers or the good of society interfere with what he does?

The answer should be obvious: students who want a teacher, rather than a mere dispenser of information or skill, want someone who will take an interest in their good, a relation substantially warmer than that necessary for the guarded exchanges of the marketplace of ideas (or the republic of thieves). An amoral or immoral person has no reason to take an interest in another's good except insofar as it serves her own (if only by satisfying some contingent passion). A morally decent teacher always has a reason to take an interest in her student's good. She can appreciate the moral context of teaching, accept its standards, and act accordingly. Students have good reason to want Mr Chips rather than Fagin. Mr Chips is likely to have their good at heart; Fagin is not.

A teacher is, then, responsible for what students do with what he teaches. If what he does affects distributive justice, the teacher may have to answer along with them. We may now turn to the second part of our problem, determining what responsibility a teacher has for distributive justice.

What responsibility for distributive justice?

Teachers normally have some responsibility for distributive justice. They are, first, responsible for distributive justice between their students. They should not, for example, give any one student too much time if others will suffer as a result. Such responsibilities are, however, administrative in this sense: they are contingent upon a certain way of organizing teaching, upon teachers being assigned several students at once. Teachers *as such* need not be responsible for distributing teaching time between their students. We can be teachers even if we have so few students that no problems of distributive justice among them arises. One can, for example, be a teacher even if one is a private tutor with one student at a time; and perhaps even if one has only one student in a lifetime.

Teachers also normally have some responsibility for distributive justice between students and strangers. For example, a teacher should not give students higher grades just to give them a competitive advantage over those who are not students. Inflating grades for that reason is unjust (as well as deceptive).

But such responsibilities for distributive justice are as administrative as those for justice between students. They exist because of the teacher's contingent role as a participant in a system of grading for certification. They are not a function of the role of teachers as such. While there can be teachers who do not grade, there can be none who transmit no knowledge, skill, judgment, or understanding.

Our question concerns the responsibility for distributive justice a teacher has as teacher, not in some contingent role associated with teaching. What is a teacher's responsibility as transmitter of information, skill, understanding, or the like? That question would be the same if the teacher had only one student in a lifetime. Would even such a teacher be entitled to give a student beneficial information, skill, or the like if she thereby put others, strangers to her, at a disadvantage or (without doing anything else morally wrong) thereby made society a worse place for everyone? Or is the teacher instead obliged to withhold what she knows, however much her student would benefit?

That is the question now. It assumes a certain context. The teaching in question must take place in a relatively just society, that is, a society (like this one) in which distributive justice is approximated but only very roughly. Some serious injustices occur and go uncorrected, not by mere accident but because of imperfections in important institutions.

Why assume this context? To assume instead a perfect society would be to rule out in advance any serious problem of distributive justice. Every teacher would teach what should be taught; no teacher need fear that the students of other teachers would be at a disadvantage because they were not being taught what his own were. Our problem could not arise.

Our problem could also not arise in a society dominated by fundamentally unjust institutions. A teacher can only hope to contribute to distributive justice if the society is more or less organized to achieve it. Social justice is a social undertaking to which individuals can contribute effectively only if most others are contributing as well. In a society rotten to the core – for example, a concentration camp – a morally decent person, an inmate or even an ordinary guard, could not rationally take considerations of distributive justice into account. Distributive justice would be beyond their reach. They would have to content themselves with preventing immediate harm to others and providing immediate benefits. They should, for example, give an extra sausage to a hungry inmate without checking to see whether anyone else in the camp is more in need, since some superior might take the sausage during the time needed to check.

A concentration camp is a society in which no one is responsible for distributive justice. That is *not* our situation. In a society like ours, there is a division of moral labor, with some roles concerned primarily with doing justice and others concerned primarily with other things. The general effect of this division is distributive justice, if only roughly and for the most part. In such a society, some injustice could be prevented if the division of labor were somewhat different. Some could also be prevented if people now and then stepped out of a role; if for example, a police officer now and then decided whether to arrest taking into account more than merely what the laws allows. In such a society, a teacher might now and then prevent an injustice (or otherwise improve society) by withholding information from a student even if the student would benefit by having it.

We have already seen that the teacher's role is, as such, to benefit her students, not to do distributive justice generally. So, our problem has narrowed to the question when, if ever, a teacher may be justified in stepping out of her role to prevent distributive injustice (or otherwise contribute to distributive justice)? We might approach this question in two ways: through actual consent of some sort, whether individual or social; or (absent that) through hypothetical consent of some sort. Let us begin with actual consent.

A teacher would certainly be entitled to step out of her role if the student expressly consented after being given enough information to make an independent decision. The express consent could not, however, be general. The teacher who asked for general consent would ask to be allowed to sacrifice the student's interest whenever she could thereby prevent distributive injustice. She would be asking permission to sacrifice the student's interest at any moment – and, indeed, at every moment – doing so would serve distributive justice. She would be asking to give up responsibility for the student's welfare. She would, in effect, be asking to be something other than the student's teacher. A teacher might have good reason to ask that, and a student might have good reason to grant it. However, the result is a new role, not a justification for occasionally stepping out of the role of teacher.

Any actual consent to withhold information must therefore be particular. It must be granted case by case (or, at least, narrow category by narrow category). In each case, the students must be given enough information to make an independent assessment. They must see the justice of what the teacher wants to do and must give permission for that reason. Getting consent in this way would mean that the students must share responsibility for distributive justice with the teacher. How can a teacher share responsibility while withholding the information in question? She cannot (in this world) give the students all the information, get their consent to withhold it, and then wipe it from their mind. Can the teacher perhaps describe it in a general way, giving the students enough information to make an independent decision but not enough so that they would know what the teacher does not want them to know? Perhaps, but it is hard to see how. The students must at the very least understand the general idea if they are to make an independent decision. The general idea, if understood, will often be enough to work out the details. If students cannot work out any of its details, the conclusion we ordinarily draw is that they do not understand the general idea. Getting consent case by case thus seems (more or less) impractical.

So, the student's *actual* consent (whether general or particular) cannot provide a way to understand how a teacher could be entitled to step out of her role in order to do distributive justice. That brings us to the other possibility, *hypothetical* consent. Might not a teacher be entitled to step out of her role whenever her student (suitably idealized) would consent to it? Or when a society as a whole would? If this is a Rawlsian question, it is one to which there is no Rawlsian answer. Rawl's hypothetical consent is (as noted in Chapter 4) designed to characterize justice in the basic structure of society, not in particular cases. The role of the teacher is probably not part of the basic structure of society. But, if it were, defining the role to allow for such departures whenever a teacher could do distributive justice would run in to the definitional stop encountered before. The role would no longer be that of teacher.

The role would also be subject to a more telling criticism. Like everyone else, teachers are only human, subject to error. They are most likely to err where they know the least. What teachers know best is how to teach. They have their students before them. The rest of the world is mostly distant country divined from poor maps. Determining what serves distributive justice and what does not is not easy, even for those working on a large scale; for example, in a legislature. Teachers cannot work on the scale a legislature can. They must work student by student, class by class. How then are they to know what, if any, effect their teaching actually has? They may, of course, know quite well its immediate effect on a particular student. They are much less likely to know much about its long-term effect on that student, and they will find it impossible to determine its effect on strangers or society as a whole. Too many variables intervene too quickly. Any teacher who supposes that his role includes doing distributive justice, not simply by such administrative acts as grading fairly, but by withholding information from students, would seem by that very belief unfit for the role. The teacher has overestimated his abilities by an ominous margin. Why free such a person from a duty to take special care for his student's welfare?

So, society as a whole has good reason not to redefine the teacher's role. Might it not, however, still have reason to allow some limited departures from the teacher's role?[9] For example, what about saying that a teacher is entitled to withhold information from a student when *certain* that the student would consent if she understood what was going to be withheld and why. The teacher would, of course, have to assume that the student is a morally decent person, one for whom distributive justice is a legitimate concern. But even assuming that, and whatever other plausible assumption the teacher might make to decide whether it is permitted to depart from the role, the departure criterion would be suspect. There would still be the problem of fallibility.

Teachers as such must contribute to distributive justice by transmitting (or *not* transmitting) information, skill, or the like to those who would benefit from it. The individual teacher's contribution to distributive justice is primarily in doing a good job as a teacher. The teacher's actual contribution to overall justice depends in part on others doing as good a job as he does. In any society much like this one, some will probably do a better job; others will do worse. That is an inevitable feature of an imperfect world. What is an individual teacher to do about that? The teacher can, of course, teach more students, publish articles describing his findings, urge accrediting bodies to require the findings to be taught, and so on. What seems plain is that the teacher should not try to make up for the failure of others by doing a worse job of teaching his own students. The students would almost certainly not benefit from that and, given imperfect knowledge both of what other teachers are doing and of what effect it all will have, neither the students nor society as a whole could want the teacher to try to gauge the effect his poor teaching would have on strangers or society as a whole. That, on the information available, the teacher is certain his students will consent if they knew what the teacher does, does not change the balance of reasons. Certainty often goes with error.

Conclusion

We can now understand what is wrong with the maxim formulated early on; and what made the objection resting on it seem so powerful. The choice is not (as the objection requires) between (a) serving my students even when, by doing so, I help to shift moral burdens to strangers and make society a somewhat worse place overall and (b) protecting society at my students' expense. In this world, I never face that choice. Since I, like other teachers, am fallible, the choice I in fact face is whether to teach a student what I know even when I *believe* doing so will have bad effects. I am prepared to say that I should teach what will benefit my students even at the *risk* of putting others at a disadvantage or making society as a whole worse off. Indeed, I am willing to allow all teachers to do that. I am, in short, willing to rely on the division of moral labor, imperfect though it is, rather than take on myself responsibility for setting things right. I have no reason to believe that, working alone and in the dark, I would do better than others have, working together in relatively good light. I am unwilling to pretend to more knowledge than I have.

This is not a decisive answer, of course. The objection might still be restated in a form I have not anticipated. The answer none the less creates a strong presumption in favor of what I do, a presumption reinforced by another consideration. I have explored many side arguments along the way, perhaps too many. Each threatened the objection. I had to work out the conception of teaching on which my answer relies in order to keep the objection plausible. The objection thus seems intimately bound to its refutation.

10

SEX AND THE
UNIVERSITY

My class in business ethics was discussing a case in which Cecily Sandwich, an engineer, told her manager that she would not obey his order to revise certain risk assessments as he indicated because the result would be misleading and therefore doing as ordered would be unethical. I asked, "What should the manager do?" A student in the back volunteered, "This broad is here to do what she's told. If she won't do that, I'd fire her, no questions asked." Though I couldn't tell whether any woman in the class took offense at the word "broad," I had no doubt that I should do something in response to the student's answer. But what?

Unlike the University of Wisconsin-Milwaukee (see Chapter 2), my university does not have a "speech code." But even if it did, the student's answer would, I think, be exempt from discipline: his answer was "an opinion...germane to the subject matter."[1] And even if it were not technically exempt, I would not report it for discipline. Reporting it would threaten the trust between teacher and students upon which case discussion depends. Students worried that a careless word in class will get them into trouble tend to maintain a nervous silence or, forced to speak, to answer without saying much. Reporting the student would put the university's secondary interest in enforcing its rules through settled procedures ahead of its primary interest in maintaining a good educational environment for all students.

There was, I think, a time when deciding how to respond to the student's answer would automatically have been treated as a question of pedagogy (the student having failed to draw on an assignment concerned with the role of professional ethics in business) or of politeness ("broad" not being a word for the classroom, certainly not for a classroom in which some of the students are women). Today, however, the question is more likely to be assigned to the highly charged category of "sexual ethics" or "gender politics."[2] What I shall argue here is that this reassignment is not helpful, that the questions gathered into that large category will be easier to resolve if redistributed to their former homes and dealt with there one at a time. Questions of sexual ethics have much less in common than a common category suggests.

Insofar as questions of sexual ethics do not have much in common, any survey of them must be a ramble. I shall try to keep from rambling too much both by only sampling the questions and by imposing a rough order. I shall begin by placing today's questions in historical context, then deal with them in three clumps: (1) questions of sexual equality, (2) questions of sexuality, and (3) questions of sexual identity. Throughout I shall be on the lookout for help formulating a response to my student's use of "broad."

Sexing the university

The preceding chapters may seem unjustifiably sparing in their treatment of sex in the university. Except for Chapter 2, there is no mention of the topic at all. Chapter 2 only mentions the topic now and then, focusing instead on some apparent conflicts between maintaining academic freedom and protecting students from racial insult; and even there, race is treated as a foil to bring out the relationship between academic freedom and academic ethics. This near silence on sex – by which I mean not only "sexual relations" (copulation with its prelude, variations, and finale)[3] but also sexual differences, sexuality, and sexual identity – is not a consequence of any lack of interest either in sex as such or in its place in the university. It is, rather, the natural, if not quite intended, consequence of my belief that sex is not, or at least should not be, important in the university, whatever its status outside.

This belief may seem quixotic. I am, after all, writing in a language that virtually requires me, whether inside the university or outside, to categorize by sex every person I wish to speak of. Each must be "he" or "she," biology (more or less) deciding which. I am also writing at a time that we might justifiably label sex-crazed. Our commerce seems organized on the principle that "sex sells"; or, at least, that it sells better than efficiency, safety, durability, or even beauty. Our literature, theater, and music all emphasize sex to a degree having few rivals. What other time would designate as "adult" any entertainment, however juvenile, containing a few minutes of copulation?

The belief that sex does not, or at least should not, matter much in the university may also seem out of keeping with what I said in Chapter 2. After all, Chapter 2 argued that while scholars as such may be without race or history, the humans who people any university are not. But, just as each scholar arrives at the university with an historically determined race, including complicated attitudes toward members of that race and others, so each arrives with a body of determinate sex, with views, habits, and expectations about physical contact between that body and others, and (generally) with a strong interest in such contact. Indeed, to compare sex to race as I just have is to understate the importance of sex. We recognize race as a social construction. We can imagine a day when race no longer matters. We may even be able to identify societies present or past in which race does not, or did not, matter. However, we know of no society in which sex does not, or did not, matter. Sex, if not itself a vocation, is much more than a mere socially constructed inconvenience for education.[4] A university that does not take account of sex merely closes its eyes to danger.

Universities have, I think, never done that. They have, however, responded to sex in different ways at different times. Until the nineteenth century, universities generally excluded women from their classrooms. This helped to make the classroom relatively "sex free." Those universities providing residences for students could also exclude women from much of the rest of a student's life, even forbidding a student to marry before graduation. Those universities not providing residences might seek to regulate student conduct "in town" or simply leave such regulation to the civil magistrate.[5]

Until the nineteenth century, the university's regulation of relations between the sexes was part of a larger ascetic discipline, especially in the United States. Students might also be forbidden to play ball, to drink alcoholic beverages, to form secret societies, or to read outside the curriculum. They might be required to follow a set schedule, rising every morning at a certain hour, going together to chapel for prayers, taking breakfast together, going to class together, and so on until "lights out."

That discipline slowly crumbled during the nineteenth century. In the United States, universities let in sports, converted the forbidden "secret societies" into social fraternities, scheduled parties, allowed students to drink, and even yielded to students control over what, when, and how they studied.

Letting women into the classroom may seem a natural part of this general loosening up, but it was something more. Much of the loosening up simply made the predominantly rural universities of the United States more like the urban universities of France or Germany. Indeed, some of the older universities of the United States either moved to a city during the nineteenth century or allowed a city to engross them. The admission of women was, in contrast, as new in Europe as in the United States.

Some universities (such as Oberlin College in 1837) simply began to admit women, treating them more or less as they treated male students. This "integrationist" approach rests on what was then the daring assumption that women could be educated much as men were, that no special provision need be made (apart from separate dormitories and certain courses, such as home economics, not likely to interest men). Other universities, not willing to dare so much, adopted one of two other approaches.

One of these was "separatist." Women would receive a university education, but in a university that could protect them from competition with men, from learning to act like men, and from other dangers of much contact with men. They would have a "women's university" (such as Vassar College). Such universities could not, of course, be altogether sexually segregated. The teachers (as well as the groundskeeper, janitor, chaplain, and so on) were, of necessity, generally men, especially at first. But the men would be few and safe: refined gentlemen, clergy, or aged servants, not raw youths of the same social class. The separatist approach is still common in Islamic countries.

The other non-integrationist approach was to create a "co-ordinate" women's college within a previously all-male university (as Radcliffe College was created within Harvard). Initially, the co-ordinate women's college might share only its faculty with the "men's college." Later it might share classes, administration, and even social events.

The "experiment" with women in higher education has, on the whole, been a success (though much more from our perspective than from that of those who first brought women into higher education).[6] "Integration" has become the standard form of college education in both Europe and the Americas. Few all-female (or all-male) universities remain; the "co-ordinate" colleges that remain are largely vestigial. Women have done well competing with men. In the United States, for example, about half of all college students today are women and, on average, they do about as well as the men. Only in some professional schools (such as engineering) and some graduate programs (such as doctoral programs in philosophy or physics) are women still a small minority.

However, this success has not come without cost. Women have not just entered the university; they have changed it. Some of the changes are obviously good – for example, the easier time men and women now have finding mates – but some of the changes are more equivocal. There can be no doubt that bringing women into the university has highlighted some old problems, complicated others, and even introduced a few new ones. We need only review the main questions of "sexual ethics" now under discussion in many universities to get a sense both of the advantages and the costs of admitting women into the university.

Sexual differences and equality

Perhaps the most basic question of sexual ethics under discussion today, though certainly not the most important, is the status of the remaining sexually segregated universities. Recently, the United States Supreme Court forced Virginia to allow women into state-supported military college. One interpretation of the Court's decision is that sexually segregated schools are, like racially segregated schools, inherently unequal in a society where those excluded are also those rare in positions of power.[7] That interpretation assumes, probably correctly, that a university is a place not only of education but to make the social contacts that give one a head start in life. Because women are not generally in positions of power, the contacts made in a women's college (largely with other women) tend to be less useful in life than similar contacts made with men. Women *may* individually choose to give up the advantage of being educated with men for many reasons, but (if otherwise qualified) they should not be *forced* to give it up. So (the argument runs), an exclusively women's university might be morally permissible, if the women there have chosen to give up the head start they would have acquired had they gone to a co-educational university, but an exclusively men's university would not be, since it denies women the head start they might otherwise get there.

This rationale for sexual integration raises serious questions about the moral permissibility of much sexual segregation remaining in universities. Consider, for example, the exclusively male dormitory or fraternity (where residence or membership is entirely voluntary). Dormitories and fraternities are, beside residences, places to make contacts that could give one a head start in life. While dormitories seldom stress this advantage when recruiting, fraternities frequently do. Insofar as there is truth in what they say, an exclusively male dormitory or fraternity puts women at a disadvantage later in life (when compared to otherwise similar men). So, excluding women from residence (or membership) in a male dormitory or fraternity requires a special defense.

There are at least three defenses that might be offered for the exclusively male dormitory or fraternity. One is that university students, like everyone else, have a right to form voluntary associations with anyone they choose. That right entails the right to exclude anyone they choose. This defense suffers from at least two weaknesses.[8]

One weakness may be stated as a dilemma. The right to associate must be either limited or unlimited. If unlimited, a justification relying on it would entail implausible consequences, for example, that racially segregated dormitories and fraternities are also morally permissible. If, however, the right of association is limited, the defense of all-male dormitories and fraternities is incomplete, until we have a satisfactory criterion of limitation distinguishing racial discrimination from sexual discrimination. As it stands, the defense is either implausible or incomplete.

The other weakness of this first defense is that, even without the dilemma, it would provide only a partial (or weak) justification. The defense claims *a* (moral) *right* to establish sexually segregated dormitories and fraternities; it does not claim that such segregation is (morally) right. The defense blocks interference, leaving students free to segregate if they choose; but it does not respond to the moral indictment of that choice.

The second defense of all-male fraternities and dormitories does not suffer from these weaknesses. It offers a full justification: sexually segregated residences are justified, all things considered, because they are in the interests of women, even when women are excluded against their will. Among the advantages women gain from sexually segregated residences are (it is said) better protection against rape (a "man on the floor" would automatically be suspect) and practice running their own affairs (the government of the residence – assuming some "student government" – would automatically be in the hands of women).

Though this second defense of all-male dormitories and fraternities does not suffer from the weaknesses of the first, it does suffer from a serious weakness. The defense is frankly paternalistic: it seeks to protect women from risks they may be willing to take and to force on them benefits they may think bought at too high a price. As with paternalism generally, so here: there is (a) a set of empirical claims about benefits and burdens, (b) an evaluative claim about what it would be rational to choose, and (c) a moral claim about the permissibility of making that choice for an unwilling rational agent. The paternalistic argument fails if the needed empirical claims cannot be proved (or at least made plausible enough), or if the evaluative claim is controversial, or if the person to be treated paternalistically does not fit any of the categories permitting such treatment.

Interestingly, the paternalist defense of sexual segregation we are now considering seems to fail in all three ways. Consider, first, just one of the empirical claims on which the defense sometimes relies. Are women living in sexually integrated dormitories or fraternities more likely to be raped than women living in sexually segregated dorms or sororities, less likely to be, or just as likely to be? I know of no empirical study answering that question. Is the claimed safety none the less plausible? Yes, but no more plausible than the opposite. Even if women were, for the reason given, less likely to be raped in their residence if men cannot reside there, the absence of men in the residence may still lead women to go elsewhere to meet men, places less safe than a sexually integrated dormitory or fraternity, making the overall risk of rape higher rather than lower.

Consider, next, the question of how to balance the risks and benefits. Does reason require the choice that paternalism would force on an unwilling woman? It seems not. True, reason requires that, all else being equal, a woman (or man) not risk being raped. But all else may not be equal if the cost of avoiding the risk is a cramped social life, putting off until later learning how to avoid rape in one's residence, or just reduced opportunity to learn how men act when they are at home rather than on a date. A woman might, it seems, rationally choose to risk rape to avoid such costs.

Last, consider whether the woman in question belongs to a category allowing others, those knowing what is best for her, to pre-empt her choosing otherwise. Why, in other words, not just give the information to the woman in question and let her decide for herself? To answer that question, the paternalist must claim (a) that the woman is not mature enough to make the decision, or (b) that she is not (and cannot reasonably be made) well-informed enough to make the decision, or (c) that she is in some other way unfit to make the decision on her own (for example, because the decision requires coordination that individuals cannot manage if each decides for herself). Offering a satisfactory argument showing that most college-age women satisfy even one of these claims will not be easy. Certainly, it has yet to be done.

A third defense of all-male dormitories and fraternities relies on considerations of fairness. If women have a right to live in all-female dormitories and sororities if they choose, then fairness requires that men have the corresponding right to live in all-male dormitories or fraternities if they choose. The power of this defense is obvious, its even-handed treatment of the sexes. It is, however, only a conditional power. Defenders of sexual integration may disable the argument simply by denying that women have a right to segregate "their" residences. But this easy response, though effective, overlooks a stronger one. The argument creating the initial presumption against all-male dormitories and fraternities distinguishes the role in society of all-male dormitories and fraternities from that of all-female dormitories and sororities. The all-male dormitories and fraternities give men a head start in life; the all-female dormitories or sororities do not, precisely because the social contacts women make in a women's dormitory or sorority are with other women and – in this society, as in all others – women (all else equal) are less able than men to help one in life. Since the argument for integrating all-male dormitories and fraternities is that doing so will help to equalize access to power, all-male dormitories and fraternities can only be morally permissible when men and women are more or less equal in power in the larger society – a time still far off – or when all-male dormitories and fraternities cease for some other reason to give males greater access to power.

Dormitories and fraternities are not the only university institutions that have been, and remain, largely sexually segregated; nor are they the only ones promising a head start in life. Among other such institutions, the most important are the athletic teams. I have noticed that some intramural sports – volleyball, softball, touch football, and even soccer – seem to have quietly become "co-ed" on many campuses, perhaps the natural consequence of sexually integrated dormitories. For intercollegiate sports, however, the effort has been to achieve *parity* between men's and women's teams. Some of the reasons offered in defense of this policy of "separate but equal" should be familiar from our discussion of dormitories and fraternities.

First is paternalism. Men play rough. Women on a "men's team" would risk injury that the men, larger and (supposedly) better designed for rough treatment, do not.

Second is fairness. If women were allowed to try out for the men's teams, then men should be allowed to try out for the women's teams. But, in some sports, such as basketball (where height is important) or football (where sheer mass is), allowing men to try out for the "women's team" might well mean the end of women on the "women's team." Such problems might be resolved by sex-neutral regulations, for example, a height limit in "women's basketball" or weight limit in "women's football" (as we now have weight limits for wrestling and boxing). Having such limits might have a different effect, however. If, as is widely believed, women of the same height and weight as men do not perform as well in most sports because they lack the (sexually related) upper body strength of men, setting weight and height limits might simply give men of oriental or Mediterranean ancestry something like an equal chance to play basketball or football, something they do not now have because they are, on average, so much smaller than the blacks and blonds who dominate those sports. Women might still find themselves largely excluded. We would then have two integrationist options.

One is simply to let the chips fall where they may (as we now do for height in basketball or weight in football). Women may compete with men in any intercollegiate sport, but if they fail to make the team, so be it. The resulting segregation, if any, would be *de facto* but not *de jure*.

The other integrationist option is to abolish the scarcity of intercollegiate spaces so that everyone who wants to play a certain intercollegiate sport can. One way to do that is to have a series of graded teams (much as some schools have several bands): a "varsity team" (with the best players), a "B team" (for players not good enough for the A team), a "C team" (for players not good enough for the B team), and so on until everyone who wants to play that sport on an intercollegiate team can. The varsity team might turn out to be all male, but need not. The B, C, or D team might turn out to be all female, but need not. Again, any resulting segregation would be merely *de facto*.

One objection to multiplying teams in this way is easily disposed of. The objection is that such multiplication is too expensive. The obvious response is that it need cost nothing. It only requires spreading the same amount of money over more teams, ending support of less popular sports, or both. There are at least two reasons why the fact that universities might be forced to cut the budget of relatively rich teams or end support of relatively less popular sports cannot provide an argument against this way of giving women equality without segregation. First, similar budgetary considerations arise whenever a university adds a new varsity sport or even when an old varsity sport becomes more expensive. Second, insofar as women should have had such teams available to them all along, cutting the budget of a relatively rich sport or ending support of a relatively unpopular sport to make room for women in a more popular sport simply removes an unfair advantage men until then enjoyed. It does not take from men anything they ever had a right to.

Beside the arguments for sexual segregation familiar from the last section (paternalism and equal treatment), there are two such arguments we have not seen. One – "the transition argument" – relies on group interest; the other – "the argument from chivalry" – relies on another sort of fairness.

The transition argument had its counterpart when women were first being allowed into higher education: because society made little provision for women's sports until quite recently, women cannot be expected to compete on a par with men for a while yet. They lack the specially designed equipment and methods, the training lore, and even the skilled trainers now routinely available to males. Until that "infrastructure" has grown up, women need a "league of their own." That individual women will be excluded from men's teams for which they are qualified is the price of helping women as a group reach the level of support, skill, and lore necessary to compete with men. The interests of individuals must be sacrificed for the sake of the group.

The transition argument is troubling for two reasons. First, it imposes sacrifices on women today for the benefit of future women without any way to show that the future's interests take precedence over the interests of the present. Second, the means by which the future is to be benefited do not seem necessary to achieve the end in question, that is, the full participation of women in all sports as equals. The analogy with an argument supporting sexually segregated universities when women were first entering higher education is telling. Who can show that the first women in women's colleges were better off than their counterparts in the first sexually integrated colleges? There were both advantages and disadvantages to each system, requiring just the sort of trade-offs we generally think should be left to individuals to make.[9]

That brings us to the argument from chivalry. Men in our society (it is said) are brought up to treat women more gently than they treat men. For example, for one boy to hit another, even if the one hit is smaller, is at worst "bullying"; for the same boy to hit a girl is much worse, even if she is bigger: it is "unmanly." To ask men so raised to compete against women is to give the women an unfair advantage. So, for example, a "real man" cannot tackle a woman with the same assurance he would another man. He must "pull his punches" or appear unchivalrous (to himself if not to the world). There is a corresponding problem about women on one's own team. A "real man" would not feel right putting a woman where she could be hurt; he would feel called upon to do things to protect her that he would not feel called upon to do for a male teammate.

Of course, the premise of the argument from chivalry is a pair of sex roles the movement for women's equality has been trying to end. So, the obvious response is, "Too bad if men are at a disadvantage; it's about time they learned to treat women as their equals." But, though obvious, the response is not altogether satisfactory. On the one hand, we recognize that football, basketball, or indeed almost any sport would suffer if men treated chivalrously the women on their own team or those competing against them. On the other hand, we also recognize athletic chivalry as an expression of decency, however misguided. We do not, all else equal, want people to act in ways they consider unchivalrous; we do not want them to violate their own integrity. So, we have some reason to segregate women, if only to preserve the excellence of the sport and the integrity of those who play it.

If we consider athletics, even varsity sports, unimportant, we will assign the argument from chivalry little weight and have no trouble putting women on previously all-male teams, forcing the males to be unchivalrous, redefine their notions of chivalry, or leave the team. That the sport will suffer for a time, or forever, will not deter us. If, however, we consider athletics important as such, we are likely to prefer, for now at least, sexually segregated teams. Are athletics important? Does it matter whether a team wins or not, just so long as everyone has fun? Because I am of the "fun school" of athletics, I am regularly surprised to hear students, administrators, alumni, and even some faculty talk about this or that team as if it were the university's equivalent of a nation's military, an entity upon the success of which much depends. I am less surprised, and more impressed, by those whose concern is aesthetic, not winning but breaking records or some other form of excellence. For them, basketball, football, tennis, and so on are arts. To let just anyone play varsity sports would be like letting just anyone exhibit her paintings in an art museum. To force good players into situations where they cannot play well would be like forcing great artists to paint blindfolded and then exhibit the results beside their best work.

Here, then, the question of sexual segregation within the university merges into another question, one long debated in the United States; the role of athletics in the university.[10] Because that question is beyond the subject of this chapter, we must leave it for other questions of sexual ethics.

Sexuality

In the United States, most universities provide health insurance and medical care to students. The health insurance is voluntary, with students paying a premium only if they want the coverage. Medical care, in contrast, is generally funded out of student fees. Students must pay for the medical care whether they use it or not; indeed, whether they want it or not.

Universities provide health insurance to students as a service. Because students form an especially healthy "risk pool" (and the university provides some health care without charging the insurance company), the rate students pay is quite low, much lower than they would pay for comparable insurance bought individually or through any other group. That, I think, is sufficient reason for the university to provide health insurance. Less clear is why universities provide medical care, whether through a student clinic, infirmary, or full health service. Why not let students find physicians in just the way faculty and staff do? The most common answer parallels the argument for socialized medicine. Providing medical care on campus conveniently assures that students will have physicians available who understand their special health problems; forcing all students to participate assures a low per capita cost; and the resulting good health of students helps to keep the cost of health insurance low.

Because universities have, for whatever reason, undertaken to provide health insurance and medical care, they must decide what medical needs to insure against and what medical care to provide. The student's sexuality is relevant to a number of such decisions. Undoubtedly, the most controversial of these decisions concern birth control and abortion.

One might suppose the controversy over birth control and abortion to arise from considerations of fairness. Whether women need birth control or an abortion generally depends on their decisions. If they abstain from sex, they will need neither. Most medical needs are not so voluntary. Since insurance is a gamble, those who can easily control the risks insured against are most likely to win, that is, to pay less in premiums than they take out in benefits; or, at least, to take out proportionately more in benefits. Those who cannot control the risks are more likely to lose. Federal law forbids insurance companies to take sex into account when setting premiums. Two people, differing only in sex, must pay the same premium. So, unless we assume that copulation is, like driving a car or playing sports, "normal risk-taking" – that is, risky behavior we cannot reasonably expect people to forgo – extending health insurance coverage to birth control and abortion unfairly burdens male students. Men have no special health needs corresponding to birth control or abortion.[11]

This question of fairness has, however, had nothing to do with controversy over extending health insurance coverage to birth control or abortion. That may be because insurance rates for students are relatively low, birth control is cheap (so whether a woman is covered for it or not is not a great matter), and abortions among students are rare enough and cheap enough not to have much effect on the cost of insurance. The controversy over such coverage has, instead, simply reflected wider social debates. So, for example, Catholic universities have a religious commitment making abortion seem the moral equivalent of murder. For them, the question of abortion coverage is primarily one of complicity in moral wrongdoing of the most serious sort. Naturally, they choose not to be implicated, leaving their students to find coverage for abortion under their parent's policy, to avoid the need for abortion, or to find the few hundred dollars an abortion would cost.

For similar but less decisive reasons, Catholic universities (and those with similar views about copulation) are not inclined to cover birth control. They have, however, no such compunctions about covering the costs associated with childbirth. They do not even have compunctions about covering those costs when the birth occurs outside marriage. That seems significant. For the purposes of insurance, at least, even Catholic universities now seem to view copulation, whether within marriage or outside, as normal risk-taking, though their principles still say something else. Even Catholic universities no longer expect students to live like nuns or monks. We are a long way from the ascetic ideal of earlier centuries.

Student medical care is likely to generate many of the same questions as student health insurance. For example, should universities provide abortions or even abortion counseling at the student health service? Such questions invite no new arguments; but others do. Consider, for example, whether the university's health service should have enough female doctors on staff so that every woman who wants a doctor of her own sex can have one. If the university did that for women, should it do the same for men, assuring that every man who wants a male doctor can have one? Providing every woman who wants a female doctor with one may seem like a return to sexual segregation of the sort discussed in the last section. I do not think it is.

Why would a woman want a female doctor? One reason may be modesty, especially now that there are enough female doctors that a woman might grow up without having a male doctor. A woman may feel more comfortable having another woman examine her body than having a strange man do it. Certainly many male students feel that way about a female doctor examining them (in part, no doubt, because they have had no earlier experience of a woman examining them in that way). The other reason for providing a female doctor for those who want one – the more important, I think – is that a female doctor is (it is thought) more likely to understand the special medical problems of a woman better than a male doctor. A male doctor knows the problems from the outside; a female doctor knows them from the inside as well. Male doctors may not appreciate the sensitivity of specifically female organs, causing more discomfort than an otherwise similarly qualified woman would, and so on.

While the facts are probably less clear than these two arguments require, and may change as women become a larger part of the medical profession and medical education itself changes, what is important now is that these two arguments are (a) unconnected with the power arguments discussed in the last section, (b) nearly parallel for men and women, and (c) not such as to require segregation *de jure* (though allowing students to choose doctors by sex might produce segregation *de facto*). They are merely arguments for trying to accommodate the demand for the most appropriate doctor. These arguments would, no doubt, have little appeal where accommodating demand would disadvantage female doctors, a group we suppose already to be relatively disadvantaged. But, given the proportion of women to men in most universities, and the proportion of female to male doctors, accommodating the demand for doctors of one's own sex is likely to increase the demand for the underrepresented sex in medicine, thus contributing to equality between the sexes rather than (as with sexual segregation in the last section) working against it.

Though students are by far the largest part of the university, they are not the only part. As well as students, there are faculty and staff. Faculty and staff are employees. In the United States, health insurance normally comes through one's employer. Universities therefore have to make decisions about employee health insurance similar to those they have to make for student health insurance. They also have to decide at least one question student insurance has not yet raised, although it can; that is, the question of recognizing the enduring but not legally recognized sexual partners of the primary insured, for example, by granting the same dependent health benefits to such partners as are currently granted to a legal spouse.

Until well into this century, most universities, especially in the United States, would have had little trouble with this question, should anyone have thought to raise it. Sex inside marriage was all right; sex outside was not. Living with someone in the manner of husband and wife but without legal sanction was "living in sin," a scandal. Providing benefits to the other partner in such circumstances would have meant condoning "an affair." No university could do that. Indeed, the standard response of a university to an affair would have been to fire the faculty or staff member involved for "moral turpitude." Even tenure was no defense.

Today few universities seek to prevent all copulation outside marriage. Some universities try to be neutral on the sexual conduct of their staff, faculty, and students and leave to the criminal law and public opinion the enforcement of today's standards of sexual conduct, standards which are now much different from those of even a half century ago. But mere neutrality is difficult. For example, in the United States, universities receiving federal money must have a policy for dealing with sexual harassment. The law forbids simple neutrality (while also forbidding any distinction in treatment based merely on sex). Everywhere public opinion still demands that the university do something about certain forms of sexual conduct (though the conduct in question has changed somewhat over the years).

Some universities have responded by re-enacting parts of the criminal law. For example, IIT explicitly prohibits "harassment and/or hazing in all forms." It then defines harassment in terms of battery or assault: "striking, laying hands upon, intimidation, threatening with violence, or offering to do bodily harm to another person."[12] Taken literally, the policy would prohibit not only many forms of sexual harassment, including some too serious for the category (rape, kidnapping, or aggravated battery) but also all contact sports, all friendly pats on the back, and a good deal of common overstatement (for example, "Do that and you die" where what is obviously meant is "Please don't do that"). Of course, the policy is not to be taken literally. It begins by indicating that its concern is only those forms of harassment or hazing that are "demeaning, abusive, threatening, or alarming in nature."[13] Interpreted with that concern in mind, the policy would exempt contact sports, friendly pats on the back, and common overstatements from its prohibition. Unfortunately, whether interpreted literally or not, the policy does not include some conduct we might think sexual harassment (for example, a request for sex repeated again and again, even though each request receives an immediate and firm refusal).

Not surprisingly, then, IIT has a separate policy dealing with sexual harassment. Here "harassment [is defined as] unsolicited, offensive behavior that inappropriately asserts sexuality over status as a student or employee."[14] This policy covers a good deal of conduct not covered under the general harassment policy, but it does not cover everything we may think sexual harassment. For example, it does not cover my student's use of "broad." His conduct was, in a plain sense, solicited: it answered my question. However offensive, it did not, at least directly, assert the sexuality of anyone in the class over their status as a "student or employee [of IIT]." Indeed, it did not even assert the sexuality of Cecily Sandwich (her status as a "broad") over her status as a company employee. What it asserted, wrongly I think, was Sandwich's status as an employee over her status as an engineer. The student's use of "broad," though potentially offensive, was incidental to what he asserted and, though potentially contributing to a "hostile environment" for women, did not itself create such an environment.

Not all universities try to regulate sexual conduct simply by reenacting bits and pieces of the criminal law. Some have been more ingenious. For example, Antioch, a small rural college with a long history of liberal ideals and social activism, recently adopted a policy on sexual conduct much more coherent and complete than that of IIT. Antioch's "Sexual Offense Policy" governs "[all] sexual contact and conduct on the...campus and/or occurring with an Antioch community member [student, faculty, or staff]."[15] The Antioch policy defines sexual offense in terms of "non-consent" (or, where sexually transmitted diseases are involved, failure to inform). For consent to count, there must be a reasonably detailed discussion of each "level" of sexual activity: "Asking, 'Do you want to have sex with me?' is not enough."[16] The policy is entirely neutral concerning what sexual acts are agreed to. While the policy has been mocked for intellectualizing sex, that is actually its strength.[17] It discourages the brute groping that constitutes so much of sexuality, rewarding instead articulate agreement and the reflection necessary to achieve it. What institution, except the university, puts as much of life as possible into words, formulas, and other linguistic entities, even when doing so has no practical result beyond the pleasure of doing it well? Antioch's policy tries to bring sex into the university on the university's terms.

What effect such a policy will have on conduct remains to be seen. For now, the policy's appeal is its intentions, not its actual consequences. Indeed, if interpreted too strictly, the policy has some strange consequences. For example, suppose that I want to ask you for a date. Asking for a date is sexual conduct in a relatively straightforward, if preliminary, sense. (If this seems a stretch, you need only suppose that we are of the same sex to see how sexual my asking you for a date is.) So, presumably, I should, under the Antioch policy, have your explicit consent to ask such a question before I ask you for a date. But I cannot simply ask consent to ask you a question. "May I ask you a question?" is not specific enough. It gives no hint that sexual conduct is to follow. Yet, if I ask, "May I ask you a sexual question?" I have already asked a sexual question. Hence, I have already engaged in sexual conduct without consent; and I cannot avoid doing so, except by staying off the subject of sex altogether. That is certainly not what Antioch intends.

Antioch might avoid this paradoxical consequence by distinguishing between "conduct" and "mere words." That would be a mistake. The distinction between conduct and mere words seems even more difficult to make for sexual conduct than for other conduct. Much sexual harassment consists of nothing but words. The only sensible way to avoid the paradox is, I think, to interpret the policy as assuming certain "ground level" sexual questions which, by definition, are not offensive, however offensive they may sometimes be (for example, "May I ask you a sexual question?"). A "no" might be understood to forbid a similar question for a certain time – a week, a month, or forever – or until there is an explicit invitation.

Antioch's sexual offense policy may seem to answer a number of related questions about sexual conduct, for example, whether sexual relations between a faculty member and a student are permissible, whether sexual relations between members of the faculty or staff are permissible, and whether such relations between students are permissible when one of them has authority over the other (for example, when one student is the resident advisor, tutor, or peer counselor of the other). But it does not. These questions require independent regulation because consent, however voluntary, does not touch the fundamental problem such relations raise.

Consider the question of sexual relations between a student and a faculty member. Much of the discussion of sexual relations between students and faculty make the faculty, especially the males, sound like sexual predators and the students, especially the females, sound like victims. In fact, matters are more complicated, as the number of such relationships that end in enduring marriages suggests. Consider, for example, what Jane Gallop, now a professor of English and comparative literature, reports about her career as a graduate student:

> I wanted to get [faculty] into bed in order to make them more human, more vulnerable.... I was bowled over by their brilliance; they seemed so superior. I wanted to see them naked, to see them as like other men.[18]

She, not the faculty member, was the prime mover in the sexual relation. For her, seducing faculty was a way of giving herself the confidence to "presume she had something to say worth saying."[19] So, it seems, some copulating between faculty and students might serve education. Here, perhaps, is the place to recall those relations, praised in Plato's *Symposium*, in which a youth pairs up with an older man. The youth learns what the man has to teach, mostly about matters unrelated to sex; in return, the man finds "love," whether a mere sexual outlet, a divine passion, or an enduring friendship. Whether either youth or man exploits the other depends on the particular relationship, not on any general feature. The same may be true of Gallop's causal sex with her teachers.

Such relationships within a university are none the less troubling for at least two reasons. The first is that the student has already entered into the teacher–student relationship when, having paid the fees, he signs up for the class. From that moment, as argued in Chapter 9, the teacher has an obligation to try to benefit the student. The student does not owe his teacher anything in return (apart from fulfilling the requirements of the course), and certainly not a sexual relation. Plato's bargain is foreclosed. The Platonic

212

analogy therefore identifies the problem with the relationship, even as it helps us to understand its good side. The problem is that the student–teacher relation is a general feature of such sexual relationships. Any justification of them must take that into account.

We have reached the fundamental objection to even the sexual relationships Gallop describes. The faculty of a university are never just teachers; they are also administrators. They must apportion their time between a number of students, must treat each student fairly, and judge each, embodying that judgment in a final grade affecting both the student in question and all those in competition with her. Are there any faculty who could copulate (or even have a "less serious" sexual relation) with a student and still treat her with the same impartiality as other students? A few perhaps, those with the passions of a lizard, but even they could not prove their impartiality to those who, knowing their own passions, doubt that anyone else could be so different. Even the cold-blooded few cannot avoid a well-founded suspicion of their impartiality. So, a faculty member who has sexual relations with a student cannot serve the university or the students as they are supposed to serve them. The fundamental problem with the relationship is just what it would be if the student were not the faculty member's sex partner but his father or daughter: conflict of interest.

We can often avoid conflicts of interest. When we can, we should, if the cost is not too high. Avoiding sexual relations with students in our classes costs us relatively little. Avoiding all sexual relations with students in our university costs us more, especially if the university is distant from any substantial town and we are young and single. Avoiding all sexual relations with anyone who might some day be a student costs more still. Few of us are good at guessing the future. So, the only (morally permissible) way to be sure that no sex partner of ours will ever become one of our students is to have no sex partners.[20]

One alternative to this absolute ban on sex is to make it clear in advance – Antioch style – that the sexual relation will foreclose the normal classroom relation. The best way to make that clear is a university regulation announced loudly and often. Leaving it to individual faculty to adopt such a policy has many risks. If the faculty member waits to announce the policy until the sexual relation has begun, she denies the student the opportunity to choose to have the faculty member as a teacher rather than as a sexual partner. And, of course, waiting until the student shows up in class is worse yet; it may force the student into a last-minute scramble for a substitute course, deny her a course she needs for graduation, or otherwise harm her.[21] When a former sexual partner turns up in class even though we told her about the conflict of interest before the sexual relation began, we can still escape the threat to judgment by getting the student to transfer to another class or, when transfer is impossible or would harm the student, by having a colleague do the grading for that student.

Because this alternative is not altogether satisfactory, some may think the best policy is simply to prohibit faculty to have sexual relations with students in their university, whether the student is enrolled in their class or not. This flat prohibition, though of course preferable to a total ban on sex, is, I think, none the less both unwise in practice and unjustified in principle.

The flat prohibition is unwise because it demands too much of faculty who are also human beings living in a society in which sexual relations seem to be relatively central to life. In most universities, especially those in small towns, most of the potential sexual partners of most faculty, especially younger faculty, are students. A flat prohibition is likely to be breached often enough to come into disrepute.

The flat prohibition is also unjustified. The prohibition's purpose, preserving the impartiality of faculty judgment, can be achieved about as well merely by prohibiting faculty to have a sexual relation with a present student or to take a former sexual partner as a student. Indeed, this more limited prohibition is extensive enough to prevent even the appearance that a faculty member has used the power to grade to force a student into a sexual relation. The prohibition none the less leaves faculty and students relatively free to interact in ways that, as Gallop reminds us, are not necessarily bad for students or faculty. A prohibition limited to one's own students does not impose an unreasonable burden on faculty.

Sexual identity

As universities have tried to accommodate our changing conceptions of sexuality, they have had to rethink the privileged place of legal marriage. This rethinking has in turn forced a rethinking of sexual identity.

People have always copulated one way or another, been able or unable to bear children, and looked more like some people than others; they have also always identified themselves as, and been identified by others as, male or female. But now we have additional identifications: heterosexual, bisexual, homosexual, lesbian, transsexual, and so on. Until recently, regulating sex within the university was easy, I think, if not altogether successful, not because there was more agreement about sexual matters than there is today (though there may have been) but, primarily at least, because sex was less central to life than it is today. Celibacy seemed less demanding. Copulation was then for procreation or pleasure. Homosexual or lesbian acts might be sins ("crimes against nature"), but neither homosexuality nor lesbianism was a "way of life," a "lifestyle," or even an "identity." Indeed, even heterosexuality was not. What role should sexual identification (lifestyles or ways of life) play in the university?

Consider the question of whether to extend health insurance coverage to a "domestic partner" not recognized in law. Such partners may be divided into two kinds, same sex and opposite sex. These kinds might in turn be subdivided into those partners who copulate with one another and those who do not, but the presumption seems to be that domestic partners are, by definition, sexual partners, another sign of the times.

There seem to be two arguments against extending coverage to a same-sex partner, the "moral argument" and the "slippery slope argument." The moral argument is that the sexual relation in question is immoral ("a crime against nature") or, at least, questionable enough that universities should not condone it in staff and certainly not in faculty. The slippery slope argument is that extending coverage to a same-sex partner would require the university to do the same for domestic partners of the opposite sex.

Because the moral argument is hard to make without a religious premise, the primary argument against granting dependent benefits to domestic partners seems to be the slippery slope.[22] Why then not just slide merrily down that short slope to coverage of all domestic partners, legally recognized or not, same sex or not? Here again there is a weak moral argument concerning the propriety of copulation outside marriage, even in an enduring heterosexual domestic partnership. If a couple want to live like husband and wife, why not marry? What they are asking for are the benefits of marriage without the burdens.

There is also an economic argument. The number of heterosexual couples living together but unmarried is (probably) much larger than the number of similar homosexual couples. Hence, opening coverage to all domestic partners might increase the cost of health insurance to those primarily covered. While experience so far does not seem to show any such increase in cost, the argument's primary weakness is that it must assume the justice of the status quo. If, for example, the increase in cost, however large (short of catastrophe), were justified by considerations of fairness, then increased cost would provide no argument for keeping the present (unjust) arrangements. Justice takes precedence over (manageable) economic burdens.

There is, last, an administrative argument. Legal recognition of marriage provides a bright line between those who can be covered and those who cannot. The legal act of marriage generates a legal document identifying the partners, the marriage certificate. Mere "domestic partners" are not so easily identified. How do we distinguish, for example, between real domestic partners and those who claim to be but simply share the rent? The administrative argument, though stronger than others, is strong only until we have worked out administrative equivalents of the marriage certificate. A university might, for example, ask domestic partners to submit a notarized declaration of partnership, evidence of a common checking account, and so on. There does not seem to be any impassable barrier to developing some such procedure. So, the administrative argument is more an invitation to invention that a decisive argument against recognizing domestic partnerships not recognized in law.

This discussion of health insurance may seem parochial, an American obsession presupposing peculiar ideas about what government should and should not do. That of course is true, but it is beside the point. Concern with health insurance coverage is parochial, but the shifting conception of legitimate relationships underwriting that concern is not. A British or French university may face a similar question when, for example, a faculty member brings a companion to a department party and introduces him or her as her "domestic partner" (rather than as "friend" or "significant other"). Such an introduction has little to do with copulation but much to do with sexual identity; it is a demand for social recognition of the sexual relationship (whatever part copulation plays in it). How should the department respond? How should the university respond?

The demand for social recognition of one's sexual identity may also have something to do with some recent controversies over curriculum. For example, efforts to revise "the canon" have not emphasized arguments from quality – "Toni Morrison's *Beloved* should be on the American literature reading list because it is one of best American novels of the last half century" – but have instead emphasized arguments from representation: "Morrison's *Beloved* should be on the American literature reading list because books by women, especially black women, are underrepresented."

Why does representation matter? That is far from clear. One reason representation might be thought to matter, the need for female writers to have "role models," seems to have little empirical foundation. Certainly earlier female writers, such as Jane Austen, seem to have done well enough with many fewer female role models. Perhaps much of the appeal of the argument from role models comes from confusing role models (strictly so called) – that is, people whom we copy in detail – or from mere proofs of possibility, that is, the first few of "our kind" (something more than "mere tokens") who demonstrate the possibility of our also being allowed to do something.[23] The sexual identity of writers seems to have much less to do with their status as role models than with their status as proofs of possibility. So, for example, most of Jane Gallop's role models seem to have been men, even though she could not have been nearly so sure of an academic career had there been no women in the faculty.

Another reason representation might be thought to matter may seem more substantial: inclusion in the "canon" (it is said) grants deserved legitimacy not only to the writer included but to "her kind" (sex, sexual preference, nation, or the like). This notion of legitimacy by identification seems akin to the silliness that allows a short, overweight Chicago cabby to say "we won" when he means the Chicago Bulls won a basketball game.

That, however, is not all that is wrong with the argument from representation. The argument also presupposes a standard of adequate representation. I do not think we know what a curriculum would look like if it represented women in the numbers they deserve. Would it contain the same number of female as male writers, or be proportioned according to the ratio of female to male writers, or according to the ratio of good female to good male writers, or according to some other ratio? How do we know that the present ratio is not just about right? If considerations of quality are relevant (as I think they are), who is to judge quality? The experts (most of whom are still male)? If not the experts, who? The notion of "adequate representation" is, I think, too vague to be useful here; but, without it, the argument from representation is unusable.

The argument from representation may also be irrelevant. Would we hear much about the underrepresentation of women in the canon if as many women as men were among the experts setting the canon? If men still predominated in the canon, would not the women having voted more or less as the men did vouch for that predominance? Do we worry about the outcome when we trust the procedure?

Since the canon is set by university faculty, underlying the dispute about the canon's representativeness may be questions about hiring, promotion, and tenure of female faculty. Clearly, even today women are decidedly in the minority among faculty. Are they therefore underrepresented (because there are improper obstacles to their becoming more numerous)? Or adequately represented (because their number is the result of a fair procedure)? Or even overrepresented (because even their small number is the result of procedures unfairly rigged against men)? The assumption today – and it is, I think, still not much more than that – is that women are underrepresented, that under fair conditions women would constitute about half the faculty in every department at every rank. The problem is to identify the conditions that have brought about the underrepresentation and rectify them.

Yet, even assuming underrepresentation, there is much room for disagreement concerning both the cause of underrepresentation and the moral permissibility of the means of rectification. For example, some might argue that tenure policies are inherently unfair to women because they emphasize publication over teaching, and women, more interested in caring relationships than men, naturally prefer to teach rather than publish. Others might explain women's relative lack of publications as a byproduct of the distribution of responsibilities in the wider society. Because women have a larger part in the care of children and aged parents, they often cannot devote as much time to research and writing as can otherwise similarly qualified men.

Those two analyses, while attributing the dearth of tenured women to their lack of publications, disagree on the cause of that dearth. Agreeing on the cause will, however, not foreclose disagreement on the means of rectification. One way to rectify the dearth of tenured women may be to grant women publication handicaps so that men and women in the university have an equal chance of tenure. However, such handicaps require taking into account sexual identity rather than the actual domestic burdens under which the scholar operates. That may seem unfair even to some who agree that unfair distribution of domestic burdens causes "underpublication" and underpublication causes underrepresentation. Another way to rectify the dearth of tenured women is to treat the sexes equally and wait for society to readjust responsibilities. Our discussion of sexual identity in the university has reached the wider debate over affirmative action.

Acknowledging the connection with that wider debate does not mean that we cannot make some improvements in the condition of women in the university without settling the complex questions fueling that wider debate. What it does mean, I think, is that any defense of such improvements should rely on arguments more or less independent of affirmative action. For example, women are said to be at a disadvantage in the sciences (in part) because sexual roles encourage male and female undergraduates working together in a laboratory to divide up work so that the woman takes the notes while the man does the experiment. The simplest way to avoid this traditional division of labor is to require lab partners to exchange roles after each experiment. What is interesting about this way of improving the condition of women in the university is that it also improves the education of men; that is, the education both of those men who tend to avoid "dirty work" and of those men who tend to avoid writing. The way to defend this way of improving the condition of women is to emphasize everyone's need to experience taking notes and everyone's need to experience doing the experiment. The problem women have here is not really a "women's problem." Our focus on sex simply highlights another sort of problem, though one disproportionately harming women.[24]

Back to Cecily Sandwich

I divided the category of sexual ethics into three parts – sexual equality, sexuality, and sexual identity – primarily for coherence of exposition. As should be clear by now, the differences between problems grouped together in any of these subdivisions can be as great as differences between problems in one subdivision and another. My purpose throughout was in part to make clear how diverse the problems assigned to the category of sexual ethics can be. In part, too, my purpose was to show how little guidance understanding any of the large problems so assigned would give in dealing with the student comment with which I began this chapter. Like many problems now assigned to the category of sexual ethics, this one has more to do with teaching than with sex. Let me make that point by completing my story.

As I looked over the class, I was pretty sure that "broad" did not offend the women there, or even surprise them. They certainly did not look offended or surprised, and after three or four years at IIT, where they constituted a relatively small minority (about 20 percent of students), they should, I thought, be "battle hardened."

What was chiefly wrong with my student's use of "broad," I thought, was that it was his way of distancing himself from Cecily's position. He might not be able to dismiss her concerns so easily if he thought of her as an engineer, that is, as a member of a profession bound by a code of ethics. After all, he too was an engineer. So, my initial response was, "That's no broad, that's an engineer." He looked a bit shaken, but didn't respond. I had intended to add something about the origin of "broad" (pregnant cow). Giving the origin of a word often makes students more careful in their use of it. But before I could slip into that digression, another student broke in, taking discussion in another direction. We never got back to "broad."

Until near the end of the class hour, I thought my response had failed. Then the student, long silent, announced that he had changed his mind: Cecily was doing what an engineer with her opinion should do; the manager should respect her judgment, but he should also "shop around" for another engineer to sign off on the revised assessment.[25] I heard nothing more of "broad" that semester.

By responding to the student's thoughtlessness, his failure to think of Cecily as an engineer, I also responded to the question of sexual ethics that thoughtlessness seemed to raise. I believe that most practical questions of sexual ethics in the university are best handled in some such way as this, taking care of education and letting the sex take care of itself; or, at least, are best so handled when the standard in question is more or less settled. Where the standard is not yet settled, we should continue the discussion, treating our disagreements about ethics as we should treat other academic disagreements, that is, as disputes about arguments, evidence, and procedure. We should take most care to remain civil with those we think most confused or ignorant, to assume mistake rather than malice – as I have tried to do throughout this book.

NOTES

1 THE ETHICS BOOM, PHILOSOPHY AND THE UNIVERSITY

Early versions of this chapter were presented to the Chicago Chapter of the America Society for Public Administration, 22 June 1989; the Western Michigan Chapter of the American Society of Fund Raising Executives, Grand Rapids, 21 September 1989; the Southwestern Section of the Michigan Society of Professional Engineers, Kalamazoo, 3 October 1989; and the Center for Ethics Studies, Marquette University, Milwaukee, Wisconsin, 27 October 1989. I should like to thank those present, and my colleagues at IIT, especially, Sohair ElBaz and Jing Li, for helping me to fit the pieces together.

1 The first recorded use of "medical ethics" in this sense (or any other) seems to be the title of Thomas Percival's 1803 text, *Medical Ethics*.
2 I give priority to the very successful Samuel Gorovitz *et al.* (eds), *Moral Problems in Medicine*, Englewood Cliffs, N.J., Prentice, 1976. But, in fairness, I should mention two other texts that appeared the same year: another philosophical anthology, James M. Humber and Robert F. Almeder (eds), *Biomedical Ethics and the Law*, New York, Plenum P., 1976; and a survey by Howard Brody, *Ethical Decisions in Medicine*, Boston, Little, 1976. Several more texts appeared the following year. Medical ethics had come of age.
3 See, for example, the famous exchange beginning with Monroe Freedman, "Professional Responsibility of the Criminal Defense Lawyer," *Michigan Law Review*, 1966, vol. 64, pp. 1,469–84. The philosophically sophisticated literature – much of it the work of philosopher-lawyers – was only beginning to appear the year I first taught legal ethics. See, for example, Richard Wasserstrom, "Lawyers as Professionals: Some Moral Issues," *Human Right*, 1975, vol. 5, pp. 1–24.
4 The best of these, Vern Countryman and Ted Finman (eds), *The Lawyer in Modern Society*, Boston, Little, 1966, begins with the observation that "law teaching focuses on law almost to the exclusion of the lawyer." I used instead Maynard E. Pirsig (ed.), *Professional Responsibility*, St. Paul, West, 1970 – a text going back to 1949 – because it had been revised for the new code. None of the texts then

available drew on the philosophical literature – understandably, I think, because even I was able to do so only with great difficulty. Less understandable is why legal ethics texts *still* do not draw on the philosophical literature to the degree medical ethics texts typically do.

5 See, for example, Robert J. Baum, *Ethics and Engineering Curricula*, Hastings-on-Hudson, NY, The Hastings Center, 1980, pp. 58. Also note Baum's observation, pp. 23: "[There] is no evidence that there were any courses specifically focusing on engineering ethics being offered outside engineering departments by non-engineering faculty prior to 1975.... As of 1979, there were probably thirty to forty such courses being offered, and at least fifty more courses are in various stages of planning." More evidence of a boom.

6 *Implementation and Enforcement of Codes of Ethics in Corporations and Associations: A Report Prepared by Opinion Research Corporation* (August 1980), Sponsored by the Ethics Resource Center, 1730 Rhode Island Avenue, NW, Washington, D.C. 20036, pp. 13 and 263.

7 Ethics Resource Center, *Ethics in American Business: Policies, Programs, and Perceptions*, Washington, D.C., Ethics Resource Center, 1994, p. 3.

8 The growth is probably not as dramatic as these raw numbers indicate. The collection will keep up to three successive codes in a file. By now, most files contain three codes. That probably was not true in 1989 and certainly not in 1981 when the collection began.

9 For example, compare par. 17 of the 1912 code ("Technical discussions and criticisms of engineering subjects should not be conducted in the public press, but before engineering societies or through technical publications") with Art. 4 of the 1979 code which almost reverses the standard ("Members shall, in fulfilling their responsibilities to the community: 1. Protect the safety, health and welfare of the public and speak out against abuses in these areas affecting the public interest"). The IEEE (originally, the American Institute of Electrical Engineers) was founded in 1884.

10 The department did have a course in "Social Philosophy" which we would now group with ethics. I do not put it in that category. Political philosophy as then conceived seemed quite separate from ethics. Today, I have trouble understanding how I could have thought so. Still, I remember discussing at length, without reference to moral theory or even moral rules, such issues as the proper limits of government or the permissibility of capital punishment (and, as interesting as these issues were, having difficulty seeing their "philosophical interest"). I thought of such issues as primarily concerned with social policy to which moral theory was largely irrelevant.

11 Hastings Center Staff, "The Teaching of Ethics in American Higher Education: An Empirical Synopsis," in *Teaching Ethics in Higher Educations*, eds Daniel Callahan and Sissela Bok, New York: Plenum P, 1980, pp. 156–7.

12 *A Selected Annotated Bibliography of Professional Ethics and Social Responsibility in Engineering*, compiled by Robert F. Ladenson *et al.*, Chicago, Center for the Study of Ethics in the Professions, Illinois Institute of Technology, 1980.

13 The closest engineering comes is the *Journal of Professional Issues in Engineering*, published by the American Society of Civil Engineers. Now in its 115th year, this slim journal was until recently concerned primarily with "professional activities" and even now is concerned with a good deal more than engineering ethics. The new journal (1994), *Science and Engineering Ethics*, while publishing much important work in engineering ethics, must be shared with the sciences which still get the lion's share of the space.

14 W.T. Reich (ed.), *Encyclopedia of Bioethics*, New York, Free Press, 1978.

15 Of course, one of philosophy's most important journals, *Ethics*, is more than a century old. But it was then – as it still is – at least as much a journal of moral theory as of applied ethics. I would describe the *Journal of Value Inquiry* in the same way. But I do think its founding in 1966 was an early sign that interest in ethics was reviving.

16 The Netherlands had three; Germany and Australia each had two; and there was one each in France, Italy, Japan, Mexico, New Zealand, and Spain.

17 For this century up to 1980, see Paul and Patricia Brantingham, *Patterns in Crime*, New York, Macmillan, 1984, pp. 120–30. For the 1980s, see *Report to the National on Crime and Justice, Second Edition* (March 1989), U.S. Department of Justice, Bureau of Justice Statistics, pp. 15–17. The rate of increase is startling. For example, in 1960, there were in the United States about 60 robberies a year per 100,000 inhabitants. By 1980, the rate was 245 per 100,000, a four-fold increase. Brantingham, *Patterns*, p. 122.

18 There are, of course, other potential statistics that might seem relevant here, for example, the rate of illegitimate births. But such statistics are subject to the same critique of relevance as are criminal statistics. Little of the conduct label unethical has much to do with illegitimate births. And some statistics, such as illegitimate birth, are subject to another criticism as well. The assumption is that having a child out of wedlock is morally (or ethically) wrong. Yet that very assumption is now controversial. One cannot show an age to be less moral than another simply by assuming answers to certain controversial moral questions and then showing that the age in question behaves as if it disagreed with that answer.

19 Since "professional etiquette" is often used as a pejorative these days, I should point out that *Black's Law Dictionary*, St. Paul, West, 1968, gives only this definition: "The code of honor agreed on by mutual understanding and tacitly accepted by members of the legal profession, especially by the bar," p. 654. Except for that old-fashioned word "honor," this is a good working definition of legal ethics (and, with a few changes, of professional ethics too).

20 For some sense of what that course might have been like, see Association of American Law Schools (eds), *Selected Readings on the Legal Profession*, St. Paul, West, 1962. The work of a committee of big names, this text took ten years to prepare. For the engineers' counterpart, see: Philip L. Alger *et al.* (eds), *Ethical Problems in Engineering*, New York, John Wiley, 1965.

21 For early evidence of these courses, see Jesse Hickman Bond, *The Teaching of Professional Ethics in the Schools of Law, Medicine, Journalism and Commerce in the United States*, Ph.D., University of Wisconsin, 1915; and Theodore Day Martin, *Instruction in Professional Ethics in Professional Schools for Teachers*, Ph.D., Columbia University, 1931. Both cited in Douglas Sloan, "The Teaching of Ethics in the American Undergraduate Curriculum 1876–1976," in *Ethics Teaching in Higher Education*, p. 26n.

22 Why did the old course in professional ethics survive so much longer in law schools than in other professional schools? My guess is some combination of the following factors: (a) the legal curriculum has never gotten as crowded as the curriculum of medicine, engineering, business, or most other professions (the hot question being whether to reduce the program from three years to two); (b) the subject matter of professional ethics is more like law than the subject matter of most other professions; and (c) teaching law has changed less than teaching in professions where technology has a larger part.

23 This information comes from a letter dated 14 October 1980 and addressed to Ronald Kline, now at Cornell University. Its author, a former IEEE president, confirmed all essentials (with many interesting details) in a letter to me dated 13 October 1989: "All the time we were debating this issue [the IEEE Code of Ethics], none of us was aware that the AIEE had adopted a Code of Ethics in 1912!"

24 Sloan, pp. 10–19; and Henry C. Johnson, "On Avoiding 'Single Vision and Newton's Sleep': Sketches From an Unorthodox Moral-Education History," in William M. Kuntines and Jacob L. Gewirtz (eds), *Morality, Moral Behavior, and Moral Development*, New York, John Wiley, 1984, pp. 381–99.

25 Compare Sloan, "Teaching Ethics," p. 7: "Sermons in college chapel and, not infrequently, evidences of religion drawn in a science class by a devout professor were intended to give further witness to the moral law. The mental discipline that study of the classics and mathematics was thought to impart was viewed as indispensable to the development and exercise of moral discipline. This discipline was further reinforced by the strict in loco parentis regimen of the college schedule. The entire college experience was meant, above all, to be an experience in character development and the moral life, as epitomized, secured, and brought to a focus in the moral philosophy course."

26 James McCosh, *Our Moral Nature*. Sloan, p. 9, n. 15. McCosh (1811–94), another philosophically sophisticated minister, was eighty-one when this book appeared and four years into his retirement. *Encyclopedia of Philosophy*, ed. Paul Edwards, vol. 5, New York, Macmillan, 1967, pp. 225–6 (which, by the way, does not mention *Our Moral Nature*).

27 Compare Sloan, "Teaching Ethics," p. 26: "[After 1910, the] ethics of the medical profession, of the law, of journalism, and of business were suddenly being discussed as never before....If undergraduate instruction in ethics was lacking or failing, perhaps the moral dikes could be repaired later by arousing a professional ethical sensitivity."

28 Since I have plainly found much Sloan has to say helpful, I should point out three important differences between his approach and mine that may help to explain why I am about to draw conclusions somewhat different from his. First, I am primarily concerned with the current ethics boom generally; Sloan, with the undergraduate teaching of ethics in particular. Second, I am writing primarily as a philosopher involved in the events; Sloan, as a historian. And third, I tend to be impressed by the discontinuities; Sloan, by the continuities. Sloan sometimes writes like the economist who points out (correctly) that even during the Great Depression only one-quarter of the workforce was unemployed. I am more likely to write like a worker who can still remember how depressing the Great Depression was. No doubt, each approach has its advantages.

29 Sloan, "Teaching Ethics," p. 25, provides a poignant illustration of this proselytizing attitude: "I have begun a course of ethics for lower college classes, and for two of three months have given nothing but hygiene; and I believe the pedagogic possibilities of this mode of introduction into this great domain are at present unsuspected and that, instead of the arid, speculative casuistic way, not only college but high school boys could be infected with real love of virtue and a deep aversion to every sin against the body." I do not claim that the teacher who uttered these words (G. Stanley Hall, a psychologist, president of Clark University) indoctrinated his students. What I claim is that he did not doubt the truth of the moral views with which he hoped to "infect" them. He would have seen no need for a center to study ethical questions.

30 My only evidence for this claim is the structure of many texts in applied or professional ethics, published syllabi, and what I have heard from faculty. But this is consistent with the Hastings Center's report that the new courses "stress applied rather than theoretical concerns." Hastings Center Staff, "Teaching Ethics," p. 157.

31 Hastings Center Staff, "Teaching Ethics," 157–8: Most of the courses are "oriented around specific ethical issues," taught to groups or sections of students numbering 30 or less," and "draw liberally from" the large body of recent literature on applied ethics.

32 I do not think the contrast is to be explained entirely by the spirit of the times. Contrast, for example, G. Stanley Hall's words quoted above with the almost contemporaneous words with which two philosophers began their popular textbook: "The significance of this text in Ethics lies in its effort to awaken a vital conviction of the genuine reality of moral problems and the value of reflective thought in dealing with them." John Dewey and James H. Tufts, *Ethics*, New York, Henry Hold, 1908, p. ii. While Hall sounds like he is writing from another planet, Dewey and Tuft sound like our countrymen.

33 Unlike Sloan, I do not think it fair to describe a college president who gave the senior course in moral philosophy as a philosopher simply because he taught a course called "moral philosophy." I do not even think it fair to describe in that way such "leading academic philosophers" of the mid-nineteenth century as Francis Wayland or Noah Porter (Sloan, "Teaching Ethics," p. 5). Though men like Wayland and Porter did in fact do respectable work in philosophy (among other

fields), they were trained as ministers, not philosophers; lived the life of a minister; and held a college presidency in part because they were ministers. Their teaching was an extension of their ministry. And that, I think, explains why (as Sloan says) most of those teaching moral philosophy "studiously avoided issues that involved conflict," why "their pronouncements often rose little above the level of truism," and why their lectures tended to have an "exhortative, presumptuous, rhetorical style" (Sloan, "Teaching Ethics," p. 8) – why, in short, the old course in moral philosophy was quite unlike today's course in applied ethics.

34 3,544,000 inhabitants out of 23,192,000. *Historical Statistics of the United States: Colonial Times to 1970*, Part 1, U.S. Department Commerce, Bureau of the Census (Bicentennial Edition), p. 12 (hereafter cited as *Census*).

35 *World Almanac and Book of Facts*, New York, World Almanac, 1989, pp. 538–9. No other U.S. city had even 200,000 inhabitants in 1850.

36 *Census*, p. 12.

37 30,160,000 inhabitants out of 75,955,000. *Census*, p. 11.

38 My calculation is based on 1986 estimates, *World Almanac*, p. 537.

39 For a more general discussion of these points, see my "The Moral Authority of a Professional Code," in J. Roland Pennock and John W. Chapman (eds), *NOMOS XXIX: Authority Revisited*, New York, New York University Press, 1987, pp. 302–37; "The Use of Professions," *Business Economics*, 1987, vol. 22, pp. 5–10; *Codes of Ethics in Business*, Kalamazoo, MI, Center for the Study of Ethics in Society, Western Michigan University, 1988; "Vocational Teachers, Confidentiality, and Professional Ethics," *International Journal of Applied Philosophy*, 1988, vol. 4, pp. 11–20; "Professionalism Means Putting Your Profession First," *Georgetown Journal of Legal Ethics*, 1988, vol. 2, pp. 352–66; "Thinking Like an Engineer: The Place of a Code of Ethics in the Practice of a Profession," *Philosophy and Public Affairs*, 1991, vol. 20, pp. 150–67; "Do Cops Need a Code of Ethics?," *Criminal Justice Ethics*, 1991, vol. 10, pp. 14–28; "Treating Patients with Infectious Diseases: An Essay in the Ethics of Dentistry," *Professional Ethics*, 1993, vol. 1, pp. 51–65; and "The State's Dr. Death: What's Unethical about Physicians Helping at Executions?" *Social Theory and Practice*, 1995, vol. 21, pp. 31–60.

40 Two decades ago, some philosophers were still claiming a bit more, that is, that professional ethics can be *inconsistent* with ordinary morality. See, for example, Benjamin Freedman, "A Meta-Ethics of Professional Morality," *Ethics*, 1978, vol. 89, pp. 1–19; or Alan Goldman, *The Moral Foundations of Professional Responsibility*, Totowa, N.J., Littlefield Adams, 1980, esp. pp. 38–49. I don't think anyone still holds that view.

41 For an example of the confusion that can follow if this third sense is not recognized, see John Ladd, "Collective and Individual Moral Responsibility in Engineering: Some Questions," in Vivian Weil (ed.), *Beyond Whistleblowing: Defining Engineers' Responsibilities*, Chicago, Center for the Study of Ethics in the Professions, Illinois Institute of Technology, 1983, pp. 90–113. "Ethics, sometimes called 'critical morality,' is," he claims, "logically prior to all these institutions and

social mechanisms of control [like law or the 'value-system' of some group]....The principles of ethics (or morals), in contrast, are not the kind of thing that can be arbitrarily created, changed or rescinded....[T]hey are 'discovered' rather than created by fiat. They are established through argument and persuasion, not by imposition by an external social authority." pp. 102–3. Having equated ethics both with the study of morality ("critical morality") and with morality itself (note the parentheses containing "or morals"), Ladd can only contrast law's imposition of standards with morality's "discovery" of standards by "argument and persuasion." (Moral standards, being universal, can only be discovered.) Ladd wholly misses the possibility of local (morally binding) standards that can be "recreated, changed, or rescinded" through "argument and persuasion." Ladd has, in other words, ruled out professional or applied ethics as it seems to have developed rather than argued against it possibility.

42 See, for example, entry 3c under "ethics" in *The Oxford English Dictionary* (1933): "The rules of conduct recognized in certain associations or departments of human life." Though the first example under this definition is 1789 (Bentham's distinction between "private ethics" and the "art of legislation"), the first use in the sense of local rules is 1864; the first involving a profession is 1884 (from Australia!): "*Ethics, medical,* the laws of the duties of medical men to the public, to each other, and to themselves in regard to the exercise of their profession." Curiously, there is no reference to Percival's 1803 text. Marcus Singer seems to have been the first philosopher to note in print this new sense. See his "Recent Trends and Future Prospects in Ethics." *Metaphilosophy*, 1981, vol. 12, pp. 207–23. I should like to thank William Starr for calling my attention to Singer's paper.

2 ACADEMIC FREEDOM, ACADEMIC ETHICS, AND PROFESSIONAL ETHICS

Earlier versions of this chapter were presented at the Philosophy Colloquium, Illinois Institute of Technology, 27 February 1991; at Miami University, Oxford, Ohio, 16 April 1991; at a joint meeting of the Society for Philosophy and Public Affairs and the Association for the Philosophy of Education, Chicago, 25 April 1991; and at the College of Charleston, Charleston, South Carolina, 20 January 1992. I should like to thank all those who participated in the discussions that followed, but especially my official commentators in Chicago, Marcia Baron and Edmond Pincoffs, for many helpful comments. I should also like to thank Al Gini, Emilie Kadish, Mortimer Kadish, and Richard Lipke for written comments on one or another draft; Robert Ladenson for originally suggesting the topic and helping me see its dimensions; and Sohair ElBaz for helping me find many references I might otherwise have missed.

1 Carolyn J. Mooney, "N.Y. City College Panel Weighs Academic Freedom, Inflammatory Racial Views of 2 Faculty Members," *Chronicle of Higher Education*, May 23, 1990, pp. A13ff. I have simplified the facts a bit to ease exposition in this case and the one to follow. I

have therefore deprived those involved of their identity as well. For those interested in a fuller version of the story, one more favorable to Professor A, see *Levin v. Harleston*, 770 F. Supp. 895 (S.D.N.Y., 1991), especially pp. 899–918.

2 John Camper, "Loyola Struggling to Handle New Racial Tensions: Professor's Remark Sets Off Firestorm," *Chicago Tribune*, Sunday 15 April 1990, Section 2, pp. 1ff; and Jim Bowman, "Watch More than P's and Q's," *Chicago Tribune*, 21 April 1990, Section 1, p. 12. While I have relied for this vignette on the newspaper articles cited here, I have also discussed the case with Professor B. He asked me to say, first, that the facts were themselves in dispute and, second, that he was cleared of all wrongdoing.

3 All this is quite sketchy. For a fuller statement of my views, see especially the following works: "Thinking Like an Engineer: The Place of a Code of Ethics in the Practice of a Profession," *Philosophy and Public Affairs*, 1991, vol. 20, pp. 150–67; "Professionalism Means Putting Your Profession First," *Georgetown Journal of Legal Ethics*, 1988, vol. 2, pp. 341–57; "Vocational Teachers, Confidentiality, and Professional Ethics," *International Journal of Applied Philosophy*, 1988, vol. 4, pp. 11–20; "The Use of Professions," *Business Economics*, 1987, vol. 22, pp. 5–10; and "The Moral Authority of a Professional Code," *NOMOS*, 1987, vol. 29, pp. 302–37.

4 I mean this in the sense that Ronald Dworkin does in *Law's Empire*, Cambridge, M.A., Harvard University Press, 1986. The place Dworkin assigns cases in the law corresponds more or less to the place I assign ethics cases in the development of any ethics literature.

5 I must say that I am inclined to reject the claim that crisis as such can explain current interest in academic ethics. The academy seems to have gone from one crisis to another for as long as I can remember. The McCarthy era was all but over when I started my first year, but the House Un-American Activities Committee was still a central concern of many students and faculty I knew. Soon, however, concern shifted to student rights. Then came the Vietnam war, ending with police and soldiers shooting live ammunition at students on campus. Four students were killed at Kent State and a half dozen more at Jackson State. After that, during the long years of academic depression, many institutions tried to manage themselves like businesses, dismantling unprofitable departments and turning many promising scholars out into a world that did not need their skills. Compared to those crises, the present crisis, if that is what it is, seems mild. Consider, for example, Howard J. Ehrlich, *Campus Ethnoviolence and the Policy Options: Institute Report*, vol. 4, Baltimore, M.D., National Institute Against Prejudice and Violence, 1990. His record of campus incidents for the years 1986–8 (and other evidence of widespread discrimination), though not inconsequential, seems tame compared to what (I suspect) he could have produced for the year 1960, 1970, and perhaps even 1980.

6 Steven M. Cahn, *Saints and Scamps: Ethics in Academia*, Totowa, N.J., Rowman and Littlefield, 1986. Other recent additions to this literature include Charles J. Sykes, *ProfScam: Professors and the Demise of Higher Education*, Washington, D.C., Regnery Gateway, 1988; Bruce

Wilshire, *The Moral Collapse of the University: Professionalism, Purity and Alienation*, Albany, N.Y., SUNY Press, 1989; Murray Sperber, *College Sport, Inc.: The Athletic Department vs. the University*, New York, Henry Holt, 1990; Roger Kimball, *Tenured Radicals: How Politics Has Corrupted Our Higher Education*, New York, Harper and Row, 1990; Dinesh D'Souza, "Illiberal Education," *Atlantic Monthly*, 1991, vol. 267, pp. 51–79; and, of course, Allan Bloom, *The Closing of the American Mind*, New York, Simon and Schuster, 1987. These works, though numerous, do not, strictly speaking, constitute a literature (hence my scarce quotes). A literature is cumulative, participants acknowledging one another's work, whether to draw on it, refute it, or improve it. Usually, a contribution to the "literature" of homily presents itself as a lone voice crying in the desert.

7 See, for example, the exchange between two Stanford professors, Charles R. Lawrence III, "Acknowledging the Victim's Cry," and Gerald Gunther, "Freedom for the Thought We Hate," in *Academe*, 1990, vol. 76, pp. 10–4. For thoughtful defense of treating questions of academic freedom as questions of ordinary workplace rights, see Robert Ladenson, "Is Academic Freedom Necessary?" *Law and Philosophy*, 1986, vol. 5, pp. 59–87.

8 Edward Shils, *The Academic Ethic: Report of a Study Group of the International Council on the Future of the University*, Chicago, University of Chicago Press, 1983. Among important examples of earlier work in this category, I would put the following: *Academic Freedom: The Scholar's Place in Modern Society*, Hans Baade and Robinson Everett (eds), Dobbs Ferry, N.Y., Oceana Publications, 1964; *Academic Freedom and Tenure: A Handbook of the American Association of University Professors*, Louis Joughin (ed.), Madison, WI, University of Wisconsin Press, 1969, especially the essays collected at the back; *The Concept of Academic Freedom*, Edmund L. Pincoffs (ed.), Austin, TX, University of Texas Press, 1972; and many of the papers in *The Ethics of Teaching and Scientific Research*, Sidney Hook, Paul Kurtz, and Miro Todorovich (eds), Buffalo, N.Y., Prometheus Books, 1977. On the other hand, I would not put in that category *Morality, Responsibility, and the University: Studies in Academic Ethics*, Steven M. Cahn (ed.), Philadelphia, PA: Temple University Press, 1990. Cahn the editor has made a significant contribution to academic ethics, as I use that term here, even if Cahn the writer has not. Much will be learned from comparing the papers in his collection with earlier work. Other recent contributions to the still tiny literature include: Louis G. Lombardi, "Character v. Codes: Models for Research Ethics," *International Journal of Applied Philosophy*, 1990, vol. 5, pp. 21–8; John Martin Rich, *Professional Ethics in Education*, Springfield, I.L., Charles C. Thomas, 1984; and Mary Ellen Waithe and David T. Ozar, "The Ethics of Teaching Ethics," *Hastings Center Report*, 1990, vol. 20, pp. 17–21.

9 Shils, *The Academic Ethic*, p. 12.

10 *AAUP Policy Documents and Reports*, Washington, D.C., American Association of University Professors, 1984, pp. 135–36, reprinted from *Academe*, 1969, vol. 55, pp. 86–87. Why this date for a code of ethics?

Other professions that organized about the same time as the AAUP published a code decades earlier.

11 This judgment is, however, not universal. See, for example, Page Smith, *Killing the Spirit: Higher Education in America*, New York, Viking, 1990. Curiously, thoughtful defenses of the academy (more or less) as it is are rare. One possible example, though quite old, is Carl L. Becker, "The Cornell Tradition: Freedom and Responsibility," in his *Cornell University: Founders and the Founding*, Ithaca, N.Y., Cornell University Press, 1943, pp. 193–204. (I owe this reference to Kevin Harrington.) The only recent defense I have found is Mortimer R. Kadish, *The Ethic of Higher Education*, Palo Alto, C.A., Stanford University Press, 1991. Kadish finds a principled place for much of what American universities do and offers a vocabulary adequate for discussing how much room to make for artists, poets, football players, and the like. But even Kadish's defense includes a sustained (and powerful) critique of recent developments.

12 Paragraph II of the AAUP Statement (the one concerned with teaching) does say that "[a professor] demonstrates respect for the student as an individual." This can be read as prohibiting Professor B's conduct. But I think that reading strained. Given the spirit of the Statement, the respect due to students as individuals can only mean respect-as-individual-searchers-after-knowledge, not respect in any sense sufficient to condemn what Professor B did. And, indeed, the very sentence in which this reference to respect appears, continued: "and adheres to his proper role as *intellectual* guide and counselor." *AAUP Policy Documents*, p. 135 (italics added).

13 Discriminary Conduct Policy: Regent Resolution, Racism and Discriminatory Conduct," October 1988, UMF Fac. Doc. No. 1670, Milwaukee: University of Wisconsin, 11 January 1990, p. 1. This policy applies to faculty as well as students. Most of the policies I have examined (Stanford, Michigan, and so on) apply only to students. Why?

14 UW, "Discriminatory Conduct Policy," p. 2.

15 Bernard Shaw, *The Doctor's Dilemma*, Baltimore, M.D., Penquin Books, 1954, p. 40. I am, of course, rejecting something like the "separatist thesis" defended, for example, in Benjamin Freedman, "A Meta-Ethics of Professional Morality," *Ethics*, 1978, vol. 89, pp. 1–19. Few, if any, writers on professional ethics still think that professional status can exempt one from the requirements of ordinary morality. For some of the reasons, see my "Moral Authority of a Professional Code"; Alan Gewirth, "Professional Ethics: The Separatist Thesis," *Ethics*, 1986, vol. 96, pp. 282–300; or David Luban, "The Adversary System Excuse," in *The Good Lawyer: Lawyers' Roles and Lawyers' Ethics*, Totowa, N.J., Rowman and Allanheld, 1984, pp. 84–113. The argument for institutional ethics would be much the same.

16 Compare Kadish, *The Ethic of Higher Education*, for example, pp. 109–10 (concerned with how to respond to an incident in which two drunken fraternity men accosted two black co-eds):

> Penalties…miss the essential point for an institution of higher education.…Not only had the women been assaulted, verbally if not physically; the action of liberal education had, to the

extent the malefactors had been exposed to it, failed, and the nature of the failure had been spread before the community in the character of the assault....Might the process of education have been organized not indeed to punish or even to rehabilitate the offenders but specifically to foster the development of persons for whom such miserable behavior would constitute an affront to themselves as well as to the women?"

3 THE NEW WORLD OF RESEARCH ETHICS: A PRELIMINARY MAP

This chapter began as a talk presented to Annual Spring Meeting of the Illinois Conference, American Association of University Professors, Chicago, 1 April 1989. I should also like to thank that audience of alert academics, as well as my co-panelist, Louis Lombardi, and my colleagues, Warren Schmaus and Vivian Weil, for helpful comments.

1 My italics.
2 By "recent," I mean "since 1982" (for reasons I explain in Section II below). Perhaps it is worth pointing out that engineering has not always been separated in this way. Consider, for example, Charles E. Reagan, *Ethics for Scientific Researchers*, 2nd edn., Springfield, IL, Charles C. Thomas, 1971, in which engineering examples do appear. Note too that, unlike his scientific examples, his engineering examples carry citations, indicating a pre-existing literature. That suggests yet another question I shall ask only to put aside: Why were the engineers so far ahead of the scientists in thinking about research ethics?
3 See, for example, Russell Jacoby's comments on David Abrahams in *The Last Intellectuals*, New York, Basic Books, 1987, p. 128.
4 See, for example, "Head of College Quits under Fire: Texan's Dissertation Was Found to Resemble Wife's," *New York Times*, 20 April 1969, p. 64. The historian in question, a friend of Lyndon Johnson, had just completed a term as an undersecretary at HEW. When I checked my memory of this case, I was surprised to learn that the Attorney General of Texas eventually ruled that the University of Texas could *not* revoke his doctorate, plagiarism or no. See "Ruling in Doctorate Dispute," *New York Times*, 16 September 1969, p. 26.
5 For example, one "model" for institutional policies defines "research fraud" as "a form of scientific misconduct involving deception." "Scientific" is nowhere defined. Association of American Universities, National Association of State Universities and Land-Grant Colleges, and Council of Graduate Schools, *Framework for Institutional Policies and Procedures to Deal with Fraud in Research* (4 November 1988), p. 2
6 Note that (as defined here) research ethics is not a mere department of academic ethics. Many researchers – perhaps half of all Ph.D.s – now work outside the academy. Why then have we so far had no research scandals involving non-academic researchers? Another question I ask only to put aside.
7 See, for example, Max Weber, *Wissenschaft als Beruf*, München, Duncker und Humblott, 1921; Robert Merton, "The Normative

Structure of Science," in *The Sociology of Science: Theoretical and Empirical Investigations*, Norman W. Storer (ed.), Chicago, University of Chicago Press, 1973, pp. 267–78; Talcott Parsons and Gerald M. Platt, *The American University*, Cambridge, M.A., Harvard University Press, 1973, especially Chapter 3.

8 Sigma Xi, *Honor in Science*, 2nd edn., New Haven, CT, Sigma Xi, 1986, p. 11.

9 See, for example, Peter B. Medawar, "The Strange Case of the Spotted Mice," *New York Review of Books*, 15 April 1975, p. 8; or Joseph Hixson, *The Patchwork Mouse*, Garden City, N.J., Anchor/Doubleday, 1976.

10 L.S. Hearnshaw, *Cyril Burt – Psychologist*, New York, Random House/Vintage Books, 1981.

11 William Broad and Nicholas Wade, *Betrayers of the Truth*, New York, Simon and Schuster, 1982.

12 See, for example, B.L. van der Waerden, "Mendel's Experiments," *Centaurus*, 1968, vol. 12, pp. 275–88.

13 Why has Sigma Xi's term, "honor in science" not caught on? Is "honor" – a term referring to reputation or a virtue (a certain kind of dependability) – just too old-fashioned?

14 See, for example, Sheldon Krimsky, "University Entrepreneurship and the Public Purpose," in *Biotechnology: Professional Issues and Social Concerns*, Paul DeForest *et al.* (eds), Washington, D.C., American Association for the Advancement of Science, October 1988, pp. 34–42. For a general analysis of conflict of interest, see Michael Davis, "Conflict of Interest," *Business and Professional Ethics Journal*, 1982, vol. 1, pp. 17–27; or the entry "Conflict of Interest" in *Encyclopedia of Applied Ethics*, ed. Ruth Chadwick, San Diego, CA: Academic Press, 1997, pp. 589–95.

15 *Sourcebook of Criminal Justice Statistics*, Washington, D.C., U.S. National Criminal Justice Information and Statistics Service, 1980, p. 228.

16 *Sourcebook*, p. 288.

17 The project, funded under the Ethics, Values, and Society section, National Science Foundation, was entitled *Ethics and Policy in Journal Publications* and ran from September 1985 to August 1988. The "principal Investigators" were John C. Bailar, Patricia Woolf, and the Council of Biology Editors.

18 For example, all academics are in principle subject to the Code of Ethics of the American Association of University Professors (AAUP). That code requires each faculty member "to seek and to state the truth as he sees it," "[to practice] intellectual honesty," "[to avoid] conflict of interest that may restrict his freedom of inquiry," and "[to acknowledge] academic debts." Though these requirements could be the basis for research ethics, how many academics even know they exist? (AAUP, "Statement on Professional Responsibility," *Codes of Professional Responsibility*, Rena A. Gorlin (ed.), Washington, D.C., Bureau of National Affairs, Inc., 1986.

19 My italics.

20 Consider, for example, the recent case of Shervert Frazier as described in: Morton Hunt, "Did the Penalty Fit the Crime?," *New York Times*

Magazine, 14 May 1989, pp. 36ff. Frazier was apparently guilty of negligent plagiarism of another's writing, not of research plagiarism. Yet, under Harvard's procedures, then considered among the best in force, he was so intimidated that he resigned both his Harvard professorship and his position at Belmont Hospital rather than submit to those procedures. Belmont soon rehired him. Harvard did not. My impression is that Harvard overreacted – in part perhaps to compensate for earlier failures to react enough but in part too because no one involved had a clear idea how to gauge the seriousness of Frazier's wrongdoing. (I owe this point to Carl Cohen.)

21 For a useful introduction to punishment theory, see my *How to Make the Punishment Fit the Crime*, Boulder, CO, Westview Press, 1992.

22 *Perspectives on the Professions*, Chicago, Center for the Study of Ethics in the Professions, Illinois Institute of Technology, 1989, vol. 8, pp. 4–5. That issue also includes a paper by Dow Woodward describing a course in bioethics he teaches in Stanford's Biology Department. For some other examples of courses in research ethics, see *Professional Ethics Report*, a Newsletter of the American Association for the Advancement of Science, Committee on Scientific Freedom and Responsibility, Professional Society Ethics Group, Washington, D.C., AAUP, 1989, vol. 7, p. 7.

23 For a theoretical justification of this commonsensical claim, see my "Explaining Wrongdoing," *Journal of Social Philosophy*, 1989, vol. 20, pp. 74–90.

24 Harvard has in fact adopted such a procedure. See Paul Strohm, "Professional Ethics and Scientific Misconduct," *Footnotes*, a publication of the American Association of University Professors, 1988, vol. 6, p. 1.

4 SCIENCE: AFTER SUCH KNOWLEDGE, WHAT RESPONSIBILITY?

Versions of this chapter have been presented to: the Philosophy Colloquium, Illinois Institute of Technology, 30 September 1992; the Wingspread Conference on *Knowledge and Responsibility: The Moral Role of Scientists*, Racine, Wisconsin, 9 October 1992; and the Philosophy Department, Wayne State University, 19 November 1992. I should like to thank those present, especially Bruce Russell, my commentator at Wayne, for many helpful comments. I should also like to thank the participants in the Wingspread conference for provoking the first draft and helping me to refine several of its successors; and to the editors of *Professional Ethics* for helping to give it its penultimate form.

1 Stanley Joel Rosen and Ruth Ellen Bulger, "The Social Responsibilities of Biological Scientists," *Science and Engineering Ethics*, 1997, vol. 3, pp. 137–44.

2 Albert H. Teich and Mark S. Frankel, *Good Science and Responsible Scientists* (Washington, DC, Directorate for Science and Policy Programs, American Association for the Advancement of Science, 1992, p. 15. "Stem" is, of course, ambiguous. It could mean "derives," or it could mean some weaker relation (for example, "is made reasonable

by"). Perhaps much talk that sounds like arguments attempting to derive special moral responsibility from what scientists are is, in fact, too loose to be counted in that category. Certainly, many of the examples scientists give of their special responsibilities, for example, not faking data, seem to be no more than requirements of ordinary morality ("Don't lie," "Don't cheat," and "Don't steal). Nevertheless, we will learn more about science if we try to take such talk seriously.

3 For how the professions do this, see my papers: "The Moral Authority of a Professional Code," *NOMOS*, 1987, vol. 29, pp. 302–37; "The Use of Professions," *Business Economics*, 1987, vol. 22, pp. 5–10; "Vocational Teachers, Confidentiality, and Professional Ethics," *International Journal of Applied Philosophy*, 1988, vol. 4, pp. 11–20; "Professionalism Means Putting Your Profession First," *Georgetown Journal of Legal Ethics*, 1988, vol. 2, pp. 352–66; "Thinking Like an Engineer: The Place of a Code of Ethics in the Practice of a Profession," *Philosophy and Public Affairs*, 1991, vol. 20, pp. 150–167; "Do Cops Really Need a Code of Ethics," *Criminal Justice Ethics*, 1991, vol. 10, pp 14–28; "Codes of Ethics, Professions, and Conflict of Interest: A Case of an Emerging Profession, Clinical Engineering," *Professional Ethics*, 1992, vol. 1, pp. 179–95; "Treating Patients with Infectious Diseases: An Essay in the Ethics of Dentistry," *Professional Ethics*, 1993, vol. 2, pp. 51–65; or "The State's Dr. Death: What's Unethical About Physicians Helping at Executions?," *Social Theory and Practice*, 1995, vol. 21, pp. 31–60.

4 I am not here making a point about trade secrets. While "my" discovery probably is a trade secret, my relation to it may leave me free to reveal it (though not to take documents concerning it printed at my employer's expense). See, for example, *Futurecraft v. Clary Corp.*, 205 C.A. 2nd 279 (1962).

5 For what "rational best" might mean (beyond the obvious deliberation in a "cool hour"), see my "Realistic Utilitarianism and the Social Conditions of Cognitive Psychotherapy," *Social Theory and Practice*, 1987, vol. 13, pp. 237–59.

6 This distinction between rules and principles seems to go back no further than the 1967 article, "The Model of Rules," reprinted in Ronald Dworkin, *Taking Rights Seriously*, Cambridge, M.A., Harvard University Press, 1977, pp. 15–45.

7 So, on this analysis, what Ross called "prima facie duties" are principles, and an "all things considered" judgment is a weighing up of principles. The result of such a weighing up, though a duty in some sense, is not a responsibility (in our sense). Our concern is not with any considerations relevant to determining what to do but with requirements (which differ from Ross' all-things-considered judgments in not necessarily being final determinations). See, W.D. Ross, *The Right and the Good*, London, Oxford University Press, 1930, especially, pp. 19–34.

8 For more on my views on moral theory, see "The Moral Legislature: Contractualism without an Archimedean Point," *Ethics*, 1992, vol. 102, pp. 303–18. I don't think anything I say in this article depends on accepting this view in particular. I use it simply because I prefer it to any other.

9 Compare, for example, Kristin Shrader-Frechette, *Ethics of Scientific Research*, Lanham, Maryland, Rowman & Littlefield, 1994, Chapter 4, which seems to make the error of trying to derive specific "responsibilities" from general principles.

10 Lawyers and philosophers will be aware of H.L.A. Hart's extensive discussion of four senses of "responsibility" in Chapter IX of *Punishment and Responsibility*, New York, Oxford University Press, 1968. I am here interpreting "responsibility" in the first of Hart's four senses (that is, as "role-responsibility" rather than "causal-responsibility," "liability-responsibility," or "capacity responsibility"). I have, however, taken for granted some connections between these four senses: in particular, that where one has a role-responsibility (a domain of duties or assigned tasks) for such-and-such and one is causally responsible for an unfavorable outcome, one may have to bear liability or blame for the outcome. For a less familiar analysis of responsibility, but one more useful for our purposes, see Kenneth Kipnis, "Professional Responsibility and the Responsibility of Professions," in *Profits and Professions: Essays in Business and Professional Ethics*, edited by Wade L. Robinson, Michael Pritchard, and Joseph Ellin (Humana Press: Clifton, N.J., 1983), pp. 9–22. Having noted that a responsibility is always a matter of concern, he goes on to define carrying out one's "substantive responsibility" as "[giving] these matters all the attention they are due" (suggesting a principle rather than a rule), p. 10. But subsequent discussion finds him very soon talking in terms of duties, obligations, and rules. I therefore take his initial formulation to be provisional.

11 How might we derive the rule "Parents, care for your children"? Why not from the rule of individual responsibility (discussed under arguments from complicity below)? "Care for your children" seems to be no more than a special case of going out of your way to help someone when, however inadvertently, you have put them in need of help.

12 Compare, for example, Peter Singer, "Famine, Affluence, and Morality," *Philosophy and Public Affairs*, 1972, vol. 7, pp. 229–43; Alan Gewirth, *Reason and Morality*, Chicago, University of Chicago Press, 1978, pp. 217–30; Joel Feinberg, "The Moral and Legal Responsibility of the Bad Samaritan," *Criminal Justice Ethics*, 1984, vol. 3, pp. 56–66; Patricia Smith, "The Duty to Rescue and the Slippery Slope Problem," *Social Theory and Practice*, 1990, vol. 16, pp. 19–41; John M. Whelan, "Charity and the Duty to Rescue," *Social Theory and Practice*, 1991, vol. 17, pp. 441–56; David Copp, "Responsibility for Collective Inaction," *Journal of Social Philosophy*, 1991, vol. 22, pp. 71–80; and Alison McIntyre, "Guilty Bystanders? On the Legitimacy of Duty to Rescue Statutes," *Philosophy and Public Affairs*, 1994, vol. 23, pp. 157–91. The equivalent rule for the Good Samaritan argument would be something like: *Go out of your way whenever, without breach of an important duty or great loss to yourself, you can substantially help someone in great need.* As a rule, this is quite demanding. For example, given how many needy people there are in the world, and how easily I could help them, this rule would seem to require me to forego every

luxury, sending the money so saved to one or another philanthropic organization (and Singer actually so argues).

13 For some idea of the dynamics of this, see my "Avoiding the Tragedy of Whistleblowing," *Business and Professional Ethics Journal*, 1989, vol. 8, pp. 3–19.

14 Some readers may be tempted to dismiss "me" as not a "real scientist" but merely an "applied scientist," "engineer," or even "technician." There are at least four reasons not to do this. First, not only would my status as a scientist probably be recognized in my official title (for example, Senior Research Scientist), but my work would probably be presented to the public as "scientific findings." Second, I would probably be listed as a scientist by the Census. Those who think I should not be should offer a criterion for counting scientists that could plausibly exclude "me" without excluding most of the 400,000 or so people we now count as scientists. Third, "I" would have had the training characteristic of people whom we generally call scientists (Ph.D. in physics, etc.). Surely, place of employment does not alone determine who is or is not a scientist. Fourth, my work was scientific in the sense that it consisted of uncovering new knowledge in a recognized field of science (radar imaging).

15 I owe this point to Jeff McMahan. I have omitted two phrases of exception ("without breach of duty" and "without great loss") because their inclusion would mean that the rule could not apply to "me." Increased attractiveness would have been paid for by irrelevance.

16 The obvious answer to this question, "gratitude," is considered below.

17 Richard Brandt made this suggestion in an unpublished "Note on Knowledge and Responsibility" (October 1992) prepared for the Wingspread conference. For a more extensive version of it, see Bentley Glass, "The Ethics Basis of Science," *Science*, 1965, vol. 150, pp. 1, 254–61.

18 The authority in question is, of course, "epistemic authority," not political or legal.

19 The argument from gratitude does better for the (large percentage of) scientists employed in a university or other public facility. But whatever special obligations they would have as a result of that is as academics, not scientists.

20 But (Warren Schmaus has suggested) scientists may be less accountable than these others. Perhaps. But that would need to be shown. My own experience (forms for NSF, NEH, and state universities) is contrary. And, even if the claim were true, there would remain the question of what obligations less accountability imposes. Certainly, we ought to be especially careful with government money if the government trusts us in a way it does not trust others (though whether we have a moral obligation to do this is less clear). But what has that to do with speaking out in the public interest?

21 John Rawls, *A Theory of Justice*, Cambridge, MA, Harvard University Press, 1971, especially pp. 136–42 and 196–9.

22 That is not to say no one has tried to do this. See, for example, Robert M. Veatch, "Professional Medical Ethics: The Grounding of its Principles," *Journal of Medicine and Philosophy*, 1979, vol. 4, pp. 1–19.

23 This rule is vague on how much help "you" must give. While the rationale for the rule seems to require the addendum "and continue to help
until he is no worse than you found him," that would make the rule
more demanding than our purposes require. There are good reasons to
reject the rule of individual complicity here even in the vaguer (and
therefore less demanding form) I have given it. For more on such rules,
see my "Famous Violinists, Foetuses, and the Right to Continued Aid,"
Philosophical Quarterly, 1983, vol. 33, pp. 159–78; and "Strasser on
Dependence, Reliance, and Need," *Philosophical Quarterly*, 1986, vol.
36, pp. 384–91.

24 I owe this version of the argument from individual complicity to
Francis Slakey (or, rather, to my initial misunderstanding of his argument for collective responsibility to organize as a profession discussed
in the next note).

25 Francis Slakey has suggested that scientists individually might have a
moral obligation to establish an organization to prevent the misuse of
the knowledge they individually produce. This seems to be another
version of the argument from individual complicity (though one
reminding me of Kant's justification of the state). While I think scientists have many good reasons to want such an organization, I don't see
any reason to believe that they are morally *required* to form one. This
version of the argument seems even less plausible than those allowing
individuals more freedom in the choice of means to accomplish the end
in view. I have therefore felt free to dismiss it in a mere note rather than
in the text.

26 There is one important exception to this rule. Those who benefit,
however unwillingly, from a wrong may have to compensate the
wronged party – with the limit of liability being the value of the benefit
in question. The theory seems to be one of unjust enrichment rather
than tort. I ignore this exception here because I cannot see how to turn
it into an argument for special responsibility relevant to "my" case.

27 There are, however, a few exceptions to this rule (or, to save the thesis, a
few hybrids) – most notably, the American Psychological Association
and the American Institute of Chemists. These have codes of ethics,
disciplinary committees, and the like just as (other) professional societies do. They are both technical and professional. I should perhaps
add that, while a scientific society can be professional and still be scientific (because concerned with science as such), not all organizations of
scientists are scientific societies. Consider, for example, a mutual insurance company organized to provide life or health insurance only to
scientists; or a pension fund run for, and by, scientists.

28 I believe this conclusion, however surprising to some, is consistent with
the way much of the its membership views the IEEE.

29 The APS's "Guidelines for Professional Conduct" (3 November 1991)
seems instructively confused about its status. The first paragraph identifies its audience as "Society members" and the code following as mere
"guidelines" (making the document sound like the advice a technical
society would give its members). But the third paragraph begins "Each
physicist" (not "each member of the Society") and declares the rules
following to be "minimal standards" (even though they are stated with

the "should" of principle or ideal rather than the "shall" of rule). It even declares the standards as critical to the "physics profession." The Guidelines conclude, "Physicists have an individual and a collective responsibility to ensure that there is no compromise with these guidelines." The APS's "guidelines" thus end in effect as a professional code, not a set of guidelines designed merely for members. No doubt, there is an interesting story behind this confused document.

30 II. Rules of Practice 1.a, *Code of Ethics for Engineers*, National Society of Professional Engineers (March 1985). Note that this code applies not just to members of the NSPE but to engineers as such. This is one feature distinguishing this as a professional code rather than a code of a (professional) society; the same is true of the most popular engineering code of ethics, that produced by Accreditation Board of Engineering and Technology (which differs from the NSPE's in many small ways).

31 NSPE Code III.4.

32 NSPE Code, II.1. Note that the Code of Ethics of the American Sociological Association (14 August 1989) resolves this conflict differently: "Sociologists have an obligation to disseminate research findings, except those likely to cause harm to clients, collaborators, and participants, or those which are property under formal or informal agreement."

33 For interesting discussions of justified departures from justified rules, see Mortimer R. Kadish and Sanford H. Kadish, *Discretion to Disobey: A Study of Lawful Departures from Legal Rules*, Stanford, CA, Stanford University Press, 1973, especially pp. 95–140; and Bernard Gert, *Morality: A New Justification of the Moral Rules*, New York, Oxford University Press, 1988, pp. 282–303.

34 Indeed, there may have been a time, perhaps only recently passed, when scientists did not want to form a profession at all but to operate more like free artists. See, for example, William M. Evans, "Role Strain and the Norm of Reciprocity in Research Organizations," *American Journal of Sociology*, 1962, vol. 68, no. 3, pp. 346–54.

5 UNIVERSITY RESEARCH AND THE WAGES OF COMMERCE

1 See, for example, Michael Davis, "Better Communications Between Engineers and Managers: Some Ways to Prevent Ethically Hard Choices," *Science and Engineering Ethics*, 1997, vol. 3, pp. 1–42.

2 The AAAS invited all members of the panel to contribute their papers to a volume. Most did (with Sheldon Krimsky replacing Mark Lappe). The result was Part I of *Biotechnology: Professional Issues and Social Concerns*, P. DeForest, M.S. Frankel, J.S. Poindexter, and V. Weil (eds), Washington, D.C., American Association for the Advancement of Science, Committee on Scientific Freedom and Responsibility, October 1988. While all the papers are worth reading, the most relevant here are: E.L. MacCordy, "The Impact of Proprietary Arrangements on Universities," pp. 12–9; J.S. Price, "Bridging the Gap Between Academia and Industry: The Scientist's Role," pp. 20–7; and R.N. Beachy, "Reflections of an Industry Supported University Scientist,"

pp. 28–33. My contribution to the volume (pp. 49–53) is a response to what the volume's other contributors wrote, *not* my response to what the other panelists said.

3 D. Blumenthal, M. Gluck, K.S. Louis, M. Sotto, D. Wise, "University-Industry Research Relationships in Biotechnology: Implications for the University," *Science*, 1986, vol. 232, pp. 1,361–6, at p. 1,364.

4 I am, by the way, far from being the only philosopher who thinks applied ethics has done much for theory (and for philosophy generally). See, for example, S. Toulmin, "How Medicine Saved the Life of Ethics," *Perspectives in Biology and Medicine*, 1982, vol. 25, pp. 736–50.

6 OF BABBAGE AND KINGS: A STUDY OF A PLAGIARISM

I should like to thank Herman Berg for calling my attention to his case (when he cornered me after my session with Nader), for providing all the documents cited in the text, for telling me what he remembered of events where no documents existed or where they gave only an incomplete picture, for reading and commenting on many drafts of this chapter, and correcting many errors. While he has done enough to be listed as co-author of this chapter, I have (with his permission) chosen to take full responsibility for what is written here so that I would be free of the constraints of dual authorship.

1 Actually, the letter's fame is a bit more complicated. Strictly speaking, not the French version but an 1843 retranslation into English is famous. This first appeared in a translation (by the Countess of Lovelace) of Menabrea's paper on the Analytical Engine. It was in this version that the Babbage letter became famous. See *The Works of Charles Babbage*, Martin Campbell-Kelly (ed.), New York, New York University Press, 1989, vol. 1, p. 25.

2 According to Berg, the purpose of this letter was not so much to inform HSS of his discovery as to inquire whether the discovery merited a prize or, at least, a letter of praise he might use to strengthen his claim that the *Annals* should publish a report of it.

3 Why did Berg not simply publish his discovery elsewhere? He tried, but there are not many journals in the history of computing. Those he wrote advised him that the *Annals* was the appropriate place for a note correcting a claim made in Van Sinderen's article.

4 Berg always admitted that it was possible that between March 1984 and early 1989 the Quetelet letter was moved to the Royal Library (and then back to the Royal Academy), but he could find no one who knew of such a move. Recently J.A.N. Lee, "On 'Babbage and Kings' and 'How Sausage Was Made': And Now the Rest of the Story," *IEEE Annals of the History of Computing*, 1995, vol. 17, pp. 7–23, only added to the mystery. One Mme. Wellens-De Donder informed him, through a third party, that the letter was in the Royal Library from 1964 to 1985 (where Berg's letter should have found it) and then moved to the Royal Academy (Lee, "And Now," pp. 15–6). Though Berg has a document purporting to come from the Royal Academy, it must have come from the Royal Library (using Royal Academy stationery?).

5 Only three of the eleven paragraphs Berg had before him – that is, the minute's introductory paragraph and two concluding paragraphs – were independent of his discovery.

6 See Campbell-Kelly, *Works of Babbage*, vol. 1, pp. 22–7. He has since denied responsibility for such details (Lee, "And Now," p. 18).

7 Berg considered the phrase in quotes to be a smoking gun. The exact words appear in the version of Babbage's letter Berg discovered but not in any of the others. Since Bromley did not suggest that he had already discovered the original letter on his own (or knew of it in some other way), that phrase demonstrates that his first knowledge of it must have come from Berg.

8 But see Lee, "And Now," p. 19 (Campbell-Kelly's description of how editorial work was done).

9 Lee, "And Now," p. 20.

10 For a somewhat better experience with the AHA, see Stephen Nissenbaum, "The Plagiarists in Academe Must Face Formal Sanctions," *Chronicle of Higher Education*, 28 March 1990, p. A52.

11 Out of desperation, or whimsy, Berg went even farther afield in search of a forum, but with no more success. The International Court of Justice at the Hague told him they had no jurisdiction (22 March 1990), as did the International Criminal Police Organization (2 July 1992). On the assumption that religions might be concerned with a violation of the Commandment "thou shalt not steal," Berg wrote a number of religious organizations. Some did not write back. Those that did – the Rabbinical Council of America (5 November 1990), the Church of Jesus Christ of Latter-Day Saints (11 March 1991), Bob Jones, Chancellor of Bob Jones University (23 June 1992), the Archbishop of Detroit (6 July 1992), the Archbishop of Milwaukee (23 July 1992), and even the Papacy (14 June 1991) – all declined to get involved.

12 For their own attempts to explain the silence (long after the events), see the letters of Bromley and Campbell-Kelly in *Accountability in Research*, 1994, vol. 3, pp. 282–9. While the question of motive is probably impossible to settle on the basis of the information we have or are likely to get, it is, of course, crucial to the *amount* of blame we assign in individual cases; and, for an institution, to designing means of prevention as well. For my own articles on the subject, see Michael Davis, "Of Babbage and Kings: A Study of a Plagiarism Complaint," *Accountability in Research* 2, Spring 1993, pp. 273–86, and Michael Davis, "Righting the History of Mathematics," *Mathematical Intelligencer* 16, Fall 1994, pp. 21–6.

13 After I published my first article on this case, the other side began to respond in print. Though adding many interesting details, the response is most interesting for what it reveals about how intelligent people can back themselves into a bad situation without realizing what they are doing. See especially Lee, "And Now."

14 What might that other side be? A curator at the British National Museum of Science and Industry ends a long friendly letter to Berg (23 June 1990) with the observation: "My knowledge of Prof. Allan Bromley, Dr. Martin Campbell-Kelly and [one more] makes it inconceivable that any one of them would actively repress any due

acknowledgement. I feel sure that there is some simple explanation that does not impugn them and at the same time duly puts the record straight. However, I remain handicapped by the lack of any hard facts about the discovery." After receiving copies of the relevant documents, he wrote Berg again (4 November 1991): "I remain convinced that you are a casualty of a number of factors that have combined and that there is an explanation that does not impugn the integrity of the scholars associated with the field." Unfortunately, he could not say what that explanation might be. He had to wait another four years before the principals bothered to provide what his faith hoped for.

15 Bromley was quite explicit while explaining why he was not responsible for failing to credit Berg (even though Bromley's name was prominent both in the *Collected Works* and in advertisements for it): the letter had been located independently by Jim Roberts, an independent scholar in London, who knew nothing of either Berg's discovery or Bromley's possession of a copy of it. Roberts goes unacknowledged anywhere in the *Collected Works*, even though he did an extensive and careful study of all the available Babbage correspondence. Why? The reason, according to Bromley, is that it "never crossed my mind to name the many people I knew to have seen or studied these archives." Lee, "And Now," p. 18. For how this looks to another academic, see C. Muses, "The unique reach of cybernetics in our *Fin-de-Siecle*," *Kybernetes*, 1995, vol. 24, no. 7, pp. 6–20, especially pp. 16–8.

16 I must admit to having little sympathy for this view. It seems to narrow the definition of scholarly plagiarism to what can be prosecuted in court as plagiarism (essentially, a violation of copyright). For courts, "plagiarism" is a technical term. Much that academics might consider plagiarism (for example, copying a method of tabulating data or using information another develops) receives legal protection through the law of patent, trade secrets, or the·like; or none at all. In any case, the narrow definition seems wrong as a matter both of usage and of scholarly policy. "Plagiarism" comes (according to my dictionary) from the Latin word for kidnapping (or plundering, especially the taking of someone's "slaves"). "Ideas" as well as "original words or writing" can be plagiarized. Talk of "plagiarizing discoveries" seems to stretch ordinary language not at all (though perhaps "plagiarizing an invention" does). More important, in the commerce of scholarship, one's discoveries are at least as important as one's writing and, as Berg's story makes clear, just as susceptible to being plundered (that is, used without the customary payment). Most, perhaps all, arguments against plagiarism in the narrow sense seem to be arguments against plagiarism in a sense broad enough to include using another's discovery without giving credit. The issue is not what plagiarism "is" so much as what forms of conduct (plagiarism or not) should be subject to formal disciplinary procedures, or at least embodied in explicit rules, and which should be left to the less formal procedures of the research community (as much promise breaking is).

17 This letter (18 May 1989) does not in fact refer to the *Works* but to Berg's general feeling that he had somehow become "unmentionable" in Babbage circles. Yet, though it was written before publication of the

Works, the distinction it makes, even the terms in which it makes it, seem prophetic (and hence, worth quoting at this point).

18 For one recent example of what can be done, see Thomas Mallon, *Stolen Words: Forays into the Origins and Ravages of Plagiarism*, New York, Ticknor and Fields, 1989, as well as Marcel LaFollette's careful survey of scientific misconduct, *Stealing into Print: Fraud, Plagiarism, and Misconduct in Scientific Publishing*, Berkeley, University of California Press, 1992. Here perhaps is the place to thank LaFollette for calling her book to my attention and to note that her analysis seems inadequate for Berg's case. On the one hand, Berg's complaint does not fit any cell of the table on p. 42. On the other hand, Berg does not fit her categorization of accusers (whistleblower, nemesis, or press), pp. 137–55. Berg is a victim, not a nemesis or whistleblower (although he seems to think of himself as a whistleblower). His association is personal in a way characteristic neither of the whistleblower (who breaks with their associates in order to inform the public) nor of the nemesis (who undertakes to undo a wrong in which he had no previous part). Berg is in search of personal reward, though a reward he thinks justice requires and the withholding of which reveals a profound corruption in a variety of institutions. While LaFollette's analysis is an important advance in our understanding of fraud, plagiarism, and related misconduct in science, it is, nonetheless, only *a* step.

7 ETHICS ACROSS THE CURRICULUM

1 Grants #DIR 9014220 (EVS) and #DIR 9601905 (EHR).
2 For more on this distinction (and an example of where it does matter), see Chapter 2.
3 See, for example, T.R. Martin, "Do Courses in Ethics Improve the Ethical Judgment of Students?," *Business and Society*, 1981/82, vol. 21–22, pp. 17–26; James Rest, "The Major Components of Morality," in *Morality, Moral Development, and Moral Behavior*, W. Kurtines and J. Gewirtz (eds), New York, Wiley, 1985, pp. 24–38; and John Frank Rice and Carl Bryant, "A Descriptive Study of Moral and Intellectual Development," *U.S Air Force Academic Journal of Professional Military Ethics*, 1988, pp. 35–9.
4 One indication of this is the number of accrediting organizations that now recommend or require training in ethics as part of the curriculum. For example, on 2 December 1988, engineering's accrediting body added this to its criteria for accreditation: "An understanding of the *ethical, social, economic and safety considerations* in engineering practice is essential for a successful engineering career. Course work may be provided for this purpose, but as a minimum it should be the responsibility of the engineering faculty to infuse professional concepts into all engineering course work." *Criteria for Accrediting Programs in Engineering in the United States (1989–1990 Academic Year)*, sec. IV.C.2.i., New York, Accreditation Board of Engineering and Technology, Inc., pp. 8–9.
5 For a good critique of the honors system, see the entire January issue of *Perspectives on the Professions*, 1995, vol. 14.

6 I have said nothing about team-taught courses because they seem to me *not* to get ethics into class in a way at once economical, permanent, and distinct from those ways already discussed. In theory, team-teaching seems to be an extended guest lecture (who the guest is depending on how the course is listed or packaged). Having a guest around all term may solve the problem of limited time, testing, and grading, but still seems likely to leave the impression that professional ethics is optional. Why else would technical faculty need someone outside the profession to teach the profession's ethics? In practice (at IIT), on the other hand, team-taught courses have often served the same purpose as a workshop. Faculty teach a course together for a time. Once each has learned enough from the other to teach on his own (a year or two), the team dissolves. Team-teaching a particular course seldom lasts long (in part, no doubt, because using two faculty to teach one course strikes most administrators as inefficient).

7 See, for example, Richard A. Matasar, "Teaching Ethics in Civil Procedure Courses," *Journal of Legal Education*, 1989, vol. 39, pp. 587–607. Though he became dean of IIT's law school, Matasar was at the University of Iowa's College of Law when this article was published.

8 *Chicago Tribune*, February 15, 1987. But see Terrence R. Bishop, "Integrating Business Ethics into An Undergraduate Curriculum," *Journal of Business Ethics*, 1992, vol. 11, pp. 291–9.

9 Arne P. Vesilund, "Rules, Ethics, and Morals in Engineering Education," *Engineering Education*, February 1988, vol. 77, pp. 289–93.

10 See, for example, my "Explaining Wrongdoing," *Journal of Social Philosophy*, 1989, vol. 20, pp. 74–90.

11 Because even our NSF reviewers took some convincing on this point, it may be worth quoting in full the argument we made:

> Ideally, perhaps, such a stipend should not be necessary. Faculty should flock to the workshop for the sheer joy of learning or because they recognize a duty to teach ethics they cannot satisfy without special training. Our core group of professional faculty have, however, told us that the reality at IIT is different. The letters of support from the deans of professional schools and chairs of professional programs here…tell the same story. Our Provost considers the stipends to be of such importance that he has agreed to commit IIT to pay half ($15,000 a year for three years).
>
> We are not alone in thinking such a stipend necessary. Cornell annually offers a summer workshop for Cornell faculty who want to learn ethical theory. Those attending the workshop also receive a substantial stipend. When we asked Walter Lynn, one of the organizers of the program the reason for the stipend, he made four points. First, attendance at a summer workshop is outside the normal academic work year. Unlike sitting on another committee, it is an additional responsibility deserving additional compensation. Second, paying workshop participants makes clear the priority the

workshop has in the economy of the university. Third, the workshop demands a genuine commitment. Participants have the same strict obligation to prepare for the workshop as for a class they teach. The stipend seals the obligation. And fourth, faculty always have deserving alternatives, most of which pay at least as well. Unless you want to preach only to the converted, you must put ethics on a par with its competitors (teaching, research, and consultation). The stipend is an important means of outreach.

12 *National Society of Professional Engineers Annual Meeting* (Educational Division), Charleston, SC, 21 January 1992; *Association of Practical and Professional Ethics Annual Meeting*, Indianapolis, IN, 6 March 1992; *Fifth Annual Working Conference on Critical Literacy and Critical Thinking*, Chicago, 2 April 1992; *Illinois Association of Graduate Programs in Public Administration Faculty Workshop on Ideas and Issues in Professional Education: Their Implications for Public Administration*, Chicago, 11 April 1992; University of Chicago *Interdisciplinary Conference on Human-Animal Interaction*, Chicago, 29 May 1992; *American Society of Engineering Education Annual Conference*, Toledo, OH, 24 June 1992; "Engineering Ethics: What Should We Be Teaching?" (Mini-Plenary), *American Society of Engineering Education*, Edmonton, Alberta, 26 June 1994; "Integrating Ethics into Chemistry," *Illinois Association of Chemistry Teachers Annual Meeting*, Normal, IL, 21 October 1994; "Ethics in Engineering and Technology: IIT's Experiments in the Pervasive Method," *Tennessee Academy of Science Annual Meeting* (Plenary Panel), Nashville, TN, 18 November 1994: "Integrating Ethics into Technical Courses; Report on a Four Year NSF Faculty Development Project" (panel), *Association for Practical and Professional Ethics*, Arlington, VA, 4 March 1995; and "Integrating Ethics into Technical Courses: An Experiment in its Fifth Year," *Values and Conflicts in the Training of Professionals: Third International Conference on Social Values*, St. Catherine's College, Oxford, England, 22 July 1995.

13 Actually, things were a bit more complicated. The first few efforts at case writing were, I think, failures. The cases were far too sketchy; we could not even tell whether there was an ethical issue.

14 This represents a small shift in the view I expressed in "Who Should Teach Workplace Ethics?," *Teaching Philosophy*, 1990, vol. 13, pp. 21–36. When I wrote that piece, I thought making arguments to professional faculty was enough. Experience has convinced me that it is only the beginning. One needs, in addition, to give them the classroom experience that lies behind the confidence with which philosophers make those arguments.

15 The three books were: Immanuel Kant, *Foundations of the Metaphysics of Morals*, trans. by Lewis White Beck, New York, Macmillan/Library of Liberal Arts, 1990; John Stuart Mill, *Utilitarianism*, Indianapolis, IN, Library of the Liberal Arts, 1957; and James Rachels, *Elements of Moral Philosophy*, New York, McGraw-Hill, 1986. The articles are listed in notes under the day they were assigned.

16 "Co-leader" is purposefully vague. While we had proposed a workshop in which Vivian Weil, CSEP Director, and I would be co-leaders, she was on leave in Washington when the first workshop was given. Patricia Werhane, Philosophy, Loyola University of Chicago, replaced her (bringing considerable experience with the workshops sponsored by Arthur Anderson for business school faculty interested in teaching business ethics). The second and third year went as originally proposed. The three workshops were otherwise so alike that I shall ignore most differences here.

17 Michael Davis, "The Ethics Boom: What and Why?," *Centennial Review*, 1990, vol. 34, pp. 163–86 (a version of chapter 1); a part of William F. May's "Professional Ethics: Setting, Terrain, and Teacher," from *Ethics Teaching in Higher Education*, Daniel Callahan and Sisela Bok (eds), New York: Plenum Books, 1980, pp. 212–9.

18 See works cited above.

19 This case is a slightly revised version of the first part of "Falsifying Data?," from Michael Pritchard, *Teaching Engineering Ethics: A Case Study Approach*, Kalamazoo, Center for the Study of Ethics in Society, Western Michigan University, 15 June 1992, pp. 276–9, included as well in Charles E. Harris, Jr. *et al.*, *Engineering Ethics: Concepts and Cases*, Belmont, CA, Wadsworth, 1995, pp. 80–3.

20 See Chapter 8 for one version of the seven-step method.

21 Actually, this occurred only the first year. In the second and third years the case discussion ran over and crowded out this preview.

22 Rachels, *Elements*, pp. 79–103 (Mill), 104–123 (Kant), and 12–24 (relativism). After the first year, we used the second edition (1991). Rachels' book (whatever the edition) received many compliments.

23 This is my reconstruction of the test. Neither of my co-leaders presented it this formally, and each gave it a somewhat different emphasis.

24 Bernard Gert, *Morality: A New Justification of the Moral Rules*, New York: Oxford University Press, 1988, especially pp. 284–5 (for the two lists).

25 John Rawls, *A Theory of Justice*, Cambridge, MA, Harvard University Press, 1971; and David Gauthier, *Morals By Agreement*, Oxford, Clarendon Press, 1986.

26 Alasdair MacIntyre, *After Virtue*, Notre Dame, IN, University of Notre Dame Press, 1984; and Lawrence C. Becker, *Reciprocity*, London, Routledge & Kegan Paul, 1986.

27 Michael Davis, "Thinking like an Engineer: The Place of a Code of Ethics in the Practice of a Profession," *Philosophy and Public Affairs*, 1991, vol. 20, pp. 150–67; and David Luban, "The Structure of Role Morality," from *Lawyers and Justice*, Princeton, NJ, Princeton University Press, 1988, pp. 128–47. The assigned reading also included a continuation of "Catalyst B."

28 I owe this idea to Jean B. Hunter, assistant professor, Bioprocess Engineering, Cornell University.

29 James Rest, "Can Ethics Be Taught," *Easier Said Than Done*, 1988, vol. 1, pp. 22–6; Thomas Lickona, "What Does Moral Psychology Have to Say to the Teacher of Ethics?," from Callahan and Bok, *Ethics Teaching*

and Higher Education, pp. 103–32, 1980, and Davis, "Who Should Teach Workplace Ethics?"

30 For more on these issues, see Chapter 9.

31 Caroline Whitbeck, "Teaching Ethics to Scientists and Engineers: Moral Agents and Moral Problems," *Science and Engineering Ethics*, 1995, vol 1, pp. 299–308.

32 My "Explaining Wrongdoing," *Journal of Social Philosophy*, 1989, vol. 20, pp. 74–90; and John D. Arras, "Getting Down to Cases: The Revival of Casuistry in Bioethics," *Journal of Medicine and Philosophy*, 1991, vol. 16, pp. 29–51.

33 Scheduling difficulties the first year forced us to break the group into two parts for these later sessions (each group about eight). Each group met twice (with some people switching from one group to another between the first and second meeting). Since even these small groups took most of the day to make their presentations, answer questions, and receive comments, we divided the group in subsequent years even when there were no scheduling problems.

34 Some faculty have experimented with having students sign off on each problem. If they sign off and the answer is right, they get a little extra credit. If the answer is wrong, they get no credit. They are advised that, if they are not sure they are right, they should not sign off. They will then be given partial or full credit, as appropriate, but no extra credit. In this way, students are forced to consider how reliable their work is. Some faculty like to tell students what would happen in real life if they were wrong. Donald Gotterbarn, not a workshop graduate but the one from whom I got the idea of signing off, likes to tell his students what the effect of an error in their work would be.

35 Would we have had greater attendence at the continuing seminar the first semester had we had someone talk about grading ethics in, say, an engineering course? Perhaps. It would certainly have been worth a try. Unfortunately, that idea did not occur to us the first year (and we would not have known who could have given it). By the second year, faculty seem to have had colleagues with whom they could discuss their worries.

36 The first year's fifteenth official participant, the chair of Civil Engineering, became seriously ill a week before the workshop began.

37 Question 3 similarly asked about increased knowledge; Question 5 asked about increased ability to deal with ethical issues.

38 Compare FIN 525 (4 of 7 yes to question 1) and CE 340 (18 out of 23). The only real exception to this favorable pattern was Applied Thermodynamics (MAE 301). The same instructor who got a good response from his basic Thermodynamics students (MAE 205), 15 yeses to 5 noes (with 2 neutrals) to question 1, got only 9 yeses to 12 noes (and 1 neutral) for Applied Thermodynamics. The instructor's analysis of this outcome is worth quoting:

> An answer that kept recurring,...even [when] students...thought the course had helped them clarify their ideas on ethics, was that somehow they did not think ethics should be part of a course like this. Surprisingly, this answer

was most frequent in...Applied Thermodynamics, which has a substantial design component, and deals more with real applications [than in the basic thermodynamics course]. I hope to refine my approach for next semester in the following way: make ethics discussion a more obvious part of...Applied Thermodynamics: assign homework where design decisions involving human factors are specifically requested. Discuss it early in semester.

8 CASE METHOD

This chapter began as a session I gave at the Rocky Mountain Workshop for Teaching Ethics in Research, University of Wyoming, 12 July 1996. It then became a paper presented at a Philosophy Colloquium, Illinois Institute of Technology, on 15 October 1996; and then an article in *Teaching Philosophy*, 1997, vol. 20, pp. 353 – 85. I should like to thank my "students" in Laramie both for assuring me that what I said was helpful and for adding significantly to what I had to say; my colleagues in Chicago for confirming most of what I thought I had observed and for correcting a few errors; and the editor of *Teaching Philosophy* for suggesting further improvements.

1 For a good summary of that literature, with lots of references, see Bruce A. Kimball, *The Emergence of Case Method Teaching, 1872–1990s: A Search for Legitimate Pedagogy*, Bloomington, IN, The Poynter Center for the Study of Ethics and American Institutions, Indiana University, April 1995. For a sampling of the vast literature on case method in business, see Hans E. Klein (ed.), *Case Method Research and Case Method Applications: Selected Papers of the Sixth International Conference on Case Method Research and Case Method Applications*, Waltham, MA, Bentley College, 22–4 May 1989.
2 See, especially, Albert R. Jonsen and Stephen Toulmin, *The Abuse of Casuistry: A History of Moral Reasoning*, Berkeley, University of California Press, 1988; John D. Arras, "Getting Down to Cases: The Revival of Casuistry in Bioethics," *Journal of Medicine and Philosophy*, 1991, vol. 16, pp. 29–51; and Christopher Miles Coope, "Does Teaching Cases Mislead Us About Morality?," *Journal of Medical Ethics*, 1996, vol. 22, pp. 46–52.
3 The best discussions of how to use cases to teach practical ethics I have come across are: John B. Matthews, Kenneth E. Goodpaster, and Laura L. Nash, *Policies and Persons: A Casebook in Business Ethics*, 2nd edn, New York, McGraw-Hill, 1991, pp. 1–7; Tom L. Beauchamp, *Case Studies in Business, Society, and Ethics*, 3rd edn, Englewood Cliffs, NJ, Prentice-Hall, 1993), pp. 1–13; and Charles E. Harris, Michael S. Pritchard, and Michael J. Rabins, *Engineering Ethics: Concepts and Cases*, Belmont, CA, Wadsworth, 1995, pp. 125–44.
4 Indeed, there is little more than the few remarks in Caroline Whitbeck, "Teaching Ethics to Scientists and Engineers: Moral Agents and Moral Problems," *Science and Engineering Ethics*, 1995, vol. 1, pp. 299–308.

5 For some idea of this criticism, especially in the legal case method's early years, see William P. LaPiana, *Logic and Experience: The Origin of Modern American Legal Education*, New York, Oxford University Press, 1994, especially pp. 132–47.

6 See, for example, *Harvard Case Histories in Experimental Science*, vol. I, edited and with forward by James Bryant Conant, Cambridge, MA, Harvard University Press, 1957.

7 For more on this, see Stephen Toulmin, "How Medicine Saved Ethics" in *New Directions in Ethics*, edited by Joseph P. DeMarco, New York, Routledge, 1986, pp. 265–81; and Chapter 1.

8 Some, however, are quite elaborate. See, for example, the "famous violinist" in Judith Jarvis Thomson, "A Defense of Abortion," *Philosophy and Public Affairs*, 1971, vol. 1, pp. 47–66. Theologians have a comparable tradition of "parables." What connection does that tradition have with the development of the case method in practical ethics?

9 While physicians seem to have used medical cases (both living patients and published reports) for teaching centuries before Harvard's law school coined the term "case method," physicians cannot claim to have invented the case method (any more than they can claim to have coined the term). Until the last few decades, physicians did not use cases as the standard method of instruction. Instead, they relied primarily on lecture, textbook, and laboratory, reserving the study of cases for the last stage of medical education, that is, for clinical training just before or after the MD. There is, however, some connection between the physician's use of clinical cases and the law school's case method, an analogy which (along with the scientific laboratory) seems to appear regularly in early defenses of the method.

10 What connection is there between the lawyer's use of "case" and the physician's? Probably no more than etymology. A case is literally a box, file, or other container; and, by extension, whatever it holds. No doubt both lawyers and physicians kept records of their work, organized by the individual served and then by the individual's problem, in containers of some sort, that is, in "cases." Hence, it would be only natural for both lawyers and physicians to refer to one of these records – and, by extension, to the events it described – as "a case."

11 Michael Davis and Frederick A. Elliston (eds), *Ethics and the Legal Profession*, Buffalo, NY, Prometheus Books, 1986.

12 Another piece of evidence that the business school's case method is not "natural" is that there exist dozens of books for business students on how to learn by the case method. See, for example, J. Kenneth Matejka and Thomas J. Cosse, *The Business Case Method: An Introduction*, Richmond, VA, Robert F. Dame, 1981, especially the fourteen questions "students may have," pp. 39–48, and the bibliography (with a list of other books of the same type). Vivian Weil recalls that Prof. X had his own explanation of what went wrong: "This works with cynical business students" (in effect, that the problem was not that we academics were unfamiliar with the business school's case method but that we were not sufficiently cynical).

13 Compare, for example, the relatively long cases in Tom L. Beauchamp's casebook, *Case Studies in Business, Society, and Ethics*, 3rd edn,

Englewood Cliffs, NJ, Prentice Hall, 1993, with the relatively short cases in the anthology which he edited with Norman Bowie, *Ethical Theory and Business* 4th ed., Englewood Cliffs, NJ, Prentice Hall, 1993.

14 Lon Fuller, "The Case of the Speluncean Explorers," *Harvard Law Review*, 1949, vol. 62, pp. 616–45.

15 A case which includes a descriptive commentary is often called "a case study" to distinguish it from a mere case. For an example of a descriptive commentary, see Paula Wells, Hardy Jones, and Michael Davis, *Conflict of Interest in Engineering*, Dubuque, IA, Kendall/Hunt, 1986.

16 This rule is, I am afraid, only formally true. Some stories, though they can be turned into problems (in a sense), cannot be turned into problems successfully. In famous cases, students may recognize the story behind the problem, adding the ending themselves. The problem will then behave exactly like a story.

17 Whitbeck, "Moral Agents," p. 300: "The judgments offered as responses to intellectual puzzles are…just the 'kibitzing' of a critical spectator."

18 Compare Whitbeck, "Moral Agents," p. 302: "Of course, the best problem is an actual problem that a student is experiencing.… Problem statements may, if carefully crafted, simulate many features of an actual ethical problem however." The best problem is an actual problem *only if* all else is equal, that is, if the problem is on the right subject, does not involve too much risk, is of manageable size, and so on. Generally, all else is far from equal. Whitbeck is, I think, in effect wishing the classroom were the clinic.

19 Kohlbergian experiments with enhancing moral judgment, both his experiments and those of most of his successors, were done using relatively unrealistic hypotheticals. Only Muriel Bebeau has published much in which the cases used were real. And she has, I believe, done no comparison of results obtained for hypotheticals with results obtained from real (or at least realistic cases). See, for example, Muriel Bebeau, "Designing an Outcome-Based Ethics Curriculum on Moral Reasoning: Strategies and Evidence of Effectiveness," *Journal of Moral Education*, 1993, vol. 22, pp. 313–26; or Muriel Bebeau, "The Impact of a Dental Ethics Curriculum on Moral Reasoning," *Journal of Dental Education*, 1994, vol. 58, pp. 684–92. There is, then, no scientific evidence for the claim that real cases are better for teaching moral judgment than hypothetical cases. The alleged superiority of first-job over top-level cases rests on even less evidence than that. Because it is generally unwise to claim to know (in advance) what experiment will show, I do not think we should accept Whitbeck's claim that one sort of case is better than another unless she can offer unusually powerful arguments. She has yet to offer anything of the sort (and, given the great variety of ways in which students learn, I doubt she ever will).

20 For a collection of cases, many of which are multi-stage, see Michael S. Pritchard (ed.), *Teaching Engineering Ethics: A Case Study Approach*, Kalamazoo, MI, Center for the Study of Ethics in Society, Western Michigan University, 15 June 1992. Pritchard's suggestions on how to use his cases, pp. 1–22, include several useful insights into the case method.

21 Based on case developed in P. Aarne Vesilund, *Introduction to Environmental Engineering*, Boston, PWS Publishing Co., 1997.

22 Indeed, there is evidence that (something like) the "Socratic method" was used in legal education at least a half century before the case method. See, for example, William P. LaPiana, *Logic and Experience*, New York, Oxford University Press, 1994, p. 48.

23 Law professors will, of course, profess ignorance of what the courts *will* do. Generally, however, they do not profess ignorance of what the courts have done. They will often point out trends and, based on them, make predictions. They will even offer (what they will describe as) "the better view" on some controversial legal question. The better view (that is, the view they hold) may or may not be the "majority view" (the view of a majority of courts or scholars).

24 For example, when I took Criminal Law, one of the final exam questions I had to answer concerned Siamese twins, adults but still joined at the hip, one of whom had been convicted of murder and sentenced to life in prison, the other of whom was entirely innocent: could the first be sent to prison if he could not be severed from the second without causing death?

25 Business professors generally do not employ the sarcastic method. Business does not reward the lawyer's hardness. The business school's version of hardness is a kind of calculated self-serving.

26 See, for example, Moshe M. Blatt and Lawrence Kohlberg, "The Effects of Classroom Moral Discussion Upon Children's Level of Moral Judgment," *Journal of Moral Education*, 1975, vol. 4, pp. 129–61; or Robert M Liebert, "What Develops in Moral Development?," in *Morality, Moral Behavior, and Moral Judgment*, William M. Kurtines and Jacob L. Gewirtz (eds), New York, John Wiley & Sons, 1984, pp. 177–92.

27 For a (rare) casebook designed for this purpose, see Philip E. Davis (ed.), *Moral Duty and Legal Responsibility*, New York, Appleton-Century-Crofts, 1966.

28 A course can, of course, be a mixture of theoretical and practical ethics. And, indeed, in practice many "baby ethics" courses (such as Moral and Social Values) are. Such a mixed course may mix theoretical with practical uses of cases. The distinction made here may nonetheless be useful for understanding what an instructor in such a course is doing with a case at any moment.

29 While social issues courses do reach some issues belonging to political philosophy or political theory, they generally stay closer to questions of ethics (how we should act) rather than political philosophy (what government should do). Social issues courses are more likely to become a hybrid of philosophical ethics and practical ethics than of political philosophy and practical ethics.

30 Though such courses generally transmit a good deal of information (for example, how abortions are performed, how often, and by whom) and may also increase student willingness to act on what they believe to be right, the courses do not generally have either of these accomplishments among the stated purpose.

31 See Blatt and Kohlberg, "Discussion."

32 Compare Whitbeck, "Moral Agents," pp. 306–7.
33 For an example of using this method to generate a code of ethics for a profession, see Donn B. Parker, Susan Swope, and Dr. Bruce N. Baker, *Ethical Conflicts: Information and Computer Science, Technology, and Business*, Wellesley, MA, QED Information Sciences, Inc., 1990. I owe this reference to Jack Snapper.
34 For more on ethics bowl, see "Ethics Bowl at Annual Meeting," *Speaking Ethically*, 1996, vol. 5, p. 4, or contract the inventor, Robert Ladenson, Center for the Study of Ethics in the Professions, Illinois Institute of Technology, Chicago, IL 60616; phone 312–567–3474, fax 312–567–3016, or e-mail ladenson@charlie.cns.iit.edu.

9 A MORAL PROBLEM IN THE TEACHING OF PRACTICAL ETHICS

I read versions of this chapter to the Philosophy Colloquium, Illinois Institute of Technology, 17 September 1990; and to the Philosophy Department, DePaul University, 18 January 1991. I thank those present (and the editors of *Teaching Philosophy*) for their helpful comments.

1 See my "Avoiding the Tragedy of Whistleblowing," *Business and Professional Ethics Journal*, 1989, vol. 8, pp. 3–19. The problem assumes that I have this right. In fact, all I know is that I have good reason to believe I do. I should, of course, make that clear to my students.
2 Interestingly, I did not see the problem until others pointed it out. The obvious is not obvious until we see it. Here, then, is the place to thank Mishilam Groper for questioning the moral appropriateness of the advice I gave in "Reflections on the Fate of Whistleblowers," Mechanical Engineering Bi-Weekly Seminar Series, Western Michigan University (3 October 1989); and Michael Pritchard for reformulating Groper's question then and in several letters afterward – until I realized how deep it was – and for helpful comments on the first draft of what became this chapter.
3 For some evidence for this claim, see my "Who Should Teach Workplace Ethics?" *Teaching Philosophy*, 1990, vol. 13, pp. 21–38, especially n. 10.
4 For reasons to doubt this assumption, see my "Explaining Wrongdoing," *Journal of Social Philosophy*, 1989, vol. 22, pp. 74–90.
5 My point here is a moral one, but the law seems to adopt much the same view. For a recent discussion of criminal liability for aiding or assisting, see R.A. Duff, "'Can I help you?' Accessorial Liability and the Intention to Assist," *Legal Studies*, 1990, vol. 10, pp. 165–81.
6 The point seems to be quite old. Plato already raises it, for example, by putting this claim into the mouth of Gorgias: "And suppose a man who has been the pupil of a palaestra and is a skillful boxer, and in the full-ness of his strength he goes and strikes his father or mother or one of his familiars or friends, that is no reason why the trainer or master of fence should be held in detestation or banished" (*Gorgias*, p. 457). Socrates treats this claim roughly, especially when made on behalf of those teaching something more than a physical skill. I should like to thank Fay Sawyier for reminding me of this passage.

7 Compare Robert K. Fullinwider, "Moral Conventions and Moral Lessons," *Social Theory and Practice*, 1989, vol. 15, pp. 321–38.

8 Do I in fact have a stronger argument? After all, insofar as my students know that they are avoiding a morally risky job – and avoids it for morally good reasons (for example, to avoid causing others harm) – are they not (all else equal) of better character than if they took the job without realizing what they risked? The cloistered virtue I teach must include a moral sensitivity that one who does not know how to avoid morally risky jobs must lack. My students' character is therefore morally better because of what I taught. I owe this argument to Jill Gordon.

9 Compare Mortimer R. Kadish and Sanford H. Kadish, *Discretion to Disobey*, Stanford, CA, Stanford University Press, 1973.

10 SEX AND THE UNIVERSITY

A version of this chapter was presented to the Philosophy Colloquium, Illinois Institute of Technology, on 24 February 1998. I should like to thank those present, as well as Ruth Chadwick and Deborah Jones, for many helpful comments.

1 "Discriminatory Conduct Policy: Regent Resolution, Racism and Discriminatory Conduct," October 1988, UMF Fac. Doc. No. 1670, Milwaukee: University of Wisconsin, 11 January 1990, p. 1.

2 I shall hereafter avoid the term "gender" to avoid the technical distinction between "gender" and "sex" now common in gender studies but not outside, preferring ordinary language approximations of that distinction.

3 I have not chosen the term "copulation" without considering alternatives. What I want is a term that emphasizes those physical aspects of sex (both heterosexual and homosexual) most likely to be the subject of moral controversy, while remaining within the bounds of academic propriety. I rejected "making love" as too fuzzy; "having sex with" as awkward, since it has no simple noun form; and "penetration" because lesbian copulation does not require a phallus. I reserve "sexual relations" for the complex social activity in which, at least potentially, copulation is a central and reoccurring feature. My difficulty in hitting upon good terms in this discussion may suggest, what I think true, that we are in process of rearranging our understanding of sexuality.

4 I am not, please note, claiming that sex is everywhere and always the same. Much of what counts as specifically sexual conduct or sexual identity is certainly socially constructed. For example, not every society need count facial hair as masculine or child-care as women's work; nor need every society treat sex (as we commonly do) as an absolute difference rather than, say, a continuum. My point is much more modest. Given human biology, every society is more or less obliged to distinguish those who can bear children from those who cannot and those who can impregnate from those who cannot. The social construction of sex is necessary in a way the social construction of race is not.

5 Of course, women were seldom totally absent from the university. For example, even in Harvard's first decades, the president's wife had an important place in the economy of the institution. Frederick Rudolph, *The American College and University*, New York, Alfred A. Knopf, 1962, pp. 26–7.

6 The parenthesis is meant to remind us of the great gap that separates us from early supports of higher education for women. So, for example, were Ezra Cornell to visit the university to which he admitted women in 1872, he could not be happy with the "masculine" manners of today's female students, their "masculine" dress, or even their "masculine" participation in sport. That was precisely what he had to be assured would not happen. Rudolph, *American College*, 316–7.

7 *United States v. Virginia*, 116 S. Ct. 2254 (1996). So, for example, the majority opinion notes (at 2273): "The VMI Alumni Association has developed a network of employers interested in hiring VMI graduates. The Association has agreed to open its network to VMIL graduates [the women's equivalent of VMI]...but those graduates will not have the advantage afforded by a VMI degree."

8 Another weakness, no doubt, is the assimilation of university action (when it establishes a dormitory or recognizes a fraternity) to the private action of students (for example, when they club together to rent an apartment in the open market). Like individual faculty, universities as a whole have special obligations to students, obligations beyond the fair dealing every seller in the market has to every buyer. I ignore those obligations here because I have, I think, said enough about them in Chapter 9 to make a similar discussion here unnecessary.

9 How, for example, are we to balance the advantage to women of having women's universities that would seek out female faculty members, thus assuring more jobs of women with PhDs, against the advantage to women of integrated universities in which they would study under the best people in their field (most of whom might be men)?

10 Though the demands of women certainly have given that debate new life, their demands are not the only ones that have done that. The demands of the handicapped for teams of their own have added another dimension, forcing us to consider even more carefully than women's sports do what sports do for a university.

11 I ignore both vasectomies and condoms here because vasectomies are rare among students and condoms cost so little. I also ignore the birth control and abortion a male student may have to buy for his sexual partner, in part because most male students are not married (or otherwise committed to sharing such costs), but in part too because I consider the university's responsibility for sexual partners later.

12 *1996–97 Student Handbook*, Chicago, Illinois Institute of Technology, 1996, p. 72.

13 ibid.

14 *IIT Handbook*, p. 87.

15 Appendix 1, *Date Rape: Feminism, Philosophy, and the Law*, edited by Leslie Francis, University Park, PA, Pennsylvania State University Press, 1996, p. 139.

16 Francis, *Date Rape*, p. 140.

17 See especially Alan Sobel, "Antioch's 'Sexual Offense Policy': A Philosophical Exploration," *Journal of Social Philosophy* 28 (Spring 1997), 22–36.

18 Jane Gallop, *Feminist Accused of Sexual Harassment*, Durham, NC, Duke University Press, 1995, pp. 41–2.

19 ibid.

20 The words in parentheses evade an objection only a philosopher would raise; that is, that I am ignoring one other alternative, *killing* one's sexual partner immediately after having sex. That alternative, though an effective means of foreclosing later conflicts of interest, is, of course, a good example of a cure (morally) worse than the disease.

21 Compare Elliot Cohen, "Psychological Counselors-Educators: Some Conflicts of Interest, *Perspectives on the Professions* 17 (Fall 1997), 8–9.

22 The problem with religious premises here is not that they are false or otherwise illicit but that they are likely to generate arguments convincing only to co-religionists. As a philosopher, I am in search of arguments convincing to all rational persons (or, at least, all those likely to be interested in this subject). Compare my comments on religion in Chapter 1.

23 The appeal of the argument from role models does not seem to depend on empirical evidence. What appeal to the argument includes any reference to an empirical study?

24 I would take the same approach to recent concern over the sexual bias of the Scholastic Aptitude Test (SAT), a test widely used in the United States in deciding both whom to admit to the university and whom to give scholarships. Women now tend to score slightly lower on both the verbal and math sections of the SAT even though the SAT is supposed to predict first-year performance in college and women generally do slightly better in the first year than men. The cause of this anomaly seems to be a small number of questions on which men tend to do better than women. No doubt sexual bias has played a role in allowing such an anomaly to continue. Yet, the strongest objection to the use of those questions is not that they bias the SAT against women (although they do) but that they make it a less reliable indicator of first-year success than it should be. Because of that reduced reliability, some people (mostly women) who deserve to get into a better school will end up in a worse one and some who deserve a scholarship will not get it. So, using the SAT without the appropriate correction is unjust (mostly to women, but also to all others who suffer as a result).

25 This answer, though an improvement on his first, still left something out. He was still treating an engineer's judgment – and, by implication, all professional judgment – as a mere side constraint on what the manager could do. It had not yet occurred to him that he, the manager, might be wrong about what should be done, that it might be in his interests and the interests of his employer not to obscure the conflict between his judgment and that of a well-informed professional on whom he called for advice. But that insight had to wait for another day.

BIBLIOGRAPHY

Accreditation Board of Engineering and Technology, Inc. (1989) *Criteria for Accrediting Programs in Engineering in the United States (1989–1990 Academic Year)*, New York, Accreditation Board of Engineering and Technology, Inc.

Alger, Philip L. *et al.*, *Ethical Problems in Engineering* (1965) New York, John Wiley.

AAUP Policy Documents and Reports (1984) Washington, DC, American Association of University Professors.

Arras, John D. (1991) "Getting Down to Cases: The Revival of Casuistry in Bioethics", *Journal of Medicine and Philosophy*, vol. 16, pp. 29–51.

Association of American Law Schools (1962) *Selected Readings on the Legal Profession*, St. Paul, MN, West.

Association of American Universities, National Association of State Universities and Land-Grant Colleges, and Council of Graduate Schools (1988) *Framework for Institutional Policies and Procedures to Deal with Fraud in Research* (4 November).

Baade, Hans and Everett, Robinson (eds) (1964) *Academic Freedom: The Scholar's Place in Modern Society*, Dobbs Ferry, NY, Oceana Publications.

Babbage, Charles (1830) *Reflections on the Decline of Science in England*, Cambridge, Cambridge University Press.

Baum, Robert J. (1980) *Ethics and Engineering Curricula*, Hastings-on-Hudson, NY, The Hastings Center.

Beauchamp, Tom L. (1993) *Case Studies in Business, Society, and Ethics*, 3rd edn, Englewood Cliffs, NJ, Prentice Hall.

Beauchamp, Tom L. and Norman Bowie (eds) (1993) *Ethical Theory and Business*, 4th edn, Englewood Cliffs, NJ, Prentice Hall.

Bebeau, Muriel (1993) "Designing an Outcome-Based Ethics Curriculum on Moral Reasoning: Strategies and Evidence of Effectiveness", *Journal of Moral Education*, vol. 22, pp. 313–26.

—— (1994) "The Impact of a Dental Ethics Curriculum on Moral Reasoning", *Journal of Dental Education*, vol. 58, September, pp. 684–92.

Becker, Carl L. (1943) *Cornell University: Founders and the Founding*, Ithaca, NY, Cornell University Press.

Becker, Lawrence C. (1986) *Reciprocity*, London, Routledge & Kegan Paul.

Bishop, Terrence R. (1992) "Integrating Business Ethics into An Undergraduate Curriculum", *Journal of Business Ethics*, vol. 11, April, pp. 291–99.

Black's Law Dictionary (1968), St. Paul, MN, West.

Blatt, Moshe M. and Lawrence Kohlberg (1975) "The Effects of Classroom Moral Discussion Upon Children's Level of Moral Judgment", *Journal of Moral Education*, vol. 4, February, pp. 129–61.

Bloom, Allan (1987) *The Closing of the American Mind*, New York, Simon & Schuster.

Blumenthal, D., Gluck, M., Louis, K. S., Sotto, M. and Wise, D. (1986) "University-Industry Research Relationships in Biotechnology: Implications for the University," *Science*, vol. 232, June 13, pp. 1361–6.

Bond, Jesse Hickman (1915) *The Teaching of Professional Ethics in the Schools of Law, Medicine, Journalism and Commerce in the United States*, PhD dissertation, University of Wisconsin.

Bowman, Jim (1990) "Watch More than P's and Q's," *Chicago Tribune*, 21 April, Section 1, p. 12.

Brantingham, Paul and Patricia Brantingham (1984) *Patterns in Crime*, New York, Macmillan.

Broad, William and Nicholas Wade (1982) *Betrayers of the Truth*, New York, Simon & Schuster.

Brody, Howard (1976) *Ethical Decisions in Medicine*, Boston, Little.

Cahn, Steven M. (1986) *Saints and Scamps: Ethics in Academia*, Totowa, NJ, Rowman & Littlefield.

—— (ed.) (1990) *Morality, Responsibility, and the University: Studies in Academic Ethics*, Philadelphia, PA, Temple University Press.

Campbell-Kelly, Martin (ed.) (1989) *The Works of Charles Babbage*, New York, New York University Press.

Camper, John (1990) "Loyola Struggling to Handle New Racial Tensions: Professor's Remark Sets Off Firestorm," *Chicago Tribune*, Sunday, April 15, Section 2, p. 1 ff.

Cohen, Elliot (1997) "Psychological Counselors-Educators: Some Conflicts of Interest, *Perspectives on the Professions*, vol. 17, Fall, pp. 8–9.

Conant, James Bryant (ed.) (1957) *Harvard Case Histories in Experimental Science*, vol. I, Cambridge, MA, Harvard University Press, 1957.

Coope, Christopher Miles (1996) "Does Teaching Cases Mislead Us About Morality?", *Journal of Medical Ethics*, vol. 22, no. 1, pp. 46–52.

Copp, David (1991) "Responsibility for Collective Inaction", *Journal of Social Philosophy*, vol. 22, Fall, pp. 71–80.

Countryman, Vern and Ted Finman (eds) (1966) *The Lawyer in Modern Society*, Boston, Little.

Davis, Michael (1982) "Conflict of Interest," *Business and Professional Ethics Journal*, vol. 1, Summer, pp. 17–27.

—— (1983) "Famous Violinists, Foetuses, and the Right to Continued Aid", *Philosophical Quarterly*, vol. 33, Summer, pp. 159–78.

—— (1986) "Strasser on Dependence, Reliance, and Need", *Philosophical Quarterly*, vol. 36, Summer, pp. 384–91.

—— (1987a) "The Moral Authority of a Professional Code," *NOMOS XXIX: Authority Revisited*, J. Roland Pennock and John W. Chapman (eds), New York, New York University Press, pp. 302–37.

—— (1987b) "The Use of Professions," *Business Economics*, vol. 22, October, pp. 5–10.

—— (1987c) "Realistic Utilitarianism and the Social Conditions of Cognitive Psychotherapy", *Social Theory and Practice*, vol. 13, Summer, pp. 237–59.

—— (1988a) *Codes of Ethics in Business*, Kalamazoo, MI, Center for the Study of Ethics in Society, Western Michigan University.

—— (1988b) "Vocational Teachers, Confidentiality, and Professional Ethics", *International Journal of Applied Philosophy*, vol. 4, Spring, pp. 11–20.

—— (1988c) "Professionalism Means Putting Your Profession First", *Georgetown Journal of Legal Ethics*, vol. 2, Summer, pp. 352–66.

—— (1989a) "Explaining Wrongdoing," *Journal of Social Philosophy*, vol. 20, Winter, pp. 74–90.

—— (1989b) "Avoiding the Tragedy of Whistleblowing", *Business and Professional Ethics Journal*, vol. 8, Winter, pp. 3–19.

—— (1990a) "Who Should Teach Workplace Ethics?", *Teaching Philosophy*, vol. 13, March, pp. 21–36.

—— (1990b) "The Ethics Boom: What and Why?", *Centennial Review*, vol. 34, Spring, pp. 163–86.

—— (1991a) "Thinking Like an Engineer: The Place of a Code of Ethics in the Practice of a Profession", *Philosophy and Public Affairs*, vol. 20, Spring, pp. 150–67

—— (1991b) "Do Cops Need a Code of Ethics?", *Criminal Justice Ethics*, 1991, vol. 10, Summer/Fall, pp. 14–28.

—— (1992a) *How to Make the Punishment Fit the Crime*, Boulder, CO, Westview Press.

—— (1992b) "The Moral Legislature: Contractualism without an Archimedean Point", *Ethics*, 1992, vol. 102, January, pp. 303–18.

—— (1992c) "Codes of Ethics, Professions, and Conflict of Interest: A Case of an Emerging Profession, Clinical Engineering", *Professional Ethics*, vol. 1, Spring/Summer, pp. 179–95.

—— (1993a) "Treating Patients with Infectious Diseases: An Essay in the Ethics of Dentistry", *Professional Ethics*, vol. 2, Spring/Summer, pp. 51–65.

—— (1993b) "Of Babbage and Kings: A Study of a Plagiarism Complaint," *Accountability in Research* 2, Spring, pp. 273–86.

—— (1994) "Righting the History of Mathematics," *Mathematical Intelligencer* 16, Fall, pp. 21–6.

—— (1995) "The State's Dr. Death: What's Unethical About Physicians Helping at Executions?", *Social Theory and Practice*, vol. 21, Spring, pp. 31–60.

—— (1997a) "Better Communications Between Engineers and Managers: Some Ways to Prevent Ethically Hard Choices", *Science and Engineering Ethics*, vol. 3, April, pp. 1–42.

—— (1997b) "Conflict of Interest" in Ruth Chadwick (ed.) *Encyclopedia of Applied Ethics*, San Diego, CA, Academic Press, pp. 589–95.

Davis, Michael and Frederick A. Elliston (eds) (1986) *Ethics and the Legal Profession*, Buffalo, NY, Prometheus Books.

Davis, Philip E. (ed.) (1966) *Moral Duty and Legal Responsibility*, New York, Appleton-Century-Crofts.

DeForest, P., Frankel, M. S., Poindexter, J. S., and Weil, V. (eds) (1988) *Biotechnology: Professional Issues and Social Concerns*, Washington, DC, American Association for the Advancement of Science, Committee on Scientific Freedom and Responsibility, October.

Dewey, John and Tufts, James H. (1908) *Ethics*, New York, Henry Hold.

D'Souza, Dinesh (1991) "Illiberal Education", *Atlantic Monthly*, vol. 267, no. 3, pp. 51–79.

Duff, R.A. (1990) "'Can I help you?' Accessorial Liability and the Intention to Assist," *Legal Studies*, vol. 10, Fall, pp. 165–81.

Dworkin, Ronald (1977) *Taking Rights Seriously*, Cambridge, MA, Harvard University Press.

—— (1986) *Law's Empire*, Cambridge, MA, Harvard University Press.

Edwards, Paul (ed) (1967) *Encyclopedia of Philosophy*, New York, Macmillan.

Ehrlich, Howard J. (1990) *Campus Ethnoviolence and the Policy Options: Institute Report*, vol. 4, Baltimore, MD: National Institute Against Prejudice and Violence.

"Ethics Bowl at Annual Meeting", *Speaking Ethically*, 1996, vol. 5, Summer/Fall, p. 4.

Ethics Resource Center (Aug. 1980) *Implementation and Enforcement of Codes of Ethics in Corporations and Associations: A Report Prepared by Opinion Research Corporation*, Washington, DC, Ethics Resource Center.

—— (1994) *Ethics in American Business: Policies, Programs, and Perceptions*, Washington, DC, Ethics Resource Center.

Evans, William M. (1962) "Role Strain and the Norm of Reciprocity in Research Organizations", *American Journal of Sociology*, vol. 68, no. 3, pp. 346–54.

Feinberg, Joel (1984) "The Moral and Legal Responsibility of the Bad Samaritan," *Criminal Justice Ethics*, vol. 3, Winter/Spring, pp. 56–66.

Francis, Leslie (1996) *Date Rape: Feminism, Philosophy, and the Law*, University Park, PA, Pennsylvania State University Press.

Freedman, Benjamin (1978) "A Meta-Ethics of Professional Morality," *Ethics*, vol. 89, October, pp. 1–19.

Freedman, Monroe (1966) "Professional Responsibility of the Criminal Defense Lawyer," *Michigan Law Review*, vol. 64, June, pp. 1469–84.

Fuller, Lon (1949) "The Case of the Speluncean Explorers", *Harvard Law Review*, 1949, vol. 62, February, pp. 616–45.

Fullinwider, Robert K. (1989) "Moral Conventions and Moral Lessons," *Social Theory and Practice*, vol. 15, Fall, pp. 321–38.

Futurecraft v. Clary Corp., 205 C.A. 2nd 279 (1962).

Gallop, Jane (1995) *Feminist Accused of Sexual Harassment*, Durham, NC, Duke University Press.

Gauthier, David (1986) *Morals By Agreement*, Oxford, Clarendon Press.

Gert, Bernard (1988) *Morality: A New Justification of the Moral Rules*, New York, Oxford University Press.

Gewirth, Alan (1978) *Reason and Morality*, Chicago, University of Chicago Press.

—— (1986) "Professional Ethics: The Separatist Thesis," *Ethics*, vol. 96, pp. 282–300.

Glass, Bentley (1965) "The Ethics Basis of Science", *Science*, vol. 150, pp. 1254–61.

Goldman, Alan (1980) *The Moral Foundations of Professional Responsibility*, Totowa, NJ, Littlefield Adams.

Gorlin, Rena A. (ed.) (1986) *Codes of Professional Responsibility*, Washington, DC, Bureau of National Affairs, Inc.

Gorovitz, Samuel *et al.* (eds) (1976) *Moral Problems in Medicine,* Englewood Cliffs, NJ, Prentice.

Gunther, Gerald (1990) "Freedom for the Thought We Hate," *Academe*, vol. 76, December, pp. 10–2.

Harris, Charles E., Michael S. Pritchard, and Michael J. Rabins (1995) *Engineering Ethics: Concepts and Cases*, Belmont, CA, Wadsworth.

Hart, H.L.A. (1968) *Punishment and Responsibility*, New York, Oxford University Press.

Hastings Center Staff (1980), "The Teaching of Ethics in American Higher Education: An Empirical Synopsis," in Daniel Callahan and Sissela Bok (eds), *Teaching Ethics in Higher Education*, New York, Plenum Press, pp. 153–70.

"Head of College Quits under Fire: Texan's Dissertation Was Found to Resemble Wife's," *New York Times*, 20 April 1969, p. 64.

Hearnshaw, L. S. (1981) *Cyril Burt – Psychologist*, New York, Random House/Vintage Books.

Hixson, Joseph (1976) *The Patchwork Mouse*, Garden City, NJ, Anchor/Doubleday.

Hook, Sidney, Paul Kurtz, and Miro Todorovich (eds) (1977) *The Ethics of Teaching and Scientific Research*, Buffalo, NY, Prometheus Books.

Humber, James M. and Robert F. Almeder (eds) (1976) *Biomedical Ethics and the Law*, New York, Plenum Press.

Hunt, Morton (1989) "Did the Penalty Fit the Crime?" *New York Times Magazine*, May 14, pp. 36ff.

Illinois Institute of Technology (1996) *1996–97 Student Handbook*, Chicago, Illinois Institute of Technology.

Jacoby, Russell (1987) *The Last Intellectuals*, New York, Basic Books.

Johnson, Henry C. (1964) "On Avoiding 'Single Vision and Newton's Sleep': Sketches From an Unorthodox Moral-Education History," in *Morality, Moral Behavior, and Moral Development*, William M. Kuntines and Jacob L. Gewirtz (eds), New York, John Wiley, pp. 381–99.

Jonsen, Albert R. and Stephen Toulmin (1988) *The Abuse of Casuistry: A History of Moral Reasoning*, Berkeley, CA, University of California Press.

Joughin, Louis (ed.) (1969) *Academic Freedom and Tenure: A Handbook of the American Association of University Professors*, Madison, WI, University of Wisconsin Press.

Kadish, Mortimer R. (1991) *The Ethic of Higher Education*, Palo Alto, CA, Stanford University Press.

Kadish, Mortimer R. and Sanford H. Kadish (1973) *Discretion to Disobey: A Study of Lawful Departures from Legal Rules*, Stanford, CA, Stanford University Press.

Kant, Immanuel (1990) *Foundations of the Metaphysics of Morals*, trans. by Lewis White Beck, New York, Macmillan/Library of Liberal Arts.

Kimball, Bruce A. (1995) *The Emergence of Case Method Teaching, 1872–1990s: A Search for Legitimate Pedagogy*, Bloomington, IN, The Poynter Center for the Study of Ethics and American Institutions, Indiana University.

Kimball, Roger (1990) *Tenured Radicals: How Politics Has Corrupted Our Higher Education*, New York, Harper & Row.

Kipnis, Kenneth (1983) "Professional Responsibility and the Responsibility of Professions" in Wade L. Robinson, Michael Pritchard and Joseph Ellin (eds) *Profits and Professions: Essays in Business and Professional Ethics*, Clifton, N. J., Humana Press.

Klein, Hans E. (ed.) (1989) *Case Method Research and Case Method Applications: Selected Papers of the Sixth International Conference on Case Method Research and Case Method Applications*, Waltham, MA, Bentley College, 22–4 May.

Krimsky, Sheldon (1988) "University Entrepreneurship and the Public Purpose," in *Biotechnology: Professional Issues and Social Concerns*, Paul DeForest *et al.* (eds), Washington, DC, American Association for the Advancement of Science, October, pp. 34–42.

Ladd, John (1983) "Collective and Individual Moral Responsibility in Engineering: Some Questions," in *Beyond Whistleblowing: Defining Engineers' Responsibilities*, Vivian Weil (ed.), Chicago, Center for the Study of Ethics in the Professions, Illinois Institute of Technology, pp. 90–113.

Ladenson, Robert F. *et al.* (1980) *A Selected Annotated Bibliography of Professional Ethics and Social Responsibility in Engineering*, Chicago, Center for the Study of Ethics in the Professions, Illinois Institute of Technology.

—— (1986) "Is Academic Freedom Necessary?" *Law and Philosophy*, vol. 5, February, pp. 59–87.

LaFollette, Marcel (1992) *Stealing into Print: Fraud, Plagiarism, and Misconduct in Scientific Publishing*, Berkeley, CA, University of California Press.

LaPiana, William P. (1994) *Logic and Experience: The Origin of Modern American Legal Education*, New York, Oxford University Press.

Lawrence III, Charles R. (1990) "Acknowledging the Victim's Cry," *Academe*, vol. 76, December, pp. 10–2.

Lee, J.A.N. (1995) "On 'Babbage and Kings' and 'How Sausage Was Made': And Now the Rest of the Story", *IEEE Annals of the History of Computing*, vol. 17, no. 4, pp. 7–23.

Levin v. Harleston, 770 F. Supp. 895 (S.D.N.Y., 1991).

Lickona, Thomas (1980) "What Does Moral Psychology Have to Say to the Teacher of Ethics?", in Daniel Callahan and Sissela Bok, *Teaching Ethics in Higher Education* New York, Plenum Press, pp. 103–32.

Liebert, Robert M. (1984) "What Develops in Moral Development?", in *Morality, Moral Behavior, and Moral Judgment*, William M. Kurtines and Jacob L. Gewirtz (eds), New York, John Wiley & Sons, pp. 177–192.

Lombardi, Louis G. (1990) "Character v. Codes: Models for Research Ethics," *International Journal of Applied Philosophy*, vol. 5, Spring, pp. 21–8.

Luban, David (1984) "The Adversary System Excuse," in David Luban (ed.). *The Good Lawyer: Lawyers' Roles and Lawyers' Ethics*, Totowa, NJ, Rowman & Allanheld, pp. 84–113.

—— (1988) *Lawyers and Justice*, Princeton, NJ, Princeton University Press.

MacIntyre, Alasdair (1984) *After Virtue*, Notre Dame, IN, University of Notre Dame Press.

McIntyre, Alison (1994) "Guilty Bystanders? On the Legitimacy of Duty to Rescue Statutes", *Philosophy and Public Affairs*, vol. 23, Spring, pp. 157–91

Mallon, Thomas (1989) *Stolen Words: Forays into the Origins and Ravages of Plagiarism*, New York, Ticknor & Fields.

Martin, Theodore Day (1931) *Instruction in Professional Ethics in Professional Schools for Teachers*, PhD dissertation, Columbia University.

Martin, T.R. (1981/82) "Do Courses in Ethics Improve the Ethical Judgment of Students?", *Business and Society*, vol. 21–22, Winter–Spring, pp. 17–26.

Matasar, Richard A. (1989) "Teaching Ethics in Civil Procedure Courses," *Journal of Legal Education*, vol. 39, December, pp. 587–607.

Matejka, J. Kenneth and Thomas J. Cosse (1981) *The Business Case Method: An Introduction*, Richmond, VA, Robert F. Dame, Inc.

Matthews, John B., Kenneth E. Goodpaster, and Laura L. Nash (1991) *Policies and Persons: A Casebook in Business Ethics*, 2nd edn, New York, McGraw-Hill.

May, William F. (1980) "Professional Ethics: Setting, Terrain, and Teacher", in *Ethics Teaching in Higher Education*, Daniel Callahan and Sisela Bok (eds), New York, Plenum Books, pp. 205–41.

Medawar, Peter B. (1975) "The Strange Case of the Spotted Mice," *The New York Review of Books*, 15 April, p. 8.

Merton, Robert (1973) "The Normative Structure of Science," in Norman W. Storer (ed.), *The Sociology of Science: Theoretical and Empirical Investigations*, Chicago, University of Chicago Press, pp. 267–78.

Mill, John Stuart (1956) *On Liberty*, Indianapolis, IN, Library of the Liberal Arts.

—— (1957) *Utilitarianism*, Indianapolis, IN, Library of the Liberal Arts.

Mooney, Carolyn J. (1990) "N.Y. City College Panel Weighs Academic Freedom, Inflammatory Racial Views of 2 Faculty Members," *Chronicle of Higher Education*, 23 May, p. A13 ff.

Muses, C. (1995) "The Unique Reach of Cybernetics in Our *Fin-de-Siécle*", *Kybernetes*, vol. 24, no. 7, pp. 6–20.

Nissenbaum, Stephen (1990) "The Plagiarists in Academe Must Face Formal Sanctions", *Chronicle of Higher Education*, 28 March, p. A52.

Parker, Donn B., Susan Swope, and Bruce N. Baker (1990) *Ethical Conflicts: Information and Computer Science, Technology, and Business*, Wellesley, MA, QED Information Sciences, Inc.

Parsons, Talcott and Gerald M. Platt (1973) *The American University*, Cambridge, MA, Harvard University Press.

Pincoffs, Edmund L. (ed.) (1972) *The Concept of Academic Freedom*, Austin, TX, University of Texas Press.

Pirsig, Maynard E. (ed.) (1970) *Professional Responsibility*, St. Paul, MN, West.

Pritchard, Michael S. (ed.) (1992) *Teaching Engineering Ethics: A Case Study Approach*, Kalamazoo, Center for the Study of Ethics in Society, Western Michigan University.

Rachels, James (1986) *Elements of Moral Philosophy*, New York, McGraw-Hill.

Rawls, John (1971) *A Theory of Justice*, Cambridge, MA, Harvard University Press.

Reagan, Charles E. (1971) *Ethics for Scientific Researchers*, 2nd edn, Springfield, IL, Charles C. Thomas.

Regents, University of Wisconsin (1990) "Discriminary Conduct Policy: Regent Resolution, Racism and Discriminatory Conduct," Oct. 1988, UMF Fac. Doc. No. 1670, Milwaukee, University of Wisconsin, 11 January.

Reich, W.T. (ed.) (1978) *Encyclopedia of Bioethics* New York, Free Press.

Rest, James (1985) "The Major Components of Morality", in W. Kurtines and J. Gewirtz (eds), *Morality, Moral Development, and Moral Behavior*, New York, Wiley, pp. 24–38.

—— (1988) "Can Ethics Be Taught in Professional Schools: The Psychological Reseach", *Easier Said Than Done*, vol. 1, Winter, pp. 22–6.

Rice, John Frank and Carl Bryant (1988) "A Descriptive Study of Moral and Intellectual Development," *U.S Air Force Academic Journal of Professional Military Ethics*, pp. 35–9.

Rich, John Martin (1984) *Professional Ethics in Education*, Springfield, IL, Charles C. Thomas.

Rosen, Stanley Joel and Ruth Ellen Bulger (1997) "The Social Responsibilities of Biological Scientists", *Science and Engineering Ethics*, vol. 3, April, pp. 137–44.

Ross, W.D. (1930) *The Right and the Good*, London, Oxford University Press.

Rudolph, Frederick (1962) *The American College and University*, New York, Alfred A. Knopf.

"Ruling in Doctorate Dispute," *New York Times*, 16 September 1969, p. 26.

Shaw, Bernard (1954) *The Doctor's Dilemma*, Baltimore, MD, Penquin Books.

Shils, Edward (1983) *The Academic Ethic: Report of a Study Group of the International Council on the Future of the University*, Chicago, University of Chicago Press.

Shrader-Frechette, Kristin (1994) *Ethics of Scientific Research*, Lanham, MD, Rowman & Littlefield.

Sigma Xi (1986) *Honor in Science*, 2nd edn, New Haven, CN, Sigma Xi.

Singer, Marcus (1981) "Recent Trends and Future Prospects in Ethics," *Metaphilosophy*, vol. 12, July/October, pp. 207–23.

Singer, Peter (1972) "Famine, Affluence, and Morality", *Philosophy and Public Affairs*, vol. 7, Spring, pp. 229–43.

Sloan, Douglas (1980) "The Teaching of Ethics in the American Undergraduate Curriculum 1876–1976," in Sessela Bok and Daniel Callahan (eds), *Ethics Teaching in Higher Education*, New York, Plenum Press, pp. 1–57.

Smith, Page (1990) *Killing the Spirit: Higher Education in America*, New York, Viking.

Smith, Patricia (1990) "The Duty to Rescue and the Slippery Slope Problem", *Social Theory and Practice*, vol. 16, Spring, pp. 19–41.

Sobel, Alan (1997) "Antioch's 'Sexual Offense Policy': A Philosophical Exploration", *Journal of Social Philosophy*, vol. 28, Spring, pp. 22–36.

Sperber, Murray (1990) *College Sport, Inc.: The Athletic Department vs. the University*, New York, Henry Holt.

Strohm, Paul (1988) "Professional Ethics and Scientific Misconduct," *Footnotes*, a publication of the American Association of University Professors, vol. 6, Fall, p. 1.

Sykes, Charles J. (1988) *ProfScam: Professors and the Demise of Higher Education*, Washington, DC, Regnery Gateway.

Teich, Albert H. and Frankel, Mark S. (1992) *Good Science and Responsible Scientists*, Washington, DC, Directorate for Science and Policy Programs, American Association for the Advancement of Science.

Thomson, Judith Jarvis (1971) "A Defense of Abortion", *Philosophy and Public Affairs*, vol. 1, Fall, pp. 47–66.

Toulmin, Stephen (1982) "How Medicine Saved the Life of Ethics," *Perspectives in Biology and Medicine*, vol. 25, Summer, pp. 736–50.

—— (1986) "How Medicine Saved Ethics" in *New Directions in Ethics*, Joseph P. DeMarco (ed.), New York, Routledge, pp. 265–81.

United States v. Virginia, 116 S. Ct. 2254 (1996).

U.S. Department of Commerce, Bureau of the Census (1976) *Historical Statistics of the United States: Colonial Times to 1970*, Part 1, (Bicentennial Edition).

U.S. Department of Justice, Bureau of Justice Statistics (March 1989) *Report to the National on Crime and Justice, Second Edition*, Washington, DC.

U.S. National Criminal Justice Information and Statistics Service (1980) *Sourcebook of Criminal Justice Statistics*, Washington, DC.

van der Waerden, B.L. (1968) "Mendel's Experiments," *Centaurus*, vol. 12, March, pp. 275–88.

Veatch, Robert M. (1979) "Professional Medical Ethics: The Grounding of its Principles," *Journal of Medicine and Philosophy*, vol. 4, March, pp. 1–19.

Vesilund, P. Arne (1988) "Rules, Ethics, and Morals in Engineering Education", *Engineering Education*, vol. 77, February, pp. 289–93.

—— (1997) *Introduction to Environmental Engineering*, Boston, PWS Publishing Co.

Waithe, Mary Ellen and David T. Ozar, (1990) "The Ethics of Teaching Ethics," *Hastings Center Report*, vol. 20, July/August, pp. 17–21.

Wasserstrom, Richard (1975) "Lawyers as Professionals: Some Moral Issues," *Human Right*, vol. 5, Fall, pp. 1–24.

Wells, Paula, Hardy Jones, and Michael Davis (1986) *Conflict of Interest in Engineering*, Dubuque, Iowa, Kendall/Hunt.

Whelan, John M. (1991) "Charity and the Duty to Rescue", *Social Theory and Practice*, vol. 17, Fall, pp. 441–56.

Whitbeck, Caroline (1995) "Teaching Ethics to Scientists and Engineers: Moral Agents and Moral Problems", *Science and Engineering Ethics*, vol 1, July, pp. 299–308.

Wilshire, Bruce (1989) *The Moral Collapse of the University: Professionalism, Purity and Alienation*, Albany, NY, State University of New York Press.

Weber, Max (1921) *Wissenschaft als Beruf*, München, Duncker und Humblott.

Woodward, Dow (1989) "The Challenge of Understanding and Teaching Broad Aspects of Bioethics Principles", *Perspectives on the Professions*, Chicago, Center for the Study of Ethics in the Professions, Illinois.

INDEX